W9-BUI-321

VOICES FROM

SOUTHEAST ASIA

Photo: John Tenhula

VOICES FROM SOUTHEAST ASIA

Withdrawn

The Refugee Experience in the United States

10084

JOHN TENHULA

ELLIS ISLAND SERIES

MARPLE PUBLIC LIBRARY
SPROUL & SPRINGFIELD RDS.
BROOMALL, PA. 19008

HM

HOLMES & MEIER   *New York*   *London*

Published in the United States of America 1991 by
Holmes & Meier Publishers, Inc.
30 Irving Place
New York, NY 10003

Copyright © 1991 by Holmes & Meier Publishers, Inc.

All rights reserved. No part of this book may be reproduced or
transmitted in any form or by any electronic or mechanical means
now known or to be invented, including photocopying, recording,
and information storage and retrieval systems, without permission in
writing from the publishers, except by a reviewer who may quote
brief passages in a review.

BOOK DESIGN BY DALE COTTON

This book has been printed on acid-free paper.

Library of Congress Cataloging-in-Publication Data

Tenhula, John.
    Voices from Southeast Asia : the refugee experience in the
United States / John Tenhula.
        p.   cm.
    Includes bibliographical references.
    ISBN 0-8419-1110-X (cloth: acid-free paper)
    1. Indochinese Americans—Social conditions.   2. Indochinese
Americans—Cultural assimilation.   3. Indochinese Americans—
Interviews.   4. Refugees, Political—United States—Interviews.
5. Oral history.   I. Title.
E184.I43T46   1991
305.895'9073—dc20   90-40696
                                                              CIP

MANUFACTURED IN THE UNITED STATES OF AMERICA

FRONTISPIECE
Camps in "first asylum" countries, such as those in Malaysia,
Singapore, and Thailand, are temporary hosts to newly escaped
refugees, who wait there to be placed in permanent locations. Those
pictured here walk just outside the Nong Khai camp in Thailand.

THE ELLIS ISLAND SERIES

It has recently been pointed out that revisionist historiography in the United States, including the "new immigrant history" and the "new ethnic history," has fundamentally changed our historical perspective and broadened the meaning of the American experience. The Ellis Island Series was conceived as part of that revisionist wave. Each volume offers a unique new perspective on the social, cultural, and economic aspects of immigration and on the role of immigrants in shaping a pluralist, multiracial society in America.

The books in the series focus on specific immigrant groups, and examine the immigrants' experience in the United States in the light of their prior history and expectations. The scope of the series encompasses the major waves of American immigration: the movements from Britain, Ireland, and the German states during the early and mid-nineteenth century; the mass migrations from Eastern Europe and Italy at the turn of the century; and the current wave from the Third World.

Drawing on a wide range of documentation, including firsthand accounts such as letters, narratives, diaries, and oral history, the series considers the personal, psychological, and social aspects as well as the cultural, political, and economic issues accompanying migration, resettlement, and acculturation. Thus each volume explores important matters that are not often documented: What did the immigrants, or refugees, expect of life in America? What were their dreams, myths, illusions, fears, and hopes? What was it like to leave their homes and what was it like when they arrived here? How were they received and how did they fare? What did they think about and how did they feel? In these volumes, the immigrants have the opportunity to give their side of the story.

It is particularly fitting that John Tenhula's book on Southeast Asian refugees should be the first in this series. *Voices from Southeast Asia* tells the extraordinary story of a major new immigrant group that is helping to transform the cultural landscape of the United States, much as the European immigration had done in previous generations. Tenhula's work also reminds us that the conditions governing immigration have changed over the last hundred years: like many of the current newcomers, Southeast Asians are refugees, not immigrants; and the author's examination of the experiences and problems unique to refugees is especially timely and enlightening. This book is also compelling oral history; the highly personal narratives, dialogues, and poems—recounting experiences of migration, resettlement, alienation, and acculturation—present the human perspective of the new Asian immigration. Moreover, the descriptions of immigrant networks, and encounters with hostility, prejudice, and restriction, while unique and contemporary, are also reminiscent of earlier immigrant experiences. Ultimately, this volume in the Ellis Island Series chronicles the basic patterns by which generations of immigrants have formed—and continue to transform—our society. In sponsoring this series, Holmes & Meier is responding to the need to explore, understand, and rethink this fundamental aspect of the American experience.

The editors would like to express their gratitude to the late Max Holmes, who provided so much of the inspiration for this series. He was a man of extraordinary qualities who had a passionate personal and professional interest in the field of immigration and who profoundly believed in the importance of ideas.

Ira A. Glazier
Temple-Balch Institute
Philadelphia

Luigi de Rosa
Istituto Navale
Naples

Series Editors

This book is dedicated to the Southeast Asian
boat and land people who died seeking
freedom and a new life.

The world is spun to turn as heaven bids;
Men grope their way like walkers in the night.

—Nguyen Gia Thieu, 1741–1798

I dreamed a deep dream of Sayavarman. I was with all my
ancestors for the conquest of the Mekong and saw hills
north of Angkor where the Khmers conquered Champa.
My dream continued with voices that spoke in French and
then the bombing of my beloved Phnom Penh and the
devastation and destruction of all I have known this period
on earth. I awoke and thought for a long time that we are
a lost and forgotten people. Yet that was only for a short
time of history. But still we have a story to tell. I heard so
many voices. Who will listen to these stories? There are
many voices from Indochina.

—O. Pham, Cambodian refugee
San Francisco, 1986

CONTENTS

Foreword

Liv Ullmann

Voices from Southeast Asia is a very moving book filled with stories of hopes and dreams and ghosts of refugees from Vietnam, Cambodia, and Laos. It is a history of the journey of many who have come to America, those who still want to come, and the whispers of those who died trying to come.

Everyone's life is a journey. For a refugee, part of that journey is in our hands—yours and mine. I write those words thinking about the tens of thousands who have escaped Vietnam, Cambodia, and Laos since April 1975, but also of the many thousands still in camps in Thailand, Malaysia, and Hong Kong. The journey for all of the refugees has been a traumatic one, and for some, extremely difficult and with few promises of a better tomorrow.

In January 1990, as part of a human-rights fact-finding team, I visited the detention camps in Hong Kong. I call them concentration camps. What I saw shocked me. The world seems to have begun to close not only its borders but also its mind to those who are fleeing wartorn countries of Southeast Asia that continue to violate basic human rights. Most shocking was the forced repatriation to Vietnam in December 1989 of over fifty people, mostly women and children. Although this is a violation of international law, we have heard that such repatriation would become mandatory for those who were judged also to be economic refugees. And the "voices" of these people go unheard as if they, too, had been lost at sea or killed in fields mined with bombs.

But what of those who survived, who were given a second chance? *Voices from Southeast Asia* so clearly speaks to us about them—about their successful journey to a safe haven and, often, their successful transition to a new life in America. There is magic and poetry and eloquence in the statements made by the refugees interviewed for this book. In many ways my heart was lifted by their courage and determination to succeed—to not even consider failure a possibility. Many of the interviews were haunting—young people who endured so much hardship and lived to share it here—through often poignantly candid descriptions, and the very old people who would never again be sure of themselves, taken away from all that was secure and real for them. All of those interviewed seemed to talk about courage and an inner strength that manifested itself in different ways now that they have been given a chance for a new life.

Perhaps most enlightening for me were the interviews that were observations of American life. As an immigrant from Norway, I, too, could share some of those thoughts. America can be a cold and tough place in which to begin a new life and career. One is exposed to a new set of social dynamics that are unsettling: materialism, racism, differences in family structure. These interviews discuss differences between East and West. The ways in which the Vietnamese, Cambodians, and Laotians dealt with those differences were often insightful, amusing, painful, yet resourceful. And, again and again, even the refugees best describe themselves as "survivors."

The chapter expressing views of the war seemed to highlight the voices of Southeast Asian military people who never felt a part of the American military involvement. "Americans never listened to us," they keep repeating. And now, fifteen years after the war, the wounds have not yet healed, and the politicians are still not listening to the people. I am reminded of the terrible situation in Kampuchea today, with the real possibility of yet another "killing fields" in the future. Of the West's tacit support of the Pol Pot's Khmer Rouge army and their seat in the U.N. Have we learned nothing? Have we even begun to listen to the real people who must endure this possible new anguish?

Can a tragedy be avoided? These are some of the questions I asked myself when I read these interviews.

But we must not forget the refugees' stories of success and happiness. In stories that amuse, comfort—even warm us—they tell of continuing contributions to the American immigrant mosaic. Here are men, women, and children who have overcome the shock of war, dislocation, and the transfer to the States and who have begun a new life. Refugees who are contributing as new Americans. While there are many happy stories, I was very much taken by a theme repeated throughout the interviews—a deep concern for those left in the camps, those friends and family still suffering in the countries they cannot escape from. These unheard voices also echo in the reader's ear. The journey of these people may have no beginning, or end. I still believe that this journey is in our hands—yours and mine.

The author does a fine job of explaining to the reader what defines a refugee, a term which, as used today, connotes a difficult and highly political status. Refugee rights, like human rights, now seem to be interpreted in a variety of ways, thus putting in jeopardy thousands of innocent victims of war and oppression. People tend to forget that Nazi Germany or Pol Pot's Kampuchea took place so recently, that such tragedies could even exist. People tend to forget that every day lives are torn apart—lives that we can do something about. We must not turn our backs on refugees or we turn our backs on all humanity.

Many years ago, my ancestors from Scandinavia had a dream of North America as the good land. Their descendants proudly described them as strong, brave people, setting out on a journey to the unknown. But today those with similar dreams and hopes are shamed, discouraged. Why? How did we change? What happened to us? The dream did not change.

Voices from Southeast Asia shares many stories of dreams—dreams and realities that are part of the history of *all* refugees coming to a safe land, not just those from Southeast Asia. I am deeply struck by the eloquence of the voices I hear in this book.

Finally, let me share with you a poem written by a sixteen-year-old girl, Cindy Cheung from Vietnam, one of the unheard voices in a concentration camp that I recently visited in Hong Kong:

I Am Sorrow

Who will listen to my feeling?
Who will listen to my useless land?

After the war, my skin had been damaged,
There are craters in my body.
Although I was sad, sorry, and suffering
Who will listen to my feeling?
I am sad, sorry, and suffering
Who will know my feeling?
I am not sad about my harmed body
I am sorrow because of the people
who can't use me rightly.
Who will know my feeling?

ACKNOWLEDGMENTS

The idea for this book grew out of my work as a graduate student and adjunct professor at Columbia University and through my work for the National Council of Churches and the United Nations. I wish to thank the Presbyterian Church, and in particular Rev. William DuVal for a generous grant to complete this book. I also want to thank Charles W. Curtis, a former student at Columbia, and my friend Phat Mau for their research and editorial assistance in preparing the history of Vietnam, Cambodia, and Laos that appears in Appendix A. I am also grateful to Diana Bui, whose help has been invaluable. The tapes and transcripts of the interviews that follow will be donated to the Archives of Folk Culture Project, Library of Congress, Washington, D.C.

My purpose in this book has been to document through oral histories the experiences of Southeast Asian refugees who have arrived in the United States since 1975, letting them tell their stories from their own perspectives and in their own voices. In the course of completing the research and writing, I have made many friends, unfortunately too numerous to be named here, many of whom have taught me a tremendous amount about human nature and the will to survive. A special, warm note of appreciation and thanks must be given to the many people whose interviews I recorded but was unable to use here simply because of space limitations. Finally, for interviews that were included in the book, I wish to thank those who patiently, sometimes painfully, shared their stories with me.

Voices from Southeast Asia

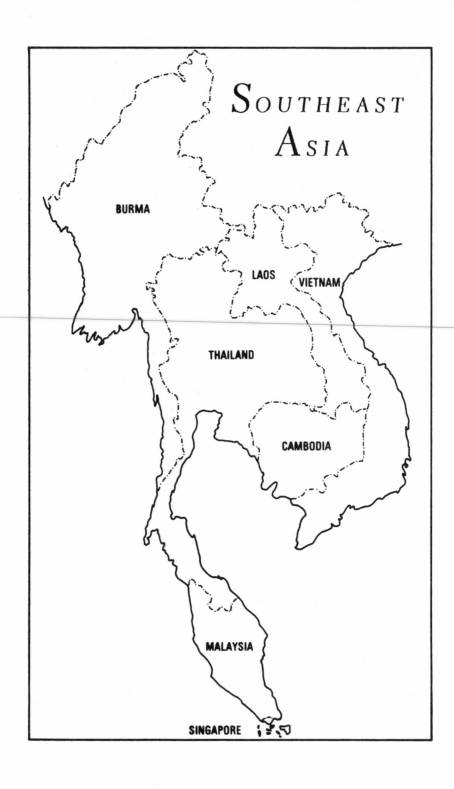

INTRODUCTION

Since the American evacuation of South Vietnam in April 1975 and the collapse of the governments in Cambodia and Laos, well over 2 million refugees have fled their homelands due to intolerable human rights violations and subsequent deteriorating economic conditions. Almost 1 million refugees from those countries have been accepted for resettlement in the United States at an estimated cost in billions of dollars. This is their story.

Many of these refugees are now American citizens and prefer to be called new Americans. They live in all fifty states and represent very diverse backgrounds of education, experience, and skills. They are in the United States because of their close collaboration with the American military during the war in Southeast Asia and because of their often fierce identification with the United States's democratic form of government.

These refugees came to the United States at the invitation and with the assistance of the federal government and in accordance with existing U.S. immigration law. They represent a wide range of distinct ethnic, cultural, and linguistic groups of people often referred to as Southeast Asian or Indochinese. Understanding those distinctions remains crucial to understanding this refugee population and their experiences.

These are not immigrants who adhered to particular annual immigration quotas and restrictions, and thus able to prepare for their departures, but homeless refugees who escaped with little or nothing but their memories, dreams, and talents. In addition, many were homeless in their own politically and economically unstable countries before their move to the United States. There are many examples of internal displacement within these war-torn countries—such as the more than 1 million Vietnamese who moved (when North and South Vietnam were created) from Hanoi to Saigon in 1954, the estimated half million Cambodians who moved into Phnom Penh before the collapse of the country to the Communists in 1975, and the increased and forced migration from rural to urban areas in all three countries during the war. The theme of forced migration is part of the Southeast Asian refugee story. Even today, large numbers of people continue to flee that region.

American sympathy and generosity during the late 1970s and early 1980s shifted as other humanitarian issues such as the African famine diverted public attention, resources, and response. Simply stated, Southeast Asian refugees are no longer a front-page issue. Yet an estimated 500,000 are in holding centers and camps awaiting some solution. In Hong Kong alone, by the end of April 1990, 54,000 Southeast Asian refugees were being kept in detention centers. After fifteen years, most of these people have no strong affiliation with the U.S. government and no immediate relatives (mother, father, sister, or brother) in this country; many have waited in camps for more than five years and probably will never be admitted to the United States Refugee Program. There are many more refugees living in camps outside their countries who still dream of being reunited with family and friends in the United States but are unable to find a country that will accept them. They simply got in line too late to meet the limited U.S. admissions quota.

This country and the world are now embarrassed by the refugees' inability to dissipate, to disappear. This change of attitude can be seen, for example, in Thailand's 1986 decision to close refugee camps on the Cambodian border and by the earlier refusal of Thailand and other governments to recognize these people as refugees, instead continuing to refer to them as "displaced" or "illegal." As one senior Thai immigration official put it, "We, too, are a poor country. There are fiscal and political limitations to our kindness. I believe a decade or more of this is enough." During the June 1989 United Nations International Conference on Indochinese Refugees, Immigration and Foreign Office officials from Britain and Hong Kong were quick to point out that their policies of granting asylum had "gone beyond all possible limits." In December 1989, Hong Kong forcibly returned Vietnamese refugees to Vietnam.

Thus, this is also a book about refugees who fear that the generous support for admission of their groups is evaporating—that further help for family and friends not yet reunited in the United States is near exhaustion. "We feel that one day Washington will simply say—no more—not one more person. We are waiting for them to tell us that we must stop. Stop. It is all we can do for you," said a Vietnamese career officer, Nguyen Van Mo.

With host governments that are usually signatories to U.N. refugee treaties, the United Nations High Commissioner for Refugees has undertaken responsibility for the major care and protection of the refugees. In terms of finding solutions to a refugee situation, the United Nations describes three possible scenarios: voluntary repatriation (going back of one's own free will) if and when possible; monetary assistance to countries housing refugees (for example, funding for the care, maintenance, and integration of refugees in Thailand); or resettlement in a new country. It is the third and ostensibly least-liked solution (because of the way it disrupts lives and affects only a small number of people) that this book describes in terms of its human consequences.

A major theme running throughout the interviews concerns American ambivalence about welcoming the oppressed who resettled here. In the late 1970s Americans were shocked by the newscasts' first televised shots of Vietnamese drowning in the South China Sea and being ignored by passing cargo ships, or being pushed back to sea in their leaky vessels off the coast of Malaysia and told to go elsewhere. Something clicked in people all over the country. American public opinion led an outcry and the response opened the gates. Over ten years later, however, those gates, as the refugees describe it, are closing. "Generosity seems to have found its limits in this country," said Le Xuan Khoa, a Vietnamese academician.

Like other immigrant and refugee groups, the Southeast Asians have experienced the United States as a country with a schizophrenic approach to its immigration policy. Americans are sympathetic to the idea of helping refugees as long as local communities remain unaffected. Americans can quickly demonstrate hospitality, and then hostility, to the idea of new members or where they choose to live. Historically all groups of refugees—and now the Southeast Asians—have challenged the American belief in an ability to provide freedom and a safe harbor for the oppressed. "Who gets in and who does not," said one refugee, is the real concern. These are questions of admission policy and, since passage of the Refugee Act of 1980, they continue to be raised—with no adequate answers.

The Southeast Asian refugees are concerned with the issue of future admissions. "If we can never return, at least we can hope to bring our family here," said My Linh Soland, an attorney from Alexandria, Virginia. This concern, continually voiced by the refugees interviewed, has direct implications for future admissions. Some of the more germane policy issues raised are discussed in the Conclusion of this book.

The very definition of "refugee" under U.S. law identifies that person as being someone who is outside his country, and having fled it, fears persecution if forced to return to that country.* Refugees are immigrants, but not all immigrants are refugees. "Immigrant" is a term often used to include any nonresident in the United States, legal or illegal. A distinction we should not forget is that refugee admission means unplanned but legal admission, according to immigration quotas, with social service benefits such as all perma-

---

*Section 101(a)(42) of the Immigration and Nationality Act as amended by the Refugee Act of 1980 defines the term "refugee" (apart from immigrant or any other admission status) as:

(A) any person who is outside any country of such person's nationality or, in the case of a person having no nationality, is outside any country in which such person last habitually resided, and who is unable or unwilling to return to, and is unable or unwilling to avail himself or herself of the protection of, that country because of persecution or a well-founded fear of persecution on account of race, religion, nationality, membership in a particular social group, or political opinion, or

(B) in such special circumstances as the President, after appropriate consultation (as defined in section 207[e] of this Act) may specify, any person who is within the country of such person's nationality, within the country in which such person is habitually residing, and who is persecuted or who has a well-founded fear of persecution on account of race, religion, nationality, membership in a particular social group, or political opinion. The term "refugee" does not include any person who ordered, incited, assisted, or otherwise participated in the persecution of any person on account of race, religion, nationality, membership in a particular social group, or political opinion.

nent residents are entitled to receive by law. Refugees fit a definition and quota, are invited to the United States, and are on their way to citizenship with full citizenship privileges. Often, however, they have special adjustment needs different from those of immigrants who enter the country under a quota in an orderly fashion, for the most part to be reunited with close family members who petitioned for their admission.

The Southeast Asians talk about American tolerance, another major theme of the interviews. During this decade of reportedly increasing numbers of incidents nationwide stemming from racial, religious, and ethnic tensions, the refugees are testing Americans' willingness to accept Asians as their neighbors and co-workers. Tensions between these groups are not unrelated to American guilt about the war, and to refugees' unhealed war wounds, including those from the loss of family and friends in Southeast Asia, and to a general inability, to date, to come to terms with the effects of the war.

Finally, we are living through a new chapter in U.S. immigration history— a peek, perhaps, into the twenty-first century. New, non-European people, with fresh ideas and work ethics that often test native-born attitudes, have their stories to tell. There is a spirit of entrepreneurship and enterprise that makes the American dream still come true for some. It is this dream that many of the people interviewed here are looking for, and that a few lucky ones have already realized.

Although refugees from Southeast Asia share many experiences with other immigrant and refugee groups, two features continue to distinguish this group. The first is the legacy of the war, of the Americans and Southeast Asians who died; the second is demographic and racial. The Southeast Asian refugees make up the largest Asian refugee group ever admitted to the United States, and the interviews repeatedly demonstrate that this is not a homogeneous group. These refugees contribute to a complex picture of diversity in terms of different cultural and linguistic skills, educational backgrounds, and even family size. "We arrived after the Statue of Liberty celebrated her one-hundredth birthday and was polished and made to look new. We are the people of the next century. We are many different peoples, and most of us can be polished and made to look new," said Quan Nguyen, a Vietnamese who was resettled in North Dakota.

These people are products of a war that the United States promoted, participated in, and lost; that experience and relationship is examined in Chapter 2. For most of the refugees interviewed, American involvement in the Southeast Asian war directly affected their lives both then and now. Some of those interviewed see America as a colonialist military power that replaced the French, a foreign occupier that continued to fight against an enemy in a military situation they never understood. "They [the Americans] did not choose to understand or listen to us in any meaningful way," said Vietnamese military officer Tran Van Tat. For others, America offered a more honest look at the inherent corruption of their own societies and offered them an opportunity to experience a different sense of values. What is clearly demonstrated in talks with former military officers is that there existed a pronounced communication barrier between the United States and the South Vietnamese, Cambodian, and Laotian military. Both sides seem never to have gained the confidence or trust in each other needed to work in a collaborative effort. Part of the difficulty of adjustment for former military people from Southeast Asia in the United States has been the very fact that they continue to see themselves as military personnel, trained only to be military people. "What do you do with an old general living in Arlington, Virginia, who doesn't want to learn English?," asked Tran Van Tat. "Do you tell him he must become like and act like the Americans, he must reach out for the American dream? All this when you know he would never be able to change in Vietnam, in his own land—least of all in America."

In Chapters 3 and 4, the refugees focus on the theme of their exodus from Southeast Asia and their move to the United States. Every individual interviewed remembers his or her escape, and the stories they share are both revealing and shocking tales of human tragedy and tough ingenuity. For many, the method of escape (over land across mine-filled borders or by way of the treacherous South China Sea) relates to the manner in which they have resettled and become part of their new communities. The first wave of refugees escaped Vietnam in late April 1975, were placed on military aircraft, transported to the United States, kept in camps, and eventually resettled. Others crossed land mines and risked stormy seas—losing family and friends in the process—only to sit and wait for months or years in crowded and hostile camps until some country offered them a resettlement opportunity. These are stories that explore the seemingly endless varieties of human patience, perseverance, and hope.

In the transfer to the United States, the refugees' experiences are difficult but not bereft of humor. The new American is put into a strange and threatening environment and expected to survive. Most do; a few do not. The refugees face possible rejection and conflict as well as failure. "I never failed before at anything," said Le Rieu Tai, a Vietnamese physician. A lot of these stories are about the conflicts and dilemmas of the move both to and within the United States, and they are often shared in a very straightforward and reflective way. "I never thought that the move to this country would be so difficult," said Dr. Le Rieu Tai. "Perhaps I was not realistic about it. Even after all of these years here, I still feel like a stranger in a strange country."

Chapter 5 traces the time-consuming process through which the refugees have become part of their new communities in the United States and have established ties to those communities. Their stories focus on how, over time, an immigrant develops roots or fails to develop roots. Critical to the entire resettlement process, as evaluated by those interviewed, are identifying needs, exploring the employment situation, and confronting the personal obstacles that each person encounters.

In the Southeast Asian refugee population, there are what resettlement agencies call "vulnerable groups," such as the elderly and widows with children, who often have not received the personalized kind of attention they need. "These are the poor souls that fall through the bureaucratic cracks," said Pauline Van Tho, a Vietnamese former senator now involved in resettlement work. Key to all of this is understanding that there are very real resettlement differences between the various "waves" of refugees—those who came out in 1975 by U.S. military evacuation or by boat or over land in 1980 or 1990. During the current period of promoting and implementing national immigration reform, critics continue to ask, "Haven't we done enough for these people?" while policymakers talk about having already absorbed America's "fair share."

Refugees report employment and English language proficiency as the two critical components needed to establish themselves in the United States. The people interviewed describe those needs and talk about handicaps—from the Vietnamese actress (self-described as Marilyn Monroe–like) who, now living in Hollywood, has lost acting roles because of her ever-so-slight mispronunciation of *th* to the elderly Laotian woman who has tried several times to learn English in a classroom situation that she describes as "not part of this world." Others talk about loss of status as well as property and material goods. Underlying the interviews is the tremendous personal strength and resilience these people possess, a determination to survive and succeed. Their hopes and accomplishments will provide vital energy for American culture, commerce, and politics. "It is a people like us, who come here and take risks and succeed and are able to sit here and talk about it, that's what it means to establish roots for me—it means I took risks, that I succeeded in most things and I put something back into this country that gave me the opportunity to be here," said businessman Nguyen Ngoc Linh.

The future as described in Chapter 6 by one immigrant is a "Janus-like person with two faces." One face looks toward getting on with his life in this new country and the other face looks to the past. "You live forever split apart. Yes, you live, but it is always a life divided." The refugees are keenly aware of current political events in the countries they left. They are still connected to friends and family who did not or could not escape, and they dream of being reunited with them or returning "home." Many share a survival guilt, as did other refugees who have come to this country. "Why did I get out and they did not, why me?" This feeling is described as a delayed response, a guilt that seems to strike after being in this country for a period of time, often after five or six years.

The future for these people is also about constant change, adjustment, and compromise. A faster or more successful integration into American society often seems to depend upon age. "After forty, you are too set, too established in your ways to learn a new language and culture—it is all too much," said Vera Chinh, a Vietnamese social worker from Sacramento. But the future involves devising plans of action to develop and fulfill immigrant potential. "There are so many potential resources in these refugees that just need to be brought out," said Vietnamese training director Pho Ba Long. At the same time, the future also entails trying to forget the painful events of the past. "I try every day to tell myself that my life is in America, not Cambodia," said businesswoman Sirathra Som. "America now, not Cambodia! Forget the past, the future is here, now. This is a very, very, very difficult thing for me to do. I work very hard at it; sometimes I succeed, sometimes I do not." I can still hear her repeating, "America now, not Cambodia!"

This is an oral history of the recent arrival of Southeast Asian newcomers to American soil. Each interview or piece of writing explores and shares with the reader something of refugee experience and personal life, or as Samphy Iep, a Cambodian resettlement worker, said, "something we would like to forget. We all have a part of us that has been torn away, something special, precious, that is gone." Together these interviews form a collective portrait of the largest refugee migration to the United States. The way these people have been welcomed and treated as they began life anew in communities around this country has a great deal to say about the American people—their levels of tolerance, their values, and their beliefs.

My method of research and interviewing was not scientific or scholarly in

any way, and assumed a greater degree of organization as the research and interviews progressed. More than 130 refugees were interviewed on tape, the interviews lasting from one to three hours each. Approximately one-third of the
individuals were interviewed a second and third time over a three-year period.
Some people chose to correspond with me after the initial interview to help
clarify or supplement their responses to certain questions I had raised. The
method of sampling was dictated, in part, by my travel and work schedule,
which has taken me to most refugee resettlement communities in some forty
states for the National Council of Churches. I simply began to compile a list
of people I wanted to interview whom I had already met or who were sug-
gested to me. This random, cross-sectional, geographic approach to interviewing had to be flexible, taking into account the jobs, language training,
and personal schedules of those being interviewed. The interviews themselves
took place in coffee shops, on park benches, in offices, and in kitchens of private homes.

Of the people interviewed, 50 percent were Vietnamese, 25 percent Cambodian, and 25 percent Laotian. The interviews were arranged by a sponsor,
friend, relative, or employer and were conducted by me in English and
French or in Vietnamese, Khmer, and Lao through paid and volunteer inter-
preters. My intention throughout was to provide a "sample" of different
groups that existed within the refugee population; this was not anything ap-
proaching an accurate cross-section, although I tried to be as attentive as possible to the varied educational backgrounds and linguistic skills of the people.

The poetry in this book is a result of discussions in which the interviewee
was encouraged to collect and write his or her thoughts about certain questions and subjects, or just write about anything that came to mind. Frequently
the person's voice came through more clearly on paper than through the mi-
crophone.

Most interviews were edited to provide the reader with a more coherent,
concise, but representative text. At the request of many of the people who
were interviewed, names have been changed for reasons of privacy. All pseu-
donyms were created arbitrarily and do not refer to any actual persons.

The general format of questions asked for all those interviewed was the following:

1. *What were your expectations before you came here? What are the realities
of life for you now?*

2. *What has been your personal experience in your move to this country?*

What specific events or experiences have influenced your life in this country?

3. *What has been the most significant personal change in your life since coming to this country?*

4. *What were the strong and the weak points of the resettlement program for you? How could it be improved?*

5. *What do you think American attitudes toward you are?*

6. *At what point do you stop being a refugee?*

These questions were chosen to afford the reader a better understanding of the dynamics of refugee migration patterns as well as an opportunity to explore the human dynamics of the refugees' situation. My questions aimed to elicit personal experiences and stories of the move to this country as well as the resettlement process in new communities—in an attempt to better understand who these people are and how Americans received them. And in response, the people interviewed shared their dreams of what they thought would exist in America as well as the reality of the new life that they found or made here.

All too often, Americans want to see immigrants and refugees as part of a heroic folk tale in which they arrive penniless on our shores and in a very short time succeed beyond their and our wildest expectations. It is a good story, but in truth the happy ending is attained by only a few. In a society geared toward quick success in terms of material possessions and gains, this refugee group has taught us that there is one very important element in the character of these people collectively, and that is their perception of time, which is very different from the Western one. "This is not a video flashback, it is our lives," said Tran Van Tho, a Vietnamese social worker. "We walk, not run. We listen and we act in a way that uses our values and education and experience, now along with American values and experiences. You run, we walk, but we will travel together."

CHAPTER 1

Photo: A. Hollmann/UNHCR

EAST AND WEST

As a means of introduction to this group, it is fair to say that Southeast Asians have forced Americans and themselves to think about the differences between the societies they represent. Refugees and Americans frequently describe values and life-styles in generalities that perpetuate myths and stereotypes; but in part these demonstrate that there are also very real differences. These contrasts in terms of general values, religion, work, and even the concept of time affected the way people worked and fought together during the war. How they live together now in the United States is also affected, and whether or not Americans have an understanding of the refugees' history and cultural values has a great deal to do with the forming of friendships and mutually satisfying work relationships across the two groups.

The following interviews discuss some real and less tangible differences between present-day life in the United States and the life the refugees left be-

◁FACING PAGE
This Hmong woman and her child,
at the Chiang Kham camp in Thailand,
fled their home in Laos during the war.

hind. They left that life behind, but for the most part did not forget it. Although those interviewed talk about contrasting spiritual values and other differences between life in the East and West, their histories and teachings can be an important part of their new lives. "Buddhism can have a modern face, you just have to look for it," said Samphy Iep, a Cambodian resettlement worker. One issue that all those interviewed have learned to identify and try to cope with is Western materialism, heightened, they say, by advertising. "The French taught us materialism," continued Samphy Iep, "but nothing like the Americans did here."

MONK PHEN ANONTHASY
East/West Values

He has kept me waiting for almost an hour, sitting on a metal folding chair in some anteroom, adjacent to his office. The temple itself is in an industrial section of Oakland. The building was most likely a garage, and you can still see the original lines of the structure. The heavy smell of incense is hanging in the air.

He must be over seventy years of age, and he is bent over as he approaches. He leads me to his office, then inside the temple. There is a feeling of quiet about this man who seems unconcerned about where he is—be it Laos or Oakland. He remains in a perfect lotus position on the hard floor and never moves. His eyes are fixed on my eyes and I felt that he has your undivided attention. A baby cries close by—but he seems not to even hear the cries.

I left Laos for Thailand in 1976 and stayed there for four years before coming to the United States. I was needed to help my people in the camps. I left Laos because Buddhism and Marxist thought cannot live together. They cannot. It is impossible! For the Communists there can be no alternatives and there can be no compromise; Communism and Buddhism could not continue in Laos, so I left. This is a political side to life that my people cannot accept. They took us—all of the monks—and they placed us in a camp. It was a prison and I was afraid they would kill us. I am here now. For me, Oakland [California] or Vientiane or Bangkok—it is the same thing. I don't even look out of the window anymore—see, it is all covered! The spirit is with you and a person is still the same person only in a different place. I do not leave the temple; for me, this is my world.

What are the differences you see between the East and West?

I would say the biggest differences between East and West are three. First, we have a different system of values as taught to us through Buddhism. It is a system of thought that affects the way we think—all of our daily activities. You never separate the spiritual from the real. It surrounds the family, the role of each member in that family, and how the family continues to reinforce those values.

Second is the day-to-day existence, the patterns of living. The housing and the places our people live in are very different here from Laos. This affects your life every day. Just look at this room. Do you think I belong here? Look, don't I look lost? Oh, but inside I'm not lost. We live close to our family members and the village system is one where you are aware of who your neighbor is and what he does. Here everything is respect for your privacy and you do not know who your neighbor is or anything about him. You see, we believe that the place of one's birth and the residence of our ancestors is very important for the continuation of our life. Land is important; it is your history, your heritage, your being. If you remove land, you remove spirit. But is this not what the American Indians believed, too? Was not land their soul?

Third, the relationship between parent and child changes too much here. This means children stop obeying parents and they leave home too quickly; also, family life has it that everyone works and you leave early in the morning and return late in the evening. Your time with your children is very short. Children should have more respect for older people. It is terrible what happens between children and older people when they come to America.

I know my people have many problems here. They come to me for discussions and advice and just to be in the temple. They come to reflect. Yesterday, a woman had a car crash and came for advice—she thought she had bad spirits, that she did something wrong. You see, she believed that she was being punished. To her, the car crash said that she was a bad woman. Buddha gives advice on all troubles. You go to Buddha for everything you need. So much discomfort has to do with the work and the language here. Materialism is the need for everyone to work for money; Lao people find it hard and they go in different directions. Capitalism does very strange things to a person's system of values. Too many material goods are here to tempt and confuse you. Money can cause so much unhappiness.

What happens to the Lao family in America?

Work forces women into a new relationship with their husbands and children. I see more women who leave their husbands, and the husbands get depressed with problems because they cannot carry on their roles within the family. Many use welfare but that is not enough money to live on, and when a person does not work, he gets depressed. It is like the air he breathes is being taken away. Work is terribly important for one's self-respect and dignity. I try to help. Buddha teaches control of oneself and to deal with the changes in life. What the Laotian communities in the United States really need are more monks; in all of San Francisco there are no monks.

And there is crime. Yes, there is much crime in Oakland. Many women tell me of rape and robbery. I try to listen to them and to help them. I suppose there is crime everywhere but I do not notice it. I spend most of my days here in the temple. I pray a lot.

MONK DONG TA
Philosophical Differences

With his worn face and studious manner, Dong Ta appears to be a scholar. He gives me the impression he is only skimming the surface of what he is explaining to me. You keep wondering what his position in Vietnamese society would have been before he fled: perhaps monk also, or a professor or aristocrat. His English is drawn out with a heavy French accent, and he constantly speaks with his hands. He is pleasant but keeps me at a distance.

It's difficult to explain the difference between Vietnamese and Americans in way of thought. It is a different value system and it shows in the different ways each group solves problems; which is to say a value system of what is important in life. For example, you can talk about the Taoist idea of harmony. For us, harmony is everything, life and death. This harmony is a sort of accommodation to whatever the problem might be. It's looking for the path that is least stressful, least confrontational. It might be what you call a shortcut to a law or regulation, but it is really a different way of looking at things, doing things.

As a Vietnamese, you learn never to clash or confront. This you always avoid. There are always quiet ways to get things accomplished, the path of least resistance. A lot of this is respect for tradition and the past. So often things do not change, they stay status quo because it was done that way and it should continue. This idea of harmony very much influences the way the Vietnamese look at the legal system in the United States. Often this is not good. Laws that say only one direction is correct cause problems for us. We want to find an easier, more efficient path to seek solutions.

Then there are the five Confucian virtues—humanity, righteousness, propriety, wisdom, and faithfulness—as models for one's daily conduct. These virtues enter into many layers and aspects of life for a Vietnamese, especially relating to family; each is very important. I understand that these are very broad philosophical issues to deal with, but they help explain some of the different ways a Vietnamese looks at life. You see, to us they are very important.

What do most Vietnamese say about Americans?

Patience—I mean, no patience. Americans are so impatient, that's what most Vietnamese say to me. They always want something at that moment—like children! The Vietnamese have a kind of internal personal strength and endurance which we call Tanh Can Cu, which is usually meant to say that there is a willingness to do things even when the hard way is the only possible way. It is a source of strength that Vietnamese take real pride in having. There is also Tan Hien Hoc, which is a love of knowledge and learning in general. You can see this in America in the way the Vietnamese try to get as much education as they can. For example, everybody here assumes his children will go to university.

In Vietnamese mythology there is a story of a very beautiful woman. It is a poem called "Kim Van Kieu," which ends in disaster for the woman, but she accepts this because it is her fate. Vietnamese think a lot about fate. This is an important difference between Americans and Vietnamese—Americans take a very pragmatic attitude toward the events that come their way. The Vietnamese give much to fate. You know it just happens that way—what you call predestination. Often this includes feeling sorry for oneself, maybe avoiding or overcoming something, and this leads to self-pity. A lot, too, has been said about the basic difference being that Americans look at the mind and Vietnamese look at the heart. Americans have a higher regard for logic and reason, and Vietnamese spend too much time being concerned with the intangible. I don't know about that.

Vietnamese society is very class-conscious, you can see that here in America. I think that the French occupation helped reinforce this notion. It's something Americans have a great deal of difficulty understanding. But you come from a society with classes, don't you? There is this myth in America that everybody is equal. Ha! Remember it was the French that gave this idea to your President Jefferson. Take as an example a Vietnamese urban professional and some rice farmer from the countryside—do you treat them the same? It is like treating a Wall Street banker the same way you would treat a poor farmer from Mississippi. These people are not equal. You may not see the differences but we do—the moment someone begins to speak, he reveals his identity and is immediately classified. For Vietnamese, this relates to the concept of Le Dien, the rules of propriety and of ceremony. We Vietnamese like ceremony. There is a great deal of emphasis on titles, educational degrees, and family names. You know what we would really like is nobility! Look at the way the Vietnamese address everybody as Mr. and Mrs., not by first name. It makes people think the Vietnamese are cold, but that's part of the character makeup. Vietnamese have the notion of *dien*, or face. But I believe all Asians have this. It preserves a part of the character as one would like it to be, which is not what is often the actual real way the situation is.

Americans always have watches—the idea of time is very important to the culture. Vietnamese have a very different concept. Vietnamese walk, we say, but Americans run. This is just part of the culture and the way people function. It means no disrespect for a person, but the idea of a precise minute of time to arrive just makes no sense to a Vietnamese. We say you live longer when you are not so concerned with this notion of time.

One obvious difference between Vietnamese and Americans has a great deal to do with the way the Vietnamese were placed here. I mean the resettlement program. Even after all these years, I talk with Vietnamese who cannot understand why American volunteers want to help Vietnamese, to help strangers. To them it is a very foreign, very strange idea. They are puzzled about why people do this. Those concepts of community spirit do not exist among Vietnamese as they do for Americans. This complicates things even more when Americans put all refugees, Cambodians, Vietnamese, and Laotians, into the same category—Indochinese—and treat everyone as if they came from the same city, not even different countries!

This idea of doing good by giving freely of your time didn't exist in Vietnam. But I don't think Vietnam is so different from most non-Western countries. I think this idea of volunteerism is something unique to American society. But I suppose when you reach a stage in life when all your material needs are met, you might want to give something, I don't know.

You see, all of this, too, has much to do with the way the Vietnamese have been influenced by the French and especially the American military. This gave us a new taste for consumer goods. The differences between Vietnamese and Americans are real, but I would not underestimate the Vietnamese ability to accommodate very well to life here. They are survivors, you see.

FATHER DOMINIC LUONG
Philosophical Coexistence

He is a high-energy Roman Catholic priest, terribly overworked. His desk is cluttered with piles of papers and reports. Two Vietnamese nuns walk in and out of the room as we talk, picking up messages or taking orders. Later we drive around in his car in a very heavy rain, and he points out where his parishioners live, telling me in flawless English a little about each of their lives in the process.

The most important thing to remember about the Vietnamese personality is our ability to coexist under different and difficult situations without losing our identity. Buddhists can celebrate Christmas because they like the pageantry and the music; Christians can celebrate the Autumn Festival because they like the community spirit and the children's activities. We Vietnamese always feared foreigners, and I think we were able to swallow—but not digest—many cultural things that were not our own. There is quite a lot of American society we will not swallow, nor accept.

There are a few diehard conservative Vietnamese who would say that Catholicism can be seen as only a product of the French colonialist legacy. I disagree with this argument because the Vietnamese who took and still take to Catholicism embrace the best of it and accept it in a Vietnamese fashion. Above anything else, the Vietnamese adopted the educational system the missionaries offered them. This is a Western system of learning that went even further than Confucian thought in terms of accomplishment and achievement. The Catholic Church offered the Vietnamese a door through education to a larger world community, and that was very important.

Does a Buddhist-Christian conflict exist in the refugee community?

Do you mean to ask if the Buddhists and Christians have antagonisms toward each other? Yes. To answer this you must go back in history. Let's just stay in recent history. You have to understand the 1954 period, when over one million people from the north of Vietnam came to the south after the separation of the country. During that time, many Buddhists were helped by Catholics in leaving. So there was this coexistence of Buddhist and Catholic community life and the beginning of some real dialogue. It really became a sort of unwritten agreement of getting along with each other. It was an accommodation. These are, of course, supposed to be both religious groups and ethical people.

Don't forget, Christians were a minority in Vietnam when in the early 1960s the Diems were in full power and pushed Catholic doctrine on the Buddhists. To be a good Vietnamese then was to be Catholic. This was wrong, but I believe the Buddhists were able to separate the political aspirations of the Diems from the activities of the Church. Most Buddhists understood the politics of it, but I would say it was a bad period of great pain for the Church. If you were Buddhist, you were officially seen as a second-class citizen. And remember that Buddhists were over ninety percent of the country.

Then, when we came here to the United States, the Catholic Church did a great deal to help resettle refugees. I believe the Buddhists saw that for the most part there was no preference given to you if you were Buddhist or Christian. At least not on the surface. It was a period of pain for everyone and no one hurt less or more because of their religious beliefs in a situation like that.

You see, another thing to keep in mind is that the Buddhists are also animists and believe very much in the importance of ancestors. They have no written code or doctrine, so most of their knowledge depends on oral description, interpretation, and storytelling to keep it alive. There is no reinforcement of ideas to keep it going. Catholicism, however, has this reinforcing mechanism for the Vietnamese here, especially in New Orleans which is a very Catholic city.

What is the Vietnamese concept of charity?

Something quite different from what the Americans believe in, I can assure you. I give sermons about global brotherhood, and the message is accepted but the application usually falls somewhat short. This idea of charity beyond the community is a foreign concept. It just doesn't happen unless the community is urged, usually forced, to do it, but it does happen. You just need to ask for it in the right way. I can give you lots of examples right here in this community.

We just raised $1,850 for earthquake victims in Nicaragua, and two years ago the church raised $13,000 to send to poor Malaysians because the boat people remember the kindness the Malaysians showed them. In the last five years, our church here had eleven nonmembers die and not have money for funeral costs; they always raised the money, no doubt about it. Last week a group of Vietnamese paid the utility bills for some poor black American families. Their color made no difference, they helped them. So the idea of giving to strangers will work, but it is on a case-by-case basis. The generosity is there, you just have to ask for it in the right way. That is my job. I could not see these things happening in Vietnam the way they happen here.

Another thing is that the Vietnamese have not forgotten the generosity and kindness of their sponsors when they first arrived. That made a big difference and impact on them. Buddhists and Catholics alike, they were forced to let strangers make decisions for them. It was a painful process. I was at home and saw the top military people being forced to give up their arms. I have seen the whole change take place in their lives. They had to depend on strangers for everything until they got their feet on the ground and got established.

What are the greatest needs of your parishioners?

Getting a good job, a good education for the children, buying the first house, first car, and just settling in.

What about their spiritual needs?

That's more complicated. The refugees coming here, most of them, rich or poor, were reduced to the same state before they left. They arrived without any of the trappings they might have possessed before being traumatized by the ordeal of getting out of the country and into a new country.

Catholic or Buddhist, they have to face the same moral crisis of displacement. This is something that penetrates every aspect of one's conscious and unconscious state. I have counseled those who feel that they are being punished for something they have done wrong in their life, others who blame the American military, and some who keep living in the past, who can only remember life on the streets of Saigon.

Then there are those who have a crisis of faith. They ask how is it that God could permit all of this suffering. They say that a real God could not let this happen. For most of these people, the pain of separation and the guilt of survival weigh heavily on their hearts. They are usually very strong individuals who reach a breaking point and stop functioning in their usual ways. They need a mending process to heal those wounds. This takes time, sometimes years, but I see these people come around. I see them return, but in that crisis period they make life very difficult for themselves and for others. It slows down their adjustment to this new country, so in the end they really hurt themselves, but most recover.

A different group are the boat people. Now, in many ways, these people lived through a hell—a series of horrible experiences that certainly separate them from the earlier refugees who were evacuated by the American military. I have heard heroic stories about how people braved the storms and in many cases reconfirmed their faith in the process. There have been many Buddhists who have told me about how Christian prayer helped them survive the sea journey. These were people who never knew about Christian prayer and they learned to pray, to hope for something that would let them live. This was a faith born new for many and renewed for others.

I have heard stories about boat people lost at sea, with no food or water, and being passed by ships that would not stop to help them, and all the while the only thing they could do was pray and feel a sense of inner strength. I can tell you too that many Buddhists here have become Christians because of this experience. All of this makes for a common spiritual survival experience that makes the person stronger and puts him in a special kind of survival category. These people are survivors.

Does the materialism of American society cause new conflicts for the Vietnamese here?

Yes. I see the way it manifests itself in conflicts between the generations. My CYO [Catholic Youth Organization] always brings this out in their free discussion. You see, I have this theory that the younger you are when you come here, the easier it is to adjust to the American society and the more difficult it will be to maintain good relationships with your parents.

The conflicts you refer to are a serious problem and they come from the young person's ability to ease himself into the new society and his parents' rigidity about changing traditional means of living. It is the parents' unwillingness or inability to bend a little. There is a quick generational clash and it is along lines of parental authority. "Like it was in Vietnam," they would say—well, that does not apply all the time. And this is not Vietnam, but for the parents it is all they have to base their authority on. Vietnam is and will be the norm. Their children see the material goods that others have and they want those things. They are somehow convinced that they need them to be accepted by their American friends. Most of the time this parent-and-child clash gets worked out, but I do hear of children who still have problems. Now, too, you have this drug problem.

Materialism in the United States is different from what was experienced in Vietnam. There is so much emphasis on the self here. That is what I notice. For the Vietnamese, he may be just as materialistic as the American, but he shares it with his family. I think if you keep all of your possessions only for yourself, they lose value.

SUZANNE PHAM
On Coming to Peace with Change

She is wearing a bright blue dress and has a very businesslike demeanor, probably a reflection of her employment at the Federal Reserve Bank in New York. We first met over ten years ago, but this is the first in-depth conversation we have had. We are in a mutual friend's twenty-first-floor office that provides a spectacular view of Wall Street.

Do you ever think about what your life would be if you had not left Vietnam?

Yes, I think about it. Not for very long, mind you. I try to block out the part that hurts. Well, I would be worse off, that's for sure, and my husband would be in a reeducation camp, where he was; and there would be no educational opportunities for my children. We would be having a terrible time, just a terrible time.

Any regrets?

I have no regrets.

What were your expectations of America?

It all happened too quickly, so I had no expectations, none! My family took to a fishing boat the afternoon of April thirtieth, we got out to the high seas, and an American ship picked us up. We didn't plan our escape—it just happened. I didn't have time to think about anything, certainly not expectations. There were hundreds of other fishing boats there, too. We were not part of the privileged class that got helicoptered out, we waded out. I think it's better to come here without expectations, then there are fewer disappointments.

Did you sacrifice anything coming here?

At first, I was very disappointed and I had very mixed emotions. So yes, I felt I had sacrificed part of who I was. But all of this is in a cloud for me. This is the question I kept asking myself some years ago: Is it a dream or reality—dream or reality? It's a tough experience. I'd go through a day asking myself at the same time, Today, am I in Vietnam or am I in America? Where am I?

I dealt with a great deal of anger at first. But I came to accept it. I came to peace with the change. There is a finality here on this subject. You know, after fourteen years you learn to come to peace with change, peace with the idea that you are uprooted. Not all refugees are able to do this. I don't know why it happened to me. It was fast. I came to peace with my new environment. I accepted it faster than my brother who still agonizes over the loss, the change. The bottom line is that all of us have been able to function, to get a job, work here and live.

Talk a bit about some cultural differences you see between life in Vietnam and America.

Oh, that's a tall order. Well, I think that first you must understand the notion

of the standard Vietnamese family. You have input here from three generations. This is a pretty established structure. Most of the time you are unable
to make decisions on your own—that's the negative. You've always got to stop
and consult with a family team. It's very tiring. On the positive side, it gives
you a tremendous amount of support and comfort. You are never alone. Remember, the decision that is made is a family decision. It's a collective one,
not your own.

I was used to it. Then I got here and discovered that not only does this system not apply, it doesn't exist here. I had mixed feelings, it was tough at first.
It was freedom, but it was a terrifying amount of responsibility. So I made
an accommodation. Sure there were a lot of differences to deal with, but I
learned by making a few bad mistakes. I spent a lot of time feeling around
to find my way. I was really lost here at first. We've been trained to seek advice
and direction, now I just had to *do* it. Anyway, they were my decisions to
make.

Let me give you an example. In Vietnam my daughter enters university and
tells me she wants to study art and not medicine. I panic. I'd go right to my
older brother, father, or uncle for advice and support. I would know the best
way to solve the problem, but you are conditioned to ask for help. So they
would give me the three options: one, cut off all money to her; two, refuse
to pay the tuition; three, let her have her way, in the hope she will change
her mind. In the end, I would have to settle with the opinion of the group.

I have an amusing story about a cultural difference. Cecilia, my daughter,
was quite young—she was five years old when she came here—she had lost
a tooth. She wanted to put it under her pillow. I thought, well, she wants to
still hold on to it. The next morning as I woke her, her first reaction was to
reach under her pillow. She looked at me and said, "It's still here!" I said, "Of
course it is, where did you expect it to be? That's where you left it." Weeks
and weeks later I learned about the Tooth Fairy. But it was that look in her
eyes, that look of disappointment that I see vividly till now. So I learned about
the Tooth Fairy, who does not exist in Vietnamese culture.

Do you still think in Vietnamese?

Oh, yes. I still think and talk in both languages, like broken chains. For me,
language will always be a problem. If I forget a word in English, I just say
it in Vietnamese.

English is part of the reason I made a career change in 1983—from social work to computers. You need a very good command of the English language in the business world. I'm not good at word politics in the office. I would never excel. I am completing my thesis in computer science now. I prefer to move up the career ladder by the technical path.

Do you see any cultural differences in the workplace?

I see it as people versus positions. By that, I mean in Vietnam it seems there is more concern for the person, the individual. In the United States, it seems you just fill a position, a slot. It's very impersonal here, very cold. Perhaps this is because the competition is so high, you get suspicious of your co-worker. In Vietnam the work environment was much more relaxed. You were able to make friends and there were very few job layoffs. Here, job layoffs, job security or insecurity seem to be the central concern. But in Vietnam you get caught up in sexism; that seems to be less prevalent here, but then there were very, very few women managers there.

Were any women liberated in Vietnam?

Oh, women's liberation. None that I knew—that is, in terms of the work-place. But remember, because of the war, a lot of women entered the work force out of need. They were drawn and pushed toward it. I would say we were a good thirty years behind the women's movement in this country. So we got a little promotion in family life—only because we earned money, worked hard, and learned to make a few decisions on our own.

I would say I feel more equal to a man in the United States, at home and work, than I did in Vietnam. I feel more important than I would in Vietnam. Don't forget this is a culture. Women are trained to think and respond in a certain way, but that is all different for me now.

What was your first great cultural shock?

It was with my sponsor, with whom I stayed for six months when I first arrived. It was the first time when I heard the young daughter of the sponsor shout back at her. When I heard this, I was in total disbelief. You see, obedience is taught to be a virtue in our culture. Well, I thought this was a terrible, horrible thing. But believe it or not, a few years later my oldest daughter shouted at me in the same way.

What did you do?

I was prepared. I'd learned enough. I was silent, controlled myself, and turned away from her.

Do you hear from friends or family still in Vietnam?

Yes, I have since I arrived here. I have fourteen years of letters. The change is evident, and in general life has improved since the end of the war. But it is hard to communicate what you mean or feel through letters. It is both a comfort and a personal pain to hold and read those letters, really. You read the words and between the lines. Their lives are very different from yours and you can't do a thing about it. It brings up the guilt, that they are still there and you are here.

Would you return to Vietnam?

I would go back only for a visit. But only if there were a diplomatic relationship between the United States and Vietnam.

SAMPHY IEP
Dreaming in My Own Language

This is our third interview in ten years. He works for the International Rescue Committee, a refugee resettlement agency in Washington, D.C., and even though he has a waiting room full of clients, he promptly takes me into a quiet office and closes the door. He is wearing the same outfit each time we have met—a fresh white short-sleeved shirt, dark green pants, and Hush Puppies. His shirt pocket is filled with pens. He appears more animated this time. We laugh a lot throughout our talk (in English). He often leans toward me as if in confidence when he wants to make a point. I start by asking him about his clients outside, waiting.

No problem. They have learned to wait. They are refugees. It is an acquired trait. Some of these people just keep coming back for every little problem.

I already checked, there is no emergency case out there to deal with, not yet. So we can talk.

Do you work with all nationalities?

Only the Indochinese. I don't work with the Poles or the Hungarians; someone else does.

Do the other non-Indochinese refugees ever ask you questions about yourself—your being a refugee?

No, not really. But they certainly know that I am a refugee. *[He laughs.]* We all understand these things, it's like an unwritten code. I suppose you could say it's something in our eyes or the way we look at each other, or maybe the way we move. It is the unwritten language.

Are they curious about your own life and experiences?

No. Look, we all escaped something—something we would like to forget. We all have a part of us that is torn away, something special, precious, that is gone. To be stateless and away from your people, your language and culture—that is a very difficult thing to live with. We do not raise those issues among ourselves. We want to come to peace with this.

   Are you asking me if they are just curious because I am Cambodian? Well, they do not care about that either. They have no time for that. I could not tell you any difference between a Hungarian or a German refugee. To me they look the same, really. So we don't ask any questions. But I am almost certain they could not tell the difference between a Cambodian and a Vietnamese.

Can Americans tell the difference between a Cambodian or Vietnamese?

Very, very few Amerians I know, maybe one or two. But listen, neither can a Vietnamese, Cambodian, or Laotian, really. I would say that eighty percent of the Indochinese refugees could not tell these groups apart if they saw these people on the street. Don't think Americans are not caring or concerned—they are just not exposed. Some say this is racist, but I do not believe it. We [Indochinese] are no different. But I must say my neighbors still confuse me with being Korean!

I suppose a lot has to do with our respect for Buddhism. We are a very tolerant people. You could say passive. But to say passive is not a positive trait, is it?

Americans are very different in the way they talk to each other, the way they communicate even among friends. In general, Cambodians are very quiet people. For example, if I had a Cambodian secretary and an American secretary, you would hear the American secretary enter this room if your back were to the door. You would not hear the Cambodian. It is movement like a cat—very quiet.

Americans like to argue, even among friends. It's this argumentative, confrontational style that seems to be the way they like to do things. I am sure it is acquired culturally. I don't think people are born like that.

When an American has a big argument and screams at another person, this is always difficult for me. You know, I have seen two people like this able to shake hands and talk friendly the very next day. They make up and are smiling. This is not possible in Cambodian culture. If we had such a blowup we would avoid that person for such a long time, perhaps for life! We would not look that person in the eyes again in the same way. Why, even our next generation might hold a grudge on behalf of our name—out of respect for us. [He laughs.] Cambodians will avoid any hurtful situation if at all possible. They will look the other way, turn their back, maybe even walk away.

How did this behavior you are describing affect their resettlement—their living in the United States?

There are misunderstandings because you are scared or too polite to say yes or no. Confusion. You see, the Vietnamese are more aggressive than we Cambodians—and the Lao are like us. Whenever the Americans talk about Indochinese, they usually mean Vietnamese. A lot is our temperament and personality; how do you change that? Americans, the Cambodians say, will finish your sentence for you. I tell them, well, don't let them, it might be the wrong thing you wish to express. Language is the difficult thing. Imagine, I taught French and English for eleven years in Cambodia before I came here. I would guess I got maybe forty percent of what people were saying to me in my first two years here. Americans swallow their words. We learned British English. Imagine coming here, and you supposedly know the language but are not able to comprehend but less than half of what you hear? It hurts.

What were your expectations when you arrived?

I had very few expectations, really. I was glad to be here. I had no ESL [English as a Second Language], no cultural orientation sessions before I arrived. My wife (we have no children) could not speak one word of English. We landed here cold.

My expectations were to get a job, to be secure financially, and most of all to forget the terrible things that happened to Cambodia. I found all I wanted. I achieved it. It could not be better. Well, perhaps; but I am happy, really. We have our own home. I am proud of my life.

For those new arrivals it is different. I see it every day. Something happened to them. Their relatives arrived here ten years ago and started sending them money. They got the idea that money was easy to come by. You know, when you sit in those camps, you begin to build survival dreams. When people get here, the dream crashes and they walk through that door. *[He points.]* I tell them to get a job, make money, learn English—then and only then, worry about school. They all want to go to school.

Do you still see yourself as a refugee?

Oh, that's a very difficult question. Give me a minute. Well, yes, I do. I am a United States citizen now, but psychologically I still feel homeless. I dream in Khmer and talk in English. That's the conflict. It won't go away. That is my difference between East and West. I dream of the Khmer Rouge, killings and murder. I talk in a different language—English—about life in the suburbs of Washington, D.C. It is quite a contrast, isn't it?

CAMBODIAN DANCER

No one understands in America
the stories my grandmother told me
    when I was very, very young.
Nobody cares about the spirits of soil and water
or even the Khmer Laos, sacred dances.

The king of Angkor, Preah Kit Mealea, sees me dance
between the pain of my world and the pleasure
     of the spiritual world.
I am white, very white. I am invisible. Now I am serene.
See me dance and hear the spirits as they call.
Feel the tranquillity inside the community life we call
     neighborhood, they call ghetto.

Now the feast of salutation to the moon.
The music and songs continue. Can you hear them?
I dance all night. I dance all night for you.
We play Chhoung and I dance and dance.

No one understands these things in my new land.
No one cares about the light.
Only the darkness.

Cambodian girl, age seventeen, Philadelphia

CHAPTER 2

Photo: Larry Burrows/Life Magazine/©Time Warner Inc.

AMERICAN
INVOLVEMENT

The United States presence in Vietnam is a complicated and convoluted story that began largely with American involvement in the Pacific region, particularly China and the East Indies, after World War II. In a real sense the history of American intervention in Vietnam is a history of the way American foreign policy shifted from viewing that small country as a means to another end. A secure Vietnam was thought to mean a secure Southeast Asia and foreign policymakers continued to support a domino theory that would thwart Communist expansion.

In an effort to ensure the need for American presence, South Vietnamese friendship and support were needed. Several problems have been reported by those interviewed. "Rarely was the term 'partnership' used in a meaningful sense when talking about South Vietnam as an ally, the very people the Americans were fighting the war to protect," said Cam Ba Dong, an ethnic

---

◁FACING PAGE
Americans operating H-21 helicopters transport
South Vietnamese troops for a surprise
attack against the Viet Cong.

Chinese from Vietnam. "We were never thought of as being equal to the Americans. We were never partners."

The U.S. decision to play a more active role in Southeast Asian "pacification" did not flow directly from American interests in the region. America's concern above all else was the political stabilization of Southeast Asia and its integration into a more systematically perceived world order, which all too often ran counter to dominant historical forces in the area, such as nationalism and, especially, pan-Asianism. These movements grew out of hostility toward the French colonialist presence, and with the nationalists' fall to Ho Chi Minh's forces in 1945, the United States entered that picture, alone.

By 1964, President Johnson's orders were to begin air attacks upon North Vietnam and in early 1965 he ordered American ground forces to enter the war. U.S. military operations grew and by 1968 one-half million soldiers were in South Vietnam, at a cost of $30 billion a year. Little more than two years after the Paris accords, the army of South Vietnam and the government that the United States had supported since 1954 collapsed, and with it any hope of achieving the military and political objectives.

Many of those interviewed said that the defeat of America's ally came with an unexpected suddenness. As the full impact of the disintegration of Saigon's army and final pullout took place, war-tragedy stories began to grow, such as the numerous South Vietnamese collaborators who were promised safety in the United States but were mistakenly left behind. "All hell came out when it was sure South Vietnam was lost. Then our American friends ran. They ran. The ship was going down fast. They fled because they knew they would lose, too," said Le Xuan Duc, a survivor of a "reeducation camp."

These events occurred almost a generation ago, but the post–Vietnam War impact on all of us is very much with us today. What happened? What occurred during the war was an inability of the White House to sell its war policy. There were too many unanswered questions, too many missing pieces. "Americans were asked to understand the Southeast Asian struggle when in theory and practice the American military never understood it," concluded Le Xuan Duc. "You never understood what exactly you were trying to accomplish and, quite frankly—of course, this is all in retrospect—neither did we."

A former high-ranking military official in the South Vietnamese army said, "You Americans came to Vietnam and waged your own war, in your own way as a kind of continuation of the Korean War, which you called a 'conflict.' You helped us without ever understanding or trying to understand what we were all about. You made us into images of capitalist-loving 'gooks,' but we were still gooks to you; we were foreign and you were unprepared to understand what we were about. Wasn't this really another 'white man's burden'? It was like a low-paying factory job for your working-class soldiers: they came and they punched their time cards, stayed the minimum number of hours required, and then they left. Now certainly there were exceptions to what I am saying—I knew of some very heroic soldiers—but they were just that, exceptions that I could count on my hand. And once you got trapped in all of the different objectives, you lost your way and told us we lost your war. How convenient! We lost your war!"

Cambodia and Laos soon followed. The sacrifices asked of the Cambodians without consultation are still fresh in the minds of many refugees. A Cambodian refugee living in New York, Dr. G. Chan, said, "We thought we were able to avoid your war, your destruction of Vietnam, but then the table turned and you came into our country and destroyed all that was once peaceful. Until we are all dead, we will never understand or forgive Kissinger for this."

One of the most important and least measurable effects of the war was the changes it forced in the attitudes of the American people toward themselves and their place in the world. Vietnam's fall still has a profound impact on the way Americans see themselves. This time there would be no ticker tape parades, no glory. This was a guilt-ridden defeat, and there were dark moments in the aftermath of the war as the nation experienced a kind of collective amnesia, with resentment and disillusionment burning below the surface. Some of those feelings are still very much felt by American Vietnam veterans and their allies, now resettled in the United States. In the end, 60,000 Americans had died, in addition to an estimated 1 million Vietnamese, 100,000 Cambodians, and 75,000 Laotians. The following interviews explore what the American military presence meant to Southeast Asians who fought with them during the war.

NGUYEN VAN MO
Army as a Career

We begin our talk in French and then turn to English. I gather he has a good sense of history, and he seems well read. He is probably sixty years old and sits very erect. He is the picture of a career officer sitting very straight in his chair, chain-smoking. His responses to my questions are immediate, as if he were still giving a military briefing. Between puffs on his cigarettes, he keeps looking at some object fixed over my shoulders. I am not able to penetrate beyond his military experiences.

Before the Americans were in Vietnam, there were the French. I was only ten years old when the war with them broke out. Inside my city, My Tho, there were the French soldiers and outside there were the Vietminh guerrillas. My village was totally controlled by the Vietminh.

When we moved to Saigon, I went to school until I joined the army in 1962. The army was my career, my life. I didn't know anything but the army. This may be hard for you to understand, but there is little else you can do in Vietnam to reach the status that I did but through the army. There was no such thing as job mobility. No one went anywhere. You stayed with your job for life, and if you were a military man, that was your job for life.

Vietnam was a corrupt system that provided no opportunities for improvement. For me, the only way was the army. It took men like me from the countryside and the city and gave us pride in who we were and the things we could accomplish. We all knew there were potentially bad things in the system, but I was not at a level where I could see the corruption or experience cheating—anything like that, at least not at first. The soldiers worked very hard, I can tell you that much, and there was a good spirit among us. This changed later on, toward the end of the war, but in the beginning we shared a kind of camaraderie that was filled with national spirit and pride in our army and our people.

Describe your interaction with the Americans.

After 1966 they were everywhere, the Americans. No decision was reached without consultation with them. That was just the way it was. At first, we did not find this so offensive, but then, especially after [the] Tet [offensive] in 1968, the demands for our accountability grew and grew. Simple joint maneuvers became political games to argue and fight over, and argue and fight over some more. We called them partners and friends but they really were not. After a time, we didn't call them partners anymore. They were our chiefs and there could be no mistake about that, no mistake at all.

After 1954, the Vietminh called the Americans My Diem, which meant

"American Diem," then they called their supporters My Ngu, or "American puppet." These were Thieu and the generals who were supposed to be puppets with their strings pulled by the Americans. Much of this noise about our Vietnamese army being a puppet was sheer nonsense. We were good soldiers but we were continually living in the shadows of the Americans. As the political and social system began to deteriorate, it seemed the army would go, too.

By 1973, we were quite demoralized and depressed. There was little we could do to improve our image or our spirit. We were slowly changing into a group of defeated soldiers. I can remember this well. How else could we feel? We were like rats on the ship that is going down because it is on fire— everything was on fire.

Most of the American soldiers grew up in Vietnam, and they soon learned guerrilla warfare, dirty warfare, there. They had images of Korea or World War II, too many war memories and movies. It was not that way at all. The war was beyond what I can describe to you. First, this was my land, my people, my future. Why should we expect the American soldiers to care for these things? Why would you care, really? Okay, there was a fight for democracy and freedom, but these are abstract concepts that have little meaning to most of us. One can only take seriously what one can comprehend, and Americans could not comprehend Vietnam. They did not know the history, the people, they never spoke our language. At least, I never saw it. So, of course, all of it was headed toward disaster; how could it do anything else?

Are you angry when you think about the war?

Angry? Of course I am angry. I am angry as hell. We lost. We were defeated miserably. We were defeated on our soil and there can be no honest answer to your question but yes, I am very angry.

Can you stop being a career soldier?

I cannot speak for others, but for myself, I cannot. I simply cannot. One is a soldier for life; they cannot take that away from me. I have no real job or purpose here in America.

GENERAL VANG MO
Past and Future

He is a very large man with jet-black hair, probably fifty years old. His very expressive, watery eyes would flash every so often. He speaks in Lao.

I am not bitter about the war, all of that is over with. But to say that I can start again fresh is simply not true. I never knew how strange our relationship was—I mean between Laos and the United States—until I came here to live. Strange in the sense that few people knew or cared about Laos, even as it related to the war effort and all of those events. This was the hardest thing for me to get over. I mean to say that so many of our people died fighting with the CIA and the American military and then later suffered terribly at the hands of the Communists. I want someone to remember it, that is all. Perhaps I am one of those life-career military men you can do nothing with now, but I don't want my people to turn into dust and blow with the wind. These were very brave soldiers that fought and died for the American and Laotian causes.

Sure, it was a collaborative war effort between the U.S. and Laos. But the war seemed so much more different then. It was real. Now it is not real, but you still live it in your mind. Every year I am here it becomes more distant, a little less real.

Would you return if you could?

Certainly. Without a doubt. You know there are some political elements here in the U.S. who fought the secret war in the mountains who want very much to return. There is a lot of talk about it, but I doubt that it will happen, really I do. Laos is not an island over there. Do you think this government would change without affecting all of the other countries like Vietnam and Cambodia and China? No, no, no. Sure, you think a great deal of returning and making your country safe for your children. To purge and eradicate Laos of the Communists forever. For some, this is now their only ambition, and I am surprised as the years go on they are still dedicated to this idea.

You see, for my people, their land is sacred. Our ancestors are buried on that land and they are part of our life. To disturb this is very dangerous, it threatens our lives and the future of new generations; that is why they want so hard to get back. I understand this passion, I understand what they want to do. For us it was more than a military event, an engagement, a conflict, a war—whatever you want to call it. It was our present and our future. That is something very precious. But that is a different question—and you can see how my answer is not probably what you are looking for, is it?

Tell me about your family.

I had two wives in Laos and had to decide which one to bring here officially as my wife. That was more of a problem for the U.S. officials than it was for me. A lot of men have more than one wife. There is a long history to this, but that is history. The other wife now lives in San Diego. I had no children by her. I have five with the wife I kept.

You must understand that there are big differences in husband-wife relationships in Laos. The wife in Laos isn't really aware of your career. She takes care of the house and the children, that is all. That is her role in life. There were long periods of time during the late 1960s that I was never in Vientiane. I was away and my wife knew nothing about my life. So there is little she can talk about with me. She was never a part of my work life then so she has little she can talk about with me now. I don't know if it would make a difference if I could share these things with her; my life would still be the same.

Have you completed the transition from Laos to the United States?

No, not really. What do you Americans say, that you cannot teach an old dog new tricks, is that it? Well, I am an old dog and after twelve years in America, I have not learned so many new tricks—I mean, of course, skills or even ideas that I could say are new. Military men are very hard to work with, very hard.

ABOUT VIETNAM

You promised us that your support for Vietnam
would make us free to become more like you.
We believed you when you talked about dominoes and power.

You divided Asia and the world according to a map
that had different boundaries.
We had to believe you, and if we didn't
your CIA killed our leaders.
This was all for our own good, you kept telling us,
But you never asked us what we were living through
with the French only some years before.
Behind the compromises and handshakes
you felt we were less than you.
Genetics? The food we ate? Why?
How could you think you were better?
You told your people that our value of life was less
than your life, so that when our people died we mourned
less or somehow felt less grief than you did?
Do you believe this to be true? These are lies.
Our tears were like your tears.
We have no memorial in the world
for our sons and daughters, mothers and children who died.
We have no memorial wall to touch
and to be silent with or to just know it is there
for our memories and our children's memories.
Your promises will not return—
yours and ours—we must go on.

Former Vietnam army captain, San Diego
[translated from Vietnamese]

GENERALS HOANG DUC NAM and TRAN VAN TAT
Starting New

*These are two former high-ranking South Vietnam generals who are
idling away their time. You get the distinct impression they miss being
dressed in military clothes. They look more often at each other than at
me, frequently asking each other questions in Vietnamese, and speaking*

to me in English and Vietnamese. They look a little bored and continu-
ally smoke cigarettes.

Hoang Duc Nam: I was the son of a military career man who, I might now
say without any disrespect, blindly followed the French, blindly. But I suppose one day my son will write about how I blindly followed the Americans,
won't he? To be honest, all of this must be weighed against the circumstances
and events of that time period. It's too easy just to say this is a success or
that is a failure because of only one person or event—especially with the
war. There were too many complex factors that were related—and so there
you are!

I came here because my whole life depended upon the Americans. They
were always in my mind. There was no question that they would always
be with South Vietnam. So, when the Communists took over, we knew the
Americans would get us out.

I came in 1975 and moved with my family to Arlington where I knew
some people in the city. They never really helped us. Out of Vietnam, they
had no power, no influence. I sell life insurance now.

What do you remember most about the Americans?

That we were always trying to figure them out. If there was one question
we asked over and over during the war, it was 'What are the Americans up
to now?' It was a question that shows the insecurity we lived with. The response would always be 'Who really knows?' If you ask me, there are many
books to be written about American and Vietnamese misunderstandings during the war. The U.S. talked of partnership, but it was not true; it was always
a one-sided avenue that we traveled on.

I knew the end was near when the 1973 peace talks began and especially
with the lack of U.S. military aid then. I remember, South Vietnam needed
$1.6 billion in military aid in 1974. The U.S. Congress gave us $700 million
and even then your Defense Department took some of that money away from
the next year. Also, your Arab gas crisis ate up all of the resources. Then
there was Watergate and President Nixon resigned. You know, the Vietnamese will never understand Watergate. What was that all about, anyway?

I never believed in Vietnamization or thought it could work. It was tried
in some ways by the French and that was a failure. Look at the Fifth Division.
When the American divisions pulled out, only one Vietnamese division was

left to cover everything. Impossible! No wonder General Minh Van Hieu could not hold out. He should not be blamed.

Tran Van Tat: I will comment on that. It was in 1966 that this Vietnamization plan was first discussed. There was little understanding—no, there was no understanding of the Vietnamese military and its philosophy toward training. American forces wanted to train the Vietnamese army in the image of American forces and that was that, no question.

Up until the end, I was convinced that the Americans would be there. Things were bad but they improved. In April 1973, when President Thieu met President Nixon in California and Nixon promised support if Hanoi violated the cease-fire—that was important. We believed Nixon. Also, how could the great U.S. admit failure? You spent $200 billion in Vietnam, 60,000 men would be dead, over 200,000 wounded, and what—up to half a million men would eventually be in Vietnam at the highest point of U.S. military involvement. Those are really fantastic statistics. The failure was the South Vietnamese and American inability to understand each other's politics and policies.

After all, what did we know about the U.S.? You were rich. You came to Vietnam and showed us how even the common soldier could be rich, with your PXs, radios, and money. So you came with your military advisers and in some ways pushed your way into our society. All we knew about the U.S. was the Marshall Plan, the anti-Communist Dulles and President Kennedy. So we thought Vietnam was a logical extension of your time in Korea.

H.D.N.: There was all this talk about cutting costs and starting a Vietnamese people's army. But honestly, how could you insist on a volunteer army when you didn't understand the way Vietnamese people thought? You wanted us to believe our farmers could plant rice and shoot Communists they caught hiding in the paddies? Remember—Nguyen Cao Ky tried to attack some of this high cost by pointing out Thieu and his friends and their corruption to Nixon, but no one listened. So as the months went on, the morale of the soldiers went out the door. How could you blame them?

T.V.T.: I thought the end began with the loss of Phuoc Long's provincial hospital in early January 1975. Then, in early March, there was Ban Me Thuot. Desertions were very high. I remember the withdrawal from Pleiku—

all of the civilians fleeing everywhere, old men and children dead by the side of the road, killed trying to escape. Then the fall of First and Second Corps, but we still hoped for the U.S. to send the B-52s. We still hoped for that.

   H.D.N.: When the Americans began to pack, that was the mental collapse for the country. We knew the Seventh Fleet was out there. It was over . . .
   We always knew America held the real power in South Vietnam. There was never any question of what really was the relationship between the U.S. and South Vietnam. The destiny of our country always rested in foreign hands, that was our fate.

FROM A VIETNAMESE GENERAL

You know that in the late 1960s the Republic of Vietnam
and the U.S. military struck a big blow
against the Communists.
My question is, why didn't the U.S. government take the
opportunity of the situation to end the war?
It would have been logical. The Viet Cong suffered a big defeat
after the Tet in 1968.
Many of their best divisions were sent to the other fronts
for reinforcements. Then there were the air attacks
every day by the U.S. in Communist territories.
This was very damaging to North Vietnamese morale.
We knew of those who escaped to the south
from the north at that time; and they assured us that if the
raids had lasted for some time and if the U.S. sent maybe
six more divisions to start a landing operation on North Vietnam
like they did at Inchon in Korea,
the outcome of the war would have been different.
We could have won. In 1970 it all tore apart.
Remember at the beginning of 1970, to everyone's
shock, Kissinger flew to Tashkent to pay a visit
to Mao, and the U.S. started its new plan.

In 1973 when the Paris Convention ended,
the nationalist Vietnam could see that the U.S.
had already completed its pullout.
It was finished.
Then the Paris agreement with the death sentence
for the Second Republic of Vietnam,
and Le Duc Tho and Kissinger
were given the Nobel Peace Prize.
This peace with honor was complete.
And here we are today.

Former South Vietnamese army general, Los Angeles
[translated from Vietnamese]

CAM BA DONG
Comparing the French and Americans

He is dressed in a crisp white shirt, red tie, and blue sports jacket. Speaking English and French, we sit on a park bench, facing each other.

My family came from Hanoi to Saigon in 1954. Then we were refugees once more in 1978 when we left Saigon by boat for the United States.

I worked for a large French importing company in Hanoi. I have been to France twice, and in many ways I believe the French gave me an education and a profession that I would not have had any other way; but they manipulated all of us and, in their own colonialist way, obtained what they wanted from the Vietnamese until they were expelled. I suppose you could say mine was a love-hate relationship with the French. I remember those days like they were yesterday. Some events in your life you never forget.

When the eight-year battle of the first Indochina war began, the Lao and the Cambodians, both under royal leadership, were able to negotiate their independence, but Viet Minh rebel groups lived in Cambodia [Khmer Rouge] and in Laos [Pathet Lao]. With the Viet Minh victory at Dienbienphu, the French withdrawal was inevitable. Now this was a time of real shock for us.

If we could not stay, then we lost everything, but if we stayed, we lost everything. For someone who worked for so long with the French and now to see them go, well, this was something quite different. We would have Ho [Chi Minh] in the north and Diem [Ngo Dinh] in the south. It was not so long after the cease-fire that the North Vietnamese from our area [who are mostly Catholic] left for the south. My wife and three children were part of this move. In 1956, because we were ethnic Chinese, the government forced us to become citizens. We never really wanted to be citizens. These first two years in South Vietnam were the most difficult ones for me.

What do you remember about the French?

I had a restaurant in Hanoi and a food business. My father began it and I lost all of it. We left the north with two suitcases and in a cloud of shock. You see, over one million people went south on those roads that could never hold that many people. We had no time to plan, although we knew what would happen if we stayed. I had some French connections through my business in Saigon. I contacted them when I arrived, but they were no help to me—they had lost all their business and were not in a position to help anybody. So we started life over. To lose it in 1975 again was too much to accept, but I did.

You understand how strong you can become but you learn to trust no one, and it makes you bitter. I am angry at the French for reasons I still do not understand. To me, the French promised us a way of life and a protection of that way of life, and they failed. They were no longer around to make us part of their life. In some ways, they were like the Americans, but the French gave me much more than the Americans.

Influenced by the French? Yes, Vietnam was very much influenced by the French from 1865 until 1945—almost eighty years of influence, control, and domination. The French kept the four-class system improved by the Chinese, and the French also made education for some more difficult to attain, and they very much restricted us to a kind of slave mentality among the Vietnamese people and to serve the French colonial economic interests. The education that was available usually depended upon the political situation of the time. So all those years of French domination created a society with but a handful of educated elites. The majority of people working in low-ranking public clerical jobs were employed to keep the colonial administrative machinery functioning. We were very much hindered in terms of education and knowledge.

SAM SON
Cambodian Secret Bombing

He is a very soft-spoken man. I try to move closer to hear his responses. His eyes never meet mine. He plays with two small coins in his hand and it appears to be difficult for him to answer my questions. There are very long pauses—reflection, maybe—before he answers my questions. He speaks in English and French.

I remember those not-so-secret bombings that destroyed my country. Really, none of that was a secret. I went to bed and I felt my bed make motions because of the bombs. My bed shook! We heard about the bombings on the radio and in the coffeehouses. It was all that we talked about. Always we talked about what would the Vietnamese do, what would the Americans do? Then it was what would the Russians do and the Chinese do? It was all speculation, but in the meantime, my bed shook.

Everything I have read or heard in this country about my people is that we are gentle and good people. If this is true, then why did the Americans and Vietnamese destroy our country? We are a people who must wander the earth. It's sad, isn't it?

If you go back to the history of my country, to the 1970s, it is a history of civil war, revolution, and invasion. We had a great leader who tried to keep us out of the war, but, you see, Sihanouk was too honest, too much of a gentleman. He was a careful strategist who found himself host to a Communist operation in the remote parts of the country. What could he really do? For him it was an eye behind his back; he saw but he did not see what was happening. Perhaps it was naive to think it would just go away. The Americans would not look the other way and that was the conflict and the end of it. We all knew Kompong Som let the Vietnamese land and then be taken to sanctuaries. So where was the surprise? There was none.

It was the sanctuaries that the Americans wanted, and it was with Nixon that the military got what it wanted, this being the opportunity to use air and ground attacks on the sanctuaries. This was the target area called Central Office for South Vietnam, the initials were COSVN. And they said it was only nine square miles, which was supposed to contain all of the enemy troops. So, on eighteen March 1969, Nixon took revenge against the Communist offensive in South Vietnam by showing Yankee strength and striking against us. I still remember the bombing; it was my bed that shook! From that day on, there were almost four thousand B-52 raids flown over this sanctuary area that grew larger all of the time. They kept this a secret from the U.S. Congress, they said, but the press knew it, we all knew it. You must imagine it was our country being blown apart.

From the first time the Americans came into contact with the Cambodians, they confused us with the Vietnamese—the politics and the culture of Vietnam. The Americans were clearly obsessed with Vietnam; all other people were to become Vietnamese. We were a different situation, a different war, and none of this counted in any way, none of it! It was all very John Wayne— bang-bang, shoot them up! That was it, John Wayne! So, it was the bombs that changed life for us. My beautiful Phnom Penh, my garden and my pagoda. And all of the time you called it a secret. It was not. It was a powerful evil force that changed our world. And I remember that it shook my bed.

NO TRUST

I remember working for the French Embassy
and reading Le Monde about the American, William Calley,
who killed all those people during 1968
in my village, the Son Tinh district
in Quangngai province. I remember hearing
what the French people said at the Embassy
and their reactions. Something about how the French
military would not have been so cruel, and
that My Lai could only be an American reaction
or something like that. I never knew what to think.
I never trusted either the French
or the Americans. Over 150 people
were shot by just this one soldier,
what about the others? Only this man is guilty?
If the GIs had had the opportunity, more people
would have been killed like that.
It made no difference if you were north or south,
they never learned the difference.

Vietnamese refugee, Baltimore
  [translated from French]

VIETNAMESE HISTORY

Vietnam. We are like a little fish afraid of the big fish,
China, to the north. So our ancestors for many reasons
moved south. Then we went—away from the land of our
father. We remember the Trung sisters and Li-bon
who led the peasants to victories
because they understood that making war against China
could not be done without support from the
people of the countryside.
Always China was too strong.
We have this foreign control as we build our country.
So we fought the French and the Americans
and our country has been built by a history
of invasions and wars against foreign invaders.
This history still continues.
Ho Chi Minh knew his people.
He was able to move this bureaucracy
and the urban elite to the countryside
prepared to resist. His people taught us to read
and opened our eyes. Then these teachers
returned to our cities. Now our French masters
lost control of our lives.
It was like at Dienbienphu. With Soviet
and Chinese weapons the Vietnamese
peasant soldiers were ready to face the Americans
and their idea of a social revolution in which free elections
would bring harmony.

Vietnamese refugee, New Orleans

LE XUAN DUC
American POWs

*He is about fifty years old, maybe older, and we talk in English. He is seated
on a bench behind his house in a neighborhood made up mostly of blacks*

and Hispanics. He appears to know most of his neighbors, waving to them.
He continues to fiddle with the buttons on his sweater as he talks. He holds
a tattered scrapbook of photos of himself and translates for me some of the
captions. We are looking at a photograph of a young boy he tells me is his
son—and from the tone of his voice, one can only assume the son is dead. I
am struck by how quickly he smiles and closes the scrapbook. "What do you
want to know?" he asks.

Some weeks after South Vietnam fell to the Communists, I was taken as "a subversive person" to a reeducation camp near Haiphong in the north. I was separated for years from my wife and children. I eventually escaped back to the south and left by boat for Malaysia. I arrived in the U.S. in 1979 with my wife and daughter; my youngest son had died of cancer in Saigon some months before.

What do you remember about the reeducation camps?

What I remember of the reeducation camp was how little food we had, the heat, and the Communist propaganda—always this Communist propaganda. But I remember most how we were starving! They were trying very hard to destroy our minds and our spirits. They didn't care if we died or if we lived. Many of us were city people, we had never worked in the country or on a farm, although this was not really a farm. They just gave us tools and sent us into the fields. It was ridiculous. Many people got very sick. There was no medicine and even the water became scarce.

I also remember the stories I heard from another man who had lived all of his life in the north. He had run into trouble with the government for some reason, I don't know what it was, but he was in the camp some months before me and when I escaped he was still there. This man said he had seen American soldiers in a camp some weeks before. He was sure that they were Americans and that they were in reasonable health, also that they spoke good Vietnamese. He described the prisoners and some of their stories, and said that there were other prisoners alive there.

There was so much concern a few years ago, well, even today, about American POWs and if they were alive and the politics of whether the U.S. government should try harder to get them out. All I can remember was this man's stories about the men he saw. So, maybe there are more of these people still alive? Maybe we will never know.

SANG SEUNSOM
Thanking America

His room is surrounded with American Western pictures. There is an Indian blanket spread across the couch. He talks a lot about his love for Texas and Americans. A constant flow of snapshots keeps coming across the coffee table through which he describes family and events—all current. A steady stream of children, his own and neighbors', keeps interrupting our conversation— something that appears not to bother him.

There is no way I blame the Americans for what happened in Laos. We brought it on ourselves. Maybe it was out of control but things just happened. It is not fair to compare it with Vietnam—that was a totally unique situation and a whole different set of circumstances. We chose a fifty-fifty coalition government and then we had to live with it. It is as simple as that. We tried to work with the Communists and it simply did not work. So we lost.

I have much respect for the United States. As the minister of education in Laos, I worked a lot with USAID [U.S. Aid for International Development] and UNESCO [United Nations Educational, Scientific and Cultural Organization] trying to bring schools and literacy to the country. We wrote, rewrote, and translated the literacy textbooks from French to Laotian. The Americans paid for everything and I tell you the absolute truth—the only thing they wanted was for the place of publication to be the Philippines and to make sure the USAID "handshake" logo went on the cover, that's all. You see, this logo was very important to them!

Well, I tried to explain to the Communists that this was the extent of my political involvement with the U.S., but they would not believe it. They wanted to purge all support for the "capitalist/imperialist sympathizers," but I remember clearly that the Americans never asked about the contents of the books and never read them. They just printed them in the Philippines with their logo upside down.

No, the Americans never did any harm to Laos and those who say so do not understand the events, that's all. You know we are an easygoing people and I don't think we could be much use to the Americans. Now, I am not speaking about the Hmong, only the lowland people.

In 1945 there was only one high school in Laos—in Vientiane, the capital. One for the entire country, and of the forty students that year, only five were

Laotian; the rest were Vietnamese. When I left, there were over twenty-five high schools and seven teacher-training colleges and there was a national education program. I think America needs to be thanked for that. I was one of nine in the Ministry of Education. I was the only one, with my wife and ten children, to escape. I know as a fact the other eight colleagues are still in reeducation camps. You know you cannot trust the Communists.

CHAPTER 3

Photo: R. Burrows/UNHCR

THE

EXODUS

The dramatic exodus from Southeast Asia seemed to have captured everyone's imagination in late April 1975. "It was the single most traumatic event of our lives," said Vietnamese doctor Le Rieu Tai. "No one will forget how he escaped." The drama of departure from that part of the world continues to this day, conjuring up scenes and names that have become familiar: boat people, sea pirates, Pilau Bidong, Pol Pot.

We in this country can recall images of the final moments of the American pullout from Vietnam: those blurry black-and-white pictures of the roof of the U.S. Embassy in Saigon, the ladder leading up to the helicopter, the closeness of the bodies pushing to get aboard; the marines guarding the front of the Embassy, people scaling the iron gates; tear gas being set off, shots being fired into the air, and people still trying to get into the compound. In other parts of the country, such as Danang and Quangngai, similar scenes were oc-

◁FACING PAGE
Having risked the sea piracy and violent weather
that have killed or injured an estimated 100,000 of those
escaping by water, Vietnamese "boat people" arrive
at the Galang Processing Centre in Indonesia.

curring. For everyone, the final moments of visible American presence were over in the early morning sunlight.

It was April 30, 7:23 A.M. Today there would be the shock, tomorrow a new government—maybe better, maybe not, but it would be a different government and there were those who were grateful for the change and for just not hearing bombs. For many, however, the time had come to leave. There was no more Republic of South Vietnam.

Although the flight from Southeast Asia is usually seen as having taken place with the dramatic exit of American ambassadors, closing of embassies, and evacuations of refugees loyal to the Americans in April and May 1975, the outflow of refugees still continues. "Slow drips of humanity seeking freedom—still seeking freedom," said one refugee interviewed in a camp in Thailand in 1982.

In April and May 1975 the United States admitted 128,000 refugees from South Vietnam, 5,000 from Cambodia, and 2,000 from Laos. These refugees were called the "first wave" out of Southeast Asia. They were transported to Guam, screened, interviewed, placed in four Stateside camps, and resettled around the country by nonprofit secular and religious agencies by the end of December. Over land and by sea a steady but small flow of about 1,500 refugees per month continued until the end of 1977. Since then, particular events in Vietnam, Cambodia, and Laos have sent forth new waves, continuing the exodus. By late 1989, Hong Kong reported 54,000 Vietnamese in camps seeking political asylum.

Vietnam

The evacuation of South Vietnam occurred suddenly, chaotically, and, as one refugee in Los Angeles described it, "without any notice. . . . Who could believe it would be over? I expected a plan. There was no evacuation policy for us. The entire corps of English translators was left behind. There was no excuse for it. We soon realized that the big ships were out there—U.S.S. *Blue Ridge, Peoria,* and *Vancouver.* Those who got out in 1975 were lucky to be in the right doorway with their bags in hand."

Immediately after the fall of the country, the Communists attempted to restructure the society. Vietnam was a poor, war-torn nation. Hundreds of thousands of people were relocated to remote reeducation camps around the country, according to no master plan or scheme. The new government reported that agricultural production would be increased by people who were not farmers, and many thousands from the south were sent north. Land and property were confiscated and all personal freedoms were curtailed. "No one knew what would happen. The Americans promised it would be a bloodbath, but something less than that happened. What would soon happen were reprisals against ethnic Chinese Vietnamese," said Nguyen T. Nguyen, a Vietnamese social worker. These were some of the conditions that made so many continue trying to escape.

The Vietnamese quickly responded to these events by leaving first by land and eventually by boat, with the exodus by boat being orchestrated by sea captains extracting gold as exit visas. The outpouring was quick: by 1979 an average of 20,000 people per month were fleeing the country for Hong Kong, Malaysia, Singapore, and Indonesia. An estimated 100,000 died in the rough waters of the South China Sea or were attacked, robbed, and raped by invading Thai pirates who had frequented those waters for centuries. "Nobody will ever be able to understand the hell we went through to get out of our country. Some things you are able to forget in life, but not this one," said Vietnamese American Quan Nguyen.

Many tried to enter Thailand by going through northern Vietnam and China. "First-asylum" countries like Thailand permitted refugees to stay only temporarily because they feared problems with their own people. Domestic unrest over the issue of refugees in places like Thailand, Malaysia, and Hong Kong would eventually manifest itself in policies of pushing back refugees across borders or shorelines and toughening criteria for defining a refugee. By the end of 1979, the flow had peaked at 60,000 Vietnamese per month fleeing the country. The United Nations estimated that between 30 to 50 percent of all boat people to date had drowned in the South China Sea. Some 167,000 ethnic Chinese Vietnamese had fled to China by the end of 1979. The flow began to lessen.

During 1980, approximately 72,000 refugees from Vietnam arrived in first-asylum countries, a marked decrease from the previous year. The United States admitted 300,000 of these refugees; from 1980 to the end of 1989 an additional 200,000 refugees would be admitted to the U.S. program. By the end of 1989, following a U.N. Geneva conference to address this continued outflow, Hong Kong, Thailand, and Malaysia firmly stated they had reached their limit of generosity.

Responding to the world outcry over drowning people, the Vietnamese government and the United Nations in late 1979 organized an "orderly departure" program which permitted people to leave the country in a systematic fashion, directly from Vietnam. Family reunification was the goal of the program; lists were submitted of those wishing to be reunited with family members outside Vietnam. Two lists were created, one by the Vietnamese government and one by the accepting governments, primarily the United States and France. What was needed was a match, an agreement, by both governments before the departure was guaranteed. The program came to a near halt in late 1985 with allegations of stalling and political maneuvering on the part of both Vietnamese and Americans, and it was reestablished in 1987. Critics of the program have charged that Vietnamese officials extorted large sums of money as exit fees. By 1985 some 85,000 people (ODP) departed from Vietnam for the United States and other resettlement countries.

Cambodia

Cambodia has always been linked with the events of Vietnam. The fall of Cambodia began with the Paris Peace Accords signed by the United States and Vietnam in January 1973. With North Vietnam and Laos temporarily in a state of cease-fire, the action then shifted to Cambodia. This placed Cambodia as the only arena open for American bombing and activity. Attempts by Cambodian leaders to maintain neutrality proved useless and Cambodia was dragged deeper into the war. "There was no way to avoid the disaster that was soon to happen. It was like some plague or horrible curse," said former supreme court judge Phat Mau.

In February 1973, American B-52s began bombing the countryside. With the escalation of the war following the peace accords, Phnom Penh soon became a city of refugees. "I never saw anything like it," said Pam Penam, now a graduate student in Washington, D.C. "One day the city began to grow, the streets always busy with people walking with all of their possessions, then a week later it was much worse. There were too many people and no place to go, and no food. We were all refugees in our own country."

As these events occurred, the Khmer Rouge began to conduct a systematic reign of terror throughout the country, a terror that eventually affected everyone. "What was happening was the slow disintegration of our society, and no one was to be excused," said Penam. Saloth Sar, a minor military figure, was to emerge as one of the world's most evil men, whose name, like Adolf Hitler's, became synonymous with heinous crimes and atrocities. He and the

Khmer Rouge, pressed by the invading Vietnamese army, would force hundreds of thousands across the Thai border, placing Thai officials in a struggle for their own national security.

The Khmer Rouge mounted a three-sided attack on Phnom Penh at the same time as the U.S. Congress demanded an end to the bombing. Route 1, the highway that connects Saigon to Phnom Penh, was attacked by the Khmer Rouge, and by April 1973 they were within mortar range of the capital. Phnom Penh was under siege for two years before it fell. It was a capital bursting apart. Utilities were stopped, refugees poured in, and foreigners poured out. Fierce fighting paralleled the total cutoff of U.S. funding when aerial attacks ceased in early August 1973. But it was not until April 12, 1975, that the U.S. Embassy, with little notice, closed and the American staff was evacuated. Saloth Sar had defeated Lon Nol, and it was then that he assumed his new name that would soon be recognized around the world—Pol Pot. He is still hiding out in the jungles of Northwest Cambodia today.

What Pol Pot attempted to do was to create the ultimate socialist revolution. He failed miserably and in the process took the lives of millions of his countrymen and, at the same time, forced additional hundreds of thousands to flee. His piecemeal Communist program for rapid change would avoid the "step" changes of traditional Marxist-Leninist doctrine; instead, the Chinese "Great Leap Forward" would be revolutionized Khmer-style and speeded up. No transition would be needed because the Khmer people would go directly to pure Communism, and to accomplish this, Pol Pot organized the starving youth and systematically cut off Cambodia from the world. There was a sinister silence as isolation became Cambodia's policy and the country a giant labor camp. There was no separation between the workplace and home, between the state and family, between family and neighbor. "The world forgot what Cambodia was," said Len Kath, a high school teacher in his native Cambodia. "It seemed to vanish from the minds of people and we became a lost people."

The Khmer Rouge captured Phnom Penh on April 17, 1975. During May and June an estimated 100,000 former government workers and sympathizers were systematically executed. With little food supply, the government began a mass evacuation plan of all cities and demanded that people become farmers. By January 1979 an estimated 3 million people had died of torture, malnutrition, and disease. The refugees who fled from Cambodia into Vietnam (150,000) and into Thailand (33,000) reported mass killings and extreme shortages of food.

After the Vietnamese invasion of Cambodia and the flight of Pol Pot to the interior in January 1979, more than 100,000 Cambodians fled into Thailand, fearing an invasion. The Thai military forced 42,000 Cambodians back across the border into Cambodia in June 1979. Others who crossed the border were kept out of the U.N. camps, although the Thai government provided them with food and supplies.

In September 1979, additional Cambodians began crossing into Thailand because of the famine. The situation in Cambodia had now reached crisis proportions. Under international pressure, the Thai government in late October 1979 altered its refugee policy and began accepting all Indochinese refugees for temporary asylum in Thailand. In late October, the International Red Cross began relief operations in Kompong Som and Phnom Penh. By February 1981, more than 141,000 tons of food and medicines and 28,000 tons of rice seed had been delivered to border points. From 1979 to 1989, an estimated one and a half million Cambodians had fled their country.

Laos

Like South Vietnam and Cambodia, Laos was excluded from the 1973 peace negotiations in Paris in 1973. In many ways this was seen as a repeat of a previous experience in which then prime minister Souvanna Phouma, like former king Savang Vatthana during the 1962 Geneva conference (which was supposed to end the military conflict escalating in Laos), was kept totally out of the picture.

The refugees interviewed describe a situation of being uninformed about changing political events. "The Western powers controlled us and kept us in the dark. What happened was exactly as could be expected. For most, this regional war was Vietnamese and Laos was just a little piece, a piece that could be done away with or ignored. Who cares about this tiny country, anyway?" said a former Laotian army colonel, Pem Ranan. "We were sacrificed." Of the three million Laotians in the country, it was the rural mountain Hmong population, however, who bore the brunt of the war. "We fought the war in Laos for the Americans. We died for your cause, your people. In looking back at the situation now, all I see are the dead and no victory, and I ask many questions. Questions I would have never asked before," continued Ranan.

There were continued rumors that described the fighting in Laos as a secret war run by the CIA, by soldiers fighting from isolated mountain bases. "The target was the Ho Chi Minh Trail and the losses were out of proportion to the population; over twenty percent of all soldiers died. In 1967 and 1968, the Hmong population was estimated at two hundred fifty thousand; of this, forty thousand soldiers were recruited by the American forces," reported former military man Colonel Vang Kran. While equipping the regular Laotian armed forces, the United States relied more heavily on the irregular units of Hmong which were trained and commanded by the CIA. Laos was a country devastated by bombs. "It rained bombs—night and day," said Ranan. By the time the air raids ended, American aircraft had dropped more than 2 million tons of bombs on Laos, a figure exceeding all the tonnage dropped during World War II. "They bombed until there was nothing more to kill—they killed all the animals and there was little to do but flee the destruction," said Ranan. On April 30, 1975, the U.S. ambassador was forced to evacuate. "Very few Laotians could leave then; and there was never an escape plan for the Laotians," added Ranan.

Laos was in a different situation from Cambodia and Vietnam after the war. It should be remembered that there had been an attempt to form a coalition government with the Communists, an attempt that fell apart in late April 1979 after the Communists successfully took over in Vietnam and Cambodia. Laos appeared near total collapse, with an estimated one-third of the population having been dislocated during the war. After their takeover, the Pathet Lao's allegiance to the North Vietnamese could easily be seen, a political relationship which remains in force today. Reprisals were swift: by the end of the year some 20,000 Laotian government officials had been sent from the capital to "reeducation camps." Organized and unorganized flight across the Mekong River into Thailand continued to increase, an exodus that still goes on. Thousands went to Thailand because of promises made by the American military "to take care of you and your family after the fall. This promise was beyond question. We all believed it and it was often repeated by our American counterparts, our American friends," said Ranan. "This, in spite of the efforts of the Thai government to call us illegal immigrants and to discourage us by such things as a 'humane deterrence' policy."

By early 1989, an estimated 400,000 Laotians had been permanently resettled by Western countries while some 10,000 were voluntarily repatriated back to Laos with U.N. assistance. From 1981 to 1989 an estimated 270,000 Laotians were admitted to the United States. Another 30,000 remain in camps in Thailand awaiting some resettlement opportunity.

A PRAYER FOR SAFE SHORE

The foam of the ocean surrounds everything.
We are lost in the open sea, looking for a
shoreline to call safety.

We float on the deep and dark ocean
like dust on a palm leaf; we wander in endless space.
Our only fear, that we do not
sleep forever on the bottom of the sea.
We are without food or water and our children and women
lie exhausted, crying, until they can cry no more.

No ship will stop. We float like we do not exist.
Lord Buddha, do you hear our voices? From every
port we are pushed out. Our distress signals rise
and rise again.

How many boats have perished? How many families are buried
beneath those waves? Find us. We are lost in the open sea,
looking for a shoreline to call safety.

Vietnamese monk, Los Angeles
[translated from Vietnamese]

POL POT

Pol Pot is a dragon in my dreams.
He never goes away.
I never knew Sihanouk or Lon Nol.
We are on the road to permanent exile.
We are walking across the border and
I see Pol Pot. He is there.
We walk across minefields like dancing
lightly on sharp glass. We travel
by our feet on the soil that is washed

with the blood of our friends.
I see Pol Pot. He is dressed
in a *sampot* drenched in blood.
I see Pol Pot in my dreams.

Cambodian merchant, age nineteen, Oakland, California

HUE THI PHAM
Baby Lift

Her voice is clear and strong. The interview, conducted in English, is punctuated by pauses and delayed by tears. Mrs. Hue Thi Pham is a petite woman with a remarkable memory. It is a difficult and painful interview for both of us.

It's difficult for me to forget the days before the baby lift, you remember, the C-5-A lift that crashed and killed two hundred and forty-three children and forty-three adults. The South Vietnam that I knew was finished. The war was over. Although the people and the soldiers were still there, the war was over and now it was time for that painful task of finishing it, like killing a wounded animal.

The big exodus was finally under way. You could see it on the streets and you could feel it in the shops in Saigon; they were empty when only a few days before they had been crowded. That week my husband had business in the U.S. Embassy and no one seemed to know where anyone was. Around Tan Son Nhut airport, thousands of what Americans called "high risk" Vietnamese were being evacuated. Everyone wanted to be "high risk" and everyone was scared. I was a medical nurse attached for some months to the U.S. Embassy but working in Hue. You see, before Hue fell to the Communists, my husband and I moved to Saigon and lived with my sister's family. Most of my work those weeks was just routine exams and outpatient casework at the Embassy dispensary. Everyone talked about the evacuation. It was like a black cloud that hung over the whole city and would not leave, like waiting for a man to die and, sitting at his bed, just waiting. I will never forget those painful feelings of waiting for events to happen, like waiting for a shoe to drop.

Tell me about the airplane crash.

The Americans wanted to evacuate a group of Vietnamese orphans. The plan was to take two thousand children from orphanages from around Saigon and send them to the United States for adoption. Nobody really knew whether these centers were within the city or where these children were from. I never understood very much about the program, just that important people in the Embassy wanted this program to work. The baby lift was supposed to be the first of many programs for the big evacuation. I was to be on the first plane going out with the children, in case they needed medical help.

It was a hot afternoon when the C-5-A plane finally took off. It took us some time to get all the children in place and strapped down to the seats. The plane was very, very crowded—there were two and three children to a seat. Some were tied together with belts. It was not an easy job and all of the crying and heat made it more difficult. It was like a chorus of cries and more cries. The adults were divided in the plane so that each of us had a certain number of children that we watched. I was up in the front of the plane, not far from the cockpit; I could actually see and hear the captain, who was American.

Just a few minutes after the plane took off, I could hear the pilot shouting into the radio. They later told us that what happened was some technical problem, a rear loading ramp became defective. Then the pilot lost control of the flaps for the wings. There was a loud, grinding noise and we could feel the plane jerk. I knew we were in big trouble, that something was wrong. Some miles out of Saigon, the pilot made a turn to go back to the airport. The plane jerked more and I couldn't make out the noises from the babies' screams. We were losing altitude. I could feel the plane going down. The emergency plan was to make the runway, but that did not work. I remember the tremendous pain in my ears and the screams.

Then the air pressure changed and it was hard to breathe. Do you know what it is like to be choked? There was no air. The emergency air masks dropped, but there were not enough for all the children. The oxygen was running out fast and the babies didn't have enough oxygen to cry or to breathe. I was getting very faint.

What I am describing took minutes but it seemed like hours. I could see the panic on the others' faces, just in their eyes. Now I was gasping for air, still trying to help share the masks with all of the children, which I knew was an impossible thing to try, but I tried many times. I could hardly breathe and we were going down. The thud noise is what I first remember, a scrape of the bottom. It was not a crash, but this thud. Then we bounced and hit another field. This big noise and a crunch; now the right wing had come off. A small explosion and a fire broke out. The smoke became heavy and very intense. I could see fire. All of this, while I was busy trying to attend to the children, some of whom had passed out. Inside, we were bounced around, falling on each other, falling on the floor. Some of the seats gave way from the floor. They said that the plane actually broke into two sections before we crashed. I don't know. What does it matter now? The fire made us all panic even more.

It was a long time before the helicopters brought in emergency medical help and supplies. We had landed in a rice paddy. There were no roads to this place, you could get there only by helicopter. No fire trucks or ambulances. That would have saved more lives. I still see the burned bodies, they will never go away from me, they are part of my memory. So many of the children were burned to death. It was hard to decide whom to help first: everyone looked critical. That was how it happened and as I remember it. That was the start of the evacuation. And for me, that was how the war ended.

LE TRAN
Pilau Bidong

We are in the first-floor apartment of a neat and orderly row house. Everything inside is painted institutional blue. It is Saturday morning and cartoons are on the television, no volume. He is a small man in stature and wears plastic thongs, gray sweatshirt, and dungarees. The day is especially muggy. "Do you want to know about my grandchildren?" he asks, in English. We finish a cup of tea and he turns off the television. The heat does not seem to affect him.

Most of us were Hoa, that is, from Chinese ancestry but born in South Vietnam and now South Vietnamese citizens. They say that there are over one million Chinese like us in Vietnam. You see, throughout history, the Vietnamese have never accepted us, and after the Communists took over it became even worse for us. You see, we are businesspeople. It is part of our history. Now we were prohibited from working; told to go to the fields and work. How can this be? My grandfather and his grandfather were silk traders, and now they tell me to go to the fields to work. Doing what? So it was soon after all this started that I decided to leave Vietnam.

I was an engineer in Saigon until April 1979, five years after the Communists took over. I ran into trouble with the electrical plant security officials. It was over a very simple thing, but then they began to have all of these requests for me to be active in the party and to be seen in the public like a role model for the other workers. There were many other small things that were so little as to make me wonder that this had all been arranged. Two weeks later, I was replaced by someone with far less experience; also, he was not even an engineer or a university graduate. He was some political monkey they had found to give them whatever it was that they wanted and could not get from me. There were also Bulgarian advisers there who wanted to cause trouble for me. Things then got worse. The security officers gave me an ultimatum: to give them money and leave Vietnam forever or to go to the work camp—this is what the Communists called "reeducation camp," which was really prison where they tried to work you to death and all the time you sang the praise of Marx. There could be no choice; I would leave.

How did you leave?

Along with sixty-two others; we bought a twenty-foot boat from a local fishing commune for $14,000. I had thought about leaving Vietnam for a long time. We had to pay local security guards another $2,500, just for the privilege to leave. All of this took much planning and much discussion. A few wanted to wait and leave after some of their business or personal things were finished. Some wanted to leave right away, and some wanted to maybe wait and see if the government might change. This last group was the most difficult because they had not yet made up their minds what to do and they caused confusion for everyone.

It took us twenty-one days to reach Malaysia. I will never forget that trip. There were so many things that could cause disaster, so many things that were unknown dangers, so many things that would mean sure death. We all were close to death. I call it a voyage through hell and I still dream of the rough waters.

Remember, this was a very small boat for so many people. The second day at sea we hit a very bad storm. It was as if we were some small toy bouncing up and down. People got sick. Children cried. Then the ship's captain admitted to us that he was not as experienced a navigator as he had claimed before we left. We were in trouble and everyone was giving directions. Everybody began to panic. Some men were trying to give directions and some men were trying to give advice. It was confusion. The sun and heat never stopped and I thought surely we would die from the heat, but just then a storm began that grew worse and worse.

A typhoon struck our waters and this added to the fears even more. Many people had never spent time in a boat and it was being bounced back and forth like it was a little stick. The strong winds began in the afternoon and by early evening we had so much water in the main section that it was constant work to remove it. People were sick and many said they were dying. No one seemed to be in charge and the captain had no control. No one listened to him. The rains did not stop and there was no place to try to stay dry. The salt water penetrated my skin and made it turn a strange color. I thought of being on land. Then, as quickly as the storm began, it ended. It was over in a matter of minutes. The water grew calmer and the sun came out.

On the seventeenth day, our food and water were gone. People began to be very sick and argue constantly. The closeness and the weather made some crazy and we had to try to ignore what the crazy ones were saying. It was just the nature of being so close. Then an old man died and this changed everybody's thoughts. He was an old man from the north and we buried him at sea.

We had heard so much about pirate ships, but we never saw any; perhaps the weather was too bad for them. Two merchant ships passed by maybe two or three kilometers but they would not stop. Some always screamed at some dangerous point that the boat was sinking, but I knew better. When we landed finally at Kuala Trengganu, the police came on board and shouted at us. They arrested us and we were taken to a camp for some days before we were sent to Pilau Bidong.

Describe Pilau Bidong for me.

From a distance, it was a tropical island. The boat ride traveled through very pretty and quiet waters. But for some distance before we landed, we could smell all of the humanity. It was the stench I remember well. The officials said over 30,000 people lived here. My first view of the land close up was of people everywhere—not just hundreds, but thousands of people. They were just standing around doing nothing, nothing. This is what first greeted me, it was this sea of people all looking at me. There were flies on everyone and everything and it was very hot.

Pilau Bidong was a society of its own. It was a little island that was only used by the fishermen, and now this entire city was on it. People tried to find some privacy but that was impossible to do. The different sections of the camp I got to know very well. All of the paths and roads were made into mud when the rainy season would come. I arrived just after a big rain. The U.N. and camp officials tried to stop people from using the trees, but this, too, was impossible. The wood was needed for many things and it went fast. Then, when it rained, it flooded from the lack of trees, you see, because of the erosion.

What was really terrible was that there was nothing to do on the island. It was boring, no work, nothing to keep us busy. Days and weeks and months of doing nothing, just sitting. I remember that there was nowhere I could go that people did not talk about the refugee-processing office and the officials that were interviewing you for resettlement to another country. This was our big hope, and we dreamed about it all night; for me, they were mostly nightmares.

Also, there was no place to go to be alone. Everyone's lives were known by everybody. No privacy. And the children were everywhere, running in and out of the tents. The day was spent talking and watching; talking and watching. There was too much time to sit and think. For me, I make problems when I have so much time. I thought about life in Vietnam before the Communists; about my family, mother and father. I relived the boat trip to Malaysia many times. It was after five months of sitting and thinking and of going through many interviews that I was finally accepted for their U.S. resettlement program. You know, this all seems so long ago.

HOA TONG
South China Sea Pirates

She talks a little about her work in Indianapolis and her family. She remembers a great deal about the war or perhaps stories about the war, and tells me that all those events happened when she was "of a very impressionable age." She is now twenty-six and a student at a local vocational training school.

I keep thinking how difficult it must be for this woman to talk with me about her escape. She has beautiful dark eyes and even more beautiful hands, which carefully massage her wrists. She is busy making tea for me and there is a quiet in the room broken only by her slightly distracting wrist-watch noise.

I am alive to tell you this story—at least I am lucky for that. I survived the escape and the Thai pirates. We spent some years in Malaysia and now live in Pittsburgh. It has not been easy to remember these events. If I had been younger or prettier, I, too, would have been taken to Ko Kra.

We left Vietnam on December 15, 1979, from Rach Gia. It was five years since the Communists took power. Things would never again be the same for us. We are really Chinese and our great-grandparents had come south from China. We were businesspeople whose lives were forever changed by the Communists. They took our property and our clothing business and then sent us to a reeducation camp in the west. We survived that. There was no future in Vietnam for us. We paid $5,000 for two places on a boat. It took some months for the plans to materialize, and then our departure was very quick. Our boat was Number SS 060. It was small—only fourteen and a half meters long and there were ninety-one people on board when we left, so you can see how very crowded it must have been.

Describe the boat journey.

The first day of the journey was uneventful. The shock of leaving, the size of the boat, and the crowd of people struck me. My husband was very, very quiet the first day; he just sat on our baggage. All of our lives were stored in the baggage we carried. All those memories. It felt so very strange to carry them around. That day, a very old woman was sick all day with the move-ment of the boat. Her moans kept us all awake. I wanted to move but there was nowhere to go. No space. We had only a little space and if we moved we would lose even that. There were six small babies that cried, cried all the time. One began, they all cried together. We were afraid of being discovered by the Vietnamese border patrol, but after the first day, we didn't need to worry a lot about that.

The second day out, the waters got rougher. Especially in the afternoon, the waters were so high that we were tossed back and forth; back and forth. The drinking water we brought got so hot and it smelled from the heat and other things. More people got sick, and the two medical doctors that were on the boat were being asked many questions and they were busy all of the time. Throughout this difficult period, I held on to my bags very tight. I was watching my husband's bags, too. Two people we knew on the ship had been robbed already. They had been asleep and when they awoke they were missing things—taken from a small bag that one of them was sleeping near, with the straps wrapped around his hands while he slept, but they cut the handles right off. Many people were so close, but no one was caught. Who knows who did it; after a while, everybody looked suspicious, guilty. That evening there was a bad argument over the distribution of drinking water and food. The ship's captain said something about wanting more money, more gold. We never understood what he wanted. Some of the crew were drinking liquor and got very drunk and loud. By the second day, I knew all of the ninety-one faces on board very well, faces I thought I had seen all my life. On the third day of the journey, we encountered three Thai pirate boats.

They were small boats. This is what we all feared, although we had not talked about it. We had all heard stories, and the people that we left behind had told us about the stories. We thought they had warned us in a funny kind of way: they were teasing us with the stories, maybe because they were jealous or they did not want us to leave Vietnam. But you always think that your escape will be different, your example will be different. From now on, the happenings will always be on my mind, engraved on my mind like a carving in a jade stone. Only this was a nightmare carved very, very deep.

We were tied to two of the three boats. There were many protests and screams by all of us, but that was useless, and under the sun, all of this energy was just lost. Some began to cry softly. It was a mixed reaction. The men could do nothing after they had screamed at the pirates. My husband and I stepped very close together; all I can remember is that I could hear his heart beat hard. We were holding each other up for support. An old woman next to me started screaming, so near to my ear; screaming about robbery and rape. She was going crazy. She had a young and pretty daughter under her old cloth that she was trying to protect. At that moment, two of our men fell into the water and the Thai pirates would not let them get back into the boat. They stayed in the water until the pirates left, holding onto the boat.

Some twenty pirates came on board and demanded gold. Gold! Gold! They screamed that they knew we had gold and they did not have time for us. If we did not give them gold, we would die in the water. For the next four hours—but it seemed so much longer—these pirates tore open our bags and our clothes. We tried to hide some rings, but it was not possible. They took our bags and spilled the contents. Our money was kept in a false bottom of the bag that my husband had constructed, but they found it. They knew exactly where to look. All of this at the same time they were teasing the young girls, the pretty girls. They were animals, not people. They were pigs, these pirates!

Two of the young and pretty girls were taken to the front of the boat and raped. Everyone heard everything, all of the screams. That is what I remember, the screams. After a while, the screams stopped, the crying stopped, and there was silence. Everyone on the boat was still, but not for long. The pirates separated twenty women and ordered them off the boat. There were many protests. Nothing helped. People even fell overboard. It was mass confusion, hysteria, and shock. They were the prettiest girls and after they were gone, all we could hear were more cries and muffled protests. They took our girls, water, and food. We were left to die. Five days later, a Norwegian ship picked us up.

The officials said the girls that the pirates stole were taken to Ko Kra island and sold into prostitution. You know it was a nightmare and everyone was part of it. You could not close your eyes. You could not close your ears. I still see the faces and hear the cries. We landed in Lampini camp as a heavy rain began.

KHMER ROUGE

It was a time of evil.
I was only thirteen when the Khmer Rouge in
my country captured it. School stopped.
Work stopped and soon life stopped. To be
persecuted by your own people is not real.
We never understood why all this happened.
We were to be ashamed of our books, of our schools,
our teachers, our education. Stop thinking.
Stop thinking. The city is evil, the country is good.
Stop thinking. Forever I will never stop thinking
about how they killed my country.

Cambodian high school student, age eighteen, Philadelphia

LEN KATH
Pol Pot

There is a great deal of noise from the street during the interview. There is a very strong aroma of sweet incense burning in the room. We drink diet sodas and he smokes cigarettes. A very amiable, jovial person, he speaks in Khmer and English.

I survived.

My leaving Cambodia I often think was a miracle granted to me. Sometimes I think it was a curse. I have been in the U.S. since 1980. Most of that time I lived here in Chicago.

I cannot explain Pol Pot. For me, December 1980 was a day of liberation for my family, but I was wrong. What replaced the killing was the hunger.

I lived in the capital like my father and grandfather. Because I was a clerk for a shipping company, I became a suspect for the Pol Pot government. My biggest problem was that I had a high school education and I wore glasses. Can you imagine? To wear glasses automatically meant you were an intellectual. So, you see, I therefore was an urban elite and then not part of the peasant revolution.

First they took my brother and then my uncle. These people were never interested in politics; they were simple workers. They were never seen again. In early 1979, I had no job. I was not able to work for many months. We had no money and little food. We decided to leave the capital and to take our chances out of the country in Thailand. We had heard many stories about the trip to Thailand.

When did you leave Cambodia?

We left with my parents and friends of my parents. My wife never told her family. We were scared because we thought we could not trust her brother and perhaps her family would disagree with our plans. So we left and since then we have not heard from them. This grieves my wife to this day very much; in some way, she feels that we should have taken them, but at the same time, this simply was not possible.

It is the gunfire at night that I remember. When I sleep, I sometimes dream of the gunfire. I really can hear the guns. We were told that these were death squads. That is what I remember most clearly. Death squads. It was like we were little candles in a storm and it was only by a strange turn that our fires did not go out. [*He blows into the air.*] Just like that.

There were no laws in the country, no justice, only chaos. Chaos everywhere. No one can explain it. They call us here a gentle people. But then I saw Pol Pot and lived through the Pol Pot regime. I saw these people not as human but as butchers. I am ashamed.

Who would ever think that we would welcome the Vietnamese army to Cambodia? For many centuries we fought each other, then we watched as they entered the country and we were glad and happy to see them. They took away the Pol Pot butchers. When the Vietnamese conquered, we hoped for the best, for anything that would be different—that would be better. Perhaps peace. But that, too, was wrong. Yes, they stopped the mass killings and then they stopped the destroying of villages; but then the hunger started. And we do not know which evil was worse. They stopped the mass graves and the unexpected violence, but the famine grew worse. So many people were without even a little food. There was hunger everywhere. Farming was not permitted when Heng Samrin took power and now the country fell apart in a different way.

There were food shortages everywhere—especially just outside the capital. Rich farm areas that now produced nothing. People tried any way they could to gather food. Things that should not be eaten, certain forest plants were consumed. No area was left untouched, no person went unaffected. My wife and I were unable to buy rice—rice! Can you believe it, a country that is so famous for rice suddenly has no rice? There was no difference between these nightmares—to be killed by Pol Pot or to be starved by Heng Samrin.

When my wife and I decided to leave, there was really no other decision to be made. If we wanted to live, we would leave. We left with twenty others and walked for eleven days to get to Thailand. We traveled mostly at night, and all along the way we heard stories of the death that seemed to be taking over the entire country. Now we were Cambodian people trapped between the Vietnamese tiger in Phnom Penh and the Khmer Rouge crocodile in the countryside. There was no safe place to be.

We left the capital at night—my wife and two small children and I. I don't know exactly how many kilometers it was to the Taphraya district near the border. You know, most of this I want to forget. I know it felt like weeks. We traveled mostly at night. The children were always hungry. My youngest son cried and cried and we thought for sure he would give us away. Many times they give such children a little opium to quiet them, but I was afraid to do this because you never know how much to give. I had heard stories about children dying from overdoses.

Tell me about the escape.

Along the way, we heard stories about those people who were killed for no reason. It seemed every day the stories became more terrible. I wanted to shut my ears and my wife's ears, but could not; I wanted to cover my children's eyes, but could not. Nobody needs to hear and see such things. When you live through this experience, the most difficult is the part where you know that you are helpless and that there is nothing you can do, nothing. We Khmer never grew up knowing such ways, such violence and hate. Now, I live to tell it; it is a cruel burden.

At Phnom Chat, about two kilometers from the Thai border, we were delayed for some weeks. I remember the date—March 31— because bombs and many explosions hit us. I remember the noise and the fire, and I can still smell the bombs and the plastic burning. The Vietnamese were attacking the camp. Everyone began to race for the border; confusion and panic were everywhere. There was some distance to travel, especially with two children. We were more like animals running from the hunter. We were helpless, not knowing if or where the shells would strike. Someone close to me was hit by a bomb fragment. I could almost touch him, I was so close. I saw him die. Then I grabbed my children closer and we ran faster.

No one knew exactly where the Thailand border was; from where we were, it could have been two places. In the direction we ran, the distance seemed to be shorter. But just as we came to the turn in the road, my friend to my side stepped on a land mine. There was an explosion and he lost his foot. It was just gone. I can hear him scream. In the confusion, my wife took the children, and as I tried to help him, they moved to the side of me and were killed by a mine bomb. The whole road now was planted with mine bombs. I knew that they were dead, but I could not believe it. I could not. All I could see was what remained of them. [*There is a very long silence.*]

Looking back toward Phnom Chat camp, all of the houses were burning and army tanks were coming toward us. They told us that two or three thousand villagers were then taken prisoner by the Vietnamese. I made it to the border and waited with the others for the police to let us enter. I will never accept the decision to leave my wife and children there. Can you imagine what my life is now? So, this is the story of my escape from Cambodia.

HA HOA THO and PHAN TU HOA
Orderly Departure Program

The interview takes longer than usual because the interpreter keeps getting interrupted by telephone calls. The husband and wife, who speak to me in Vietnamese, have just come from their English class and are excited about their lesson or some new vocabulary they have learned. Although they have been here a very short time, they seem to have a sense of confidence, even playfulness, about themselves. They insist upon having a joke translated for me before we begin. We all laugh, and our talk starts on a very upbeat note.

There was never enough food after the Communists took over, not enough rice, and never any meat. I know there are people who starved, although we did not know any of them. We heard nothing on the radio about any of this; most of the time we were too scared to turn on the radio. Food prices continued to get higher. I am a farmer and I don't like politics, but because my ancestors were from China, we had many problems with the Communists. I would never be a member of the Communist party, so they took all my property.

Tell me about the Communist takeover.

I remember when the Communists took power. I thought that peace was here and life would be different, but that did not happen; things got worse. The first time they changed the currency in early 1976, I knew life would get very bad, and I was correct. In a few months, they changed the money again and I knew positively Vietnam would only get worse for us.

All they cared about was the army, and that was what I wanted to forget. There was no peace and they took people from the cities to the country to make them farmers. Ha! Farmers without tools, food, or a place to sleep! Can you believe it? Everyone was forced to join the army. Many people came down from the north, but we never knew what they would do in the south and we never trusted them.

We wanted our children out just after the war, and we had left to go north into China, and then into Laos, and into Thailand, but that was too risky and too far. We raised money from the whole family and sent our eldest daughter and son out by boat in early 1978. This took all the money we had or could borrow. We were so afraid because the Vietnamese officials might have caught them.

We had heard about the Thai pirates and how dangerous the waters could be. But they arrived and, by letters, we continued to communicate with them. They sent us money. Most government officials kept half of the money. Well, that is how we heard about the Orderly Departure Program and the possibility of leaving Vietnam.

When did you apply for the program?

We applied in June 1980 for the Orderly Departure Program. All of our friends and neighbors knew about it; it was no secret. We met a number of people who later left Vietnam by the program. During our first interview with the Vietnamese officials, I must say they did not ask any difficult or embarrassing questions—only where we would go and some information about our children in the United States. No unpleasant things happened to us because we applied for the program. When the United Nations and the United States officials interviewed us, they wanted to see our marriage certificate and asked some general questions about our children, and that was all. No more. You know, in fact, it was very easy. I guess we were the lucky ones.

I do not know why we were accepted and others rejected. That is still a mystery. Perhaps because my family never cared about politics and never spoke about politics. We waited almost five years to leave before they stopped the program. I know we were one of the last groups to leave, because they soon stopped the program. We spent some days in Bangkok and seven months in the Philippines in a language-training program. I did not learn much English; I was not such a good student. My wife did better than I did.

What did you expect of America?

I expected a steady job and to be able to see my children go to school. I am sorry for all those people who registered for the Orderly Departure Program and then it was stopped. Leaving by this program was better than by boat. I think also of those who drowned in the sea trying to escape. My wife said that she does not expect anything here, only to live in peace and see her children grow.

VAN TRAN
Last Helicopter

A very handsome man, he laces his shoes and seems to adjust his clothes before he smiles and we start the interview. I remember his demeanor from before. He tells me about a mutual acquaintance, in English, and we begin.

I was an interpreter and a manager for a large oil company in Saigon. Then I was employed by USAID and the CIA. My wife and I had lived in Saigon near the Xa Loi pagoda, but had to visit her family in Phuvinh that day. We finally ended up at the Continental Plaza Hotel. The Communists were at the gates and Saigon went crazy. There were 1,400 Americans and 5,600 South Vietnamese that were evacuated from Saigon just before the city fell to the Communists. (I know these numbers because I read of them later.) My wife and I were lucky— I knew ours was the last helicopter to get out.

Describe the last day for me.

It was hysteria. Too many rumors and no one you could trust, not even the American boss who had invited you so many times with your wife to his house for dinner. Whom to trust? There were too many rumors to remember or forget. What I do remember was that, because the airport was closed, evacuation by commercial and military airplanes and by sea was no longer possible. We would be taken out of Saigon by marine helicopters. They called this Operation Frequent Wind.

Under the bombs, the Vietnamese air force at Tan Son Nhut fell apart. Air crews went aboard the transport planes and helicopters, trying to get out of the country as fast as they could. The ship was going down and only the weak would remain. Trying to get out of the country, some soldiers firing their weapons came over the parking area and the runway. A C-7 twin engine plane crashed; it tried to take off with only one engine. There were no fire trucks, no rescue people.

Most people at the hotel were Americans, a few French. We went out the front door across Lam Son square and gathered in front of the Tran Hung Dao statue, but we were told this landing spot now was no longer safe and we got back on the bus heading for the airport, but guards at the gates were firing at the buses. Then a 130mm North Vietnamese shell hit the terminal. Here we separated from the Americans and were told to go to the U.S. Embassy. It was impossible to travel. We should have stayed at Tan Son Nhut. It was raining very hard when we reached the Embassy. Thousands made a sea of people crowding every possible spot. We were on a list—I knew it. How we got through the crowd and into the Embassy is my secret.

All this time my wife was silent. Then she began to talk about her sister and some family members and she wanted to go back and get them, although she knew that this was impossible. Then she began to be silent and to cry. She wanted her sister to be with us. She never saw her again.

I remember it was a Thursday night. I didn't think the ten-foot wall surrounding the Embassy would hold. The Embassy was evacuated floor by floor, and as we withdrew to the roof with the marines in back of us and in front of us toward the roof of the Embassy, we could hear gunfire outside the compound. Tear gas made it difficult to breathe. My eyes burned. The gas made it difficult to see. My wife held my wrist so tight—I never knew her to be so strong. The looters were right behind us—just a floor below. The gun shots grew louder, and then— silence. Then a few screams. It was four A.M. as the chopper lifted off, and I looked out at the Saigon lights. It was a miracle that we were doing this.

PANG VANG KHANG
Mekong Crossing

He is in his late forties and dressed in American Western clothing. He tells me that his favorite singer is Elvis Presley. Our conversation is in English.

I belong to a tribe of proud people, the Hmong. We always helped the Americans in the war and now, after the war, we fight alone.

As a Chao Fa fighter, I was part of the army trying to regain Laos for all of our people. When the Vietnamese took the Phu Bia region in 1979, the resistance was gone. We had no choice; we had to go to Thailand. The yellow poison they used killed us, and today I am still sick with it. Many are sick with it.

I crossed the Mekong one night with six other soldiers, and eventually we were found and put into Ban Vinai camp. To look back it seems brave, but there was no other way. If we were caught by the Pathet Lao, we would be dead like the many at Hin Heup. They hate us because we won't give in to their demands of Communism; because we helped the Americans. They cannot control our minds. The Pathet Lao are just voices for the Vietnamese. They do what the Vietnamese tell them to do, that's all.

That night, we crossed the Mekong on bamboo floats with no stars and no moon. The next morning, we were arrested by the Thai police and were treated very badly because the Thai people do not want us. Two men from my village came with me; I went to live in the United States, but they went to Canada.

I heard some camps in Thailand treated you better, but it made no difference. What is important is that we will return. My friends and I talk a lot about this. We will return to Laos and will drive the Communists out and then we can have our land once more. I do not know if the CIA will help us like we helped them, but we will do it soon, I hope.

AFTER POL POT

This is a story of a Cambodia that no longer exists.
We were the elder statesmen from Southeast Asia, the Mon group.
We knew Burma and Tibet—long, long before your Christ was
born; long before the Temple of Jerusalem and the great tribes.

We were farmers and fishermen. We discovered fire and lived in
raised houses. Worshiping ancestors and the spirit of the earth
and waters, we venerated the serpent Naga, who was for us
a symbol of the cosmic forces and to this day has remained
a guardian spirit of Cambodia.

After Pol Pot we returned to the days of our descendants of
Kambuja—again to call our land Kampuchea.
Then the successors of Kaumdinya who discovered the
Kingdom of the Mountain—the great cosmic mountain,
which truly was the center of the universe.

This was the period of great friendship with the Chinese.
Not until they killed our beloved Chenla king in the
eighth century did we once again rise with the royal court
under the prince Jayavaram after Angkor Wat.
We grew in size and we were the power
second only to the Chinese to the north.

Then for centuries we fought the Thai people who made us slaves.
They took us from Angkor and it was a terrible massacre,
only to find the capital new that was Phnom Penh—and then
the Europeans arrived.

Our world was broken and would never return to the same.
The Vietnamese conquered and the French arrived to protect us
and to break promises. Sihanouk made us strong and Lon Nol
gave us away. Heng Samrin and Pol Pot made us a lost people.

Let no one forget that there was a Cambodia that sought peace in
a world not ready to live with peace as a strength,
not a weakness. We hear whispers in the early morning light.
We pray that the *teuodas*, the protectors of the world, will
come again to the salvation of Cambodian people.

Oan Camorth, former Cambodian journalist, Chicago
[translated from Khmer]

CHAPTER 4

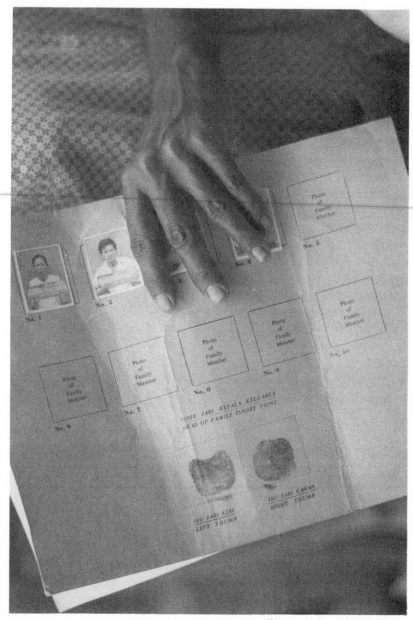

Photo: J. K. Isaac/United Nations

THE

TRANSFER

Unlike immigrants, refugees are forced to flee their countries under often life-threatening conditions. The Indochinese refugees arrived in different waves over time from 1975 to the present. The first group of Vietnamese came directly to the United States in 1975, but since that first exit, Cambodians, Laotians, and Vietnamese have gone to refugee camps in Thailand, Malaysia, Hong Kong, and other neighboring countries. More than one-half million remain in camps today. The experience of getting to the United States has been different for each group. "The move to America will always be the greatest event of my life. It happened so fast. It was like a dream that I live again and again. To move so far in so little time is frightening," said Vietnamese refugee Do Van Chi.

Psychological factors are involved in the transfer—"degrees of emotional and physical separation from home," as Do Van Chi called them—and these

---

◁FACING PAGE
A Vietnamese refugee holds an identification document issued by the United Nations at the Galang Processing Centre in Indonesia. These documents are the first step in the resettlement process.

can be different for different groups and individuals. For example, most Vietnamese in the United States can identify family and friends remaining in Vietnam and in many cases are able to write to them, but the majority of Cambodians assume their friends and relatives to be lost or dead and cannot communicate with anyone at home, even if the political situation were to change. Yet communication is possible for many Laotians, because the United States maintains diplomatic relations with the current government of Laos.

The means, the method of escape, and the circumstances accompanying it directly affect the degree and manner in which the refugees have cushioned their shock of transfer to the United States. The newcomers themselves have pointed out in these interviews that it is important to remember that unlike other immigrant and even refugee groups coming to the United States, the Southeast Asians arrived with no ethnic communities or support groups to provide them with assistance. In addition, these people collectively remain highly heterogeneous—often based on historic ethnic rivalries—and could not be expected to have available the same methods of integration into American society.

Refugees arriving since 1975 have undergone different treatment and program response by the federal government—owing in part to availability of resources, political climate, and public opinion. The people who talked with me report that in most circumstances they were not asked by the government about their own need and thus did not help define the requirements of the program. "Nobody ever asked us to help design the resettlement program— they just sent us out into all these different states and told us to get jobs," said Le Tran Han, a Vietnamese accountant in Los Angeles.

As in most refugee populations, those with the most education, experience, and exposure to the West, and the wealthiest, escaped from their country first; certainly this was the case with the Vietnamese in 1975. Subsequent waves of refugees varied tremendously, ranging from the highly educated who were unable or unwilling to leave at the end of the war to poor peasants illiterate in their own language. This diversity of backgrounds accounts for the vast differences in the individual's ability to accommodate to the transfer and eventual adjustment to the United States.

The transfer to America also varied considerably, based upon the means of escape. Following the fall of Saigon in April 1975, the first refugee wave was evacuated to Wake Island and Guam and then taken to four refugee camps in the United States. These camps were closed eight months later. For refugees who arrived after 1975, the screening and interviewing to be accepted for resettlement took place primarily in camps in Thailand, Malaysia, Hong Kong, and Singapore. The wait could be measured in months or years before acceptance for resettlement. The host countries are referred to as "first-asylum" countries, and the camps are administered by the host government and the United Nations.

The United States Resettlement Program has always given first preference to immediate family relatives—mother, father, sister, and brother. As a result, the 1975 wave set an admission as well as settlement pattern for subsequent Vietnamese arrivals. The Cambodians and Laotians would also have to establish their own communities anew. Describing the Vietnamese's camp wait, Le Tran Han said: "Pilau Bidong in Malaysia was where we were. My family at first was separated when we left, but later we found each other. I had searched the entire island for weeks. Nobody. Then months and months of waiting until we came together. Then more waiting—almost two years before we could leave the island. I saw people leave and I always asked, why not me? This was a terrible period of idle time. Time to do nothing but think about your past."

The second wave of refugees, usually referred to as the "boat people," captured world media attention for some time. These were people drowning in the South China Sea, being attacked and raped by pirates and left to die. These refugees experienced more traumatic circumstances during their escape than those who came out in 1975. In general, the later group was not as well educated and had less exposure to the West. They have been confronted with more serious problems of adjustment, and have required more attention and support in the United States. Subsequent waves came by land from Cambodia and Laos to Thailand, with a continued outpouring from Vietnam by boat.

A former academician from Vietnam, Le Xuan Khoa, commented that a successful escape depended upon a variety of considerations. "The successful move to the United States varied according to demographic factors: age, sex, education, work experience, family size, and especially language—English proficiency or the willingness to learn English." It has been the latter factor—English—that has proved to be the most critical resettlement element. All those interviewed said that language remains the major obstacle to successful adjustment in the United States. It affects all aspects of the person's life here: work, security, basic communication, everything. "You speak and understand English, or you continue to be just a stranger that lives in the dark," said one Cambodian refugee.

Some refugees with whom I spoke—especially those who volunteered the information that they were over fifty years old—maintained that it is impossible to learn a new language. A few might learn but the majority continue to struggle, although the later waves of immigrants are required to complete a six-month intensive language and acculturation program in the Philippines before they enter the United States. Then there is a large percentage of people who strive for perfection and think they simply cannot speak English, at least not well enough to get along in everyday situations. "I will never perfect the English *sh*," said one Laotian interviewed.

The U.S. refugee resettlement policy has evolved over time in a somewhat self-correcting fashion. The political and economic obstacles to admitting large numbers of Southeast Asian refugees after the American defeat in Vietnam and during an economic depression were, at best, difficult to overcome. This was not a receptive time in Congress for admission of refugees. Remember, it was President Ford who chastised Congress for not living up to its historic role when it failed to fund the evacuation of the first wave of refugees. This reaction is based in part on our loss of the war and fear of Asians, as well as the resettlement experience of a previous admission program of some 700,000 Cubans between 1960 and 1965.

The policy adopted in the 1960s for Cuban refugees was a national resettlement program to disperse them throughout the country, in part to avoid the "ghettoization" of a non-Anglo people. The program was eventually viewed by many people as a failure in that a large proportion of Cubans who had been resettled in other areas of the country returned to southern Florida within a few years. Politically, however, the program did calm south Floridian fears during its operation.

A similar set of dynamics confronted policymakers with regard to the Southeast Asian refugees. Owing to the federal urgency to close the Stateside camps before the end of 1975, a concerted effort was made to spread the refugees around the country, using the services of religious and secular voluntary agencies. "Little if any attention was given to employment matching or skills interviewing—people were simply placed with a 'sponsor' who agreed to help that individual to get settled and become economically self-sufficient in the new community," said former interpreter Van Tran.

Subsequent refugee waves received similar treatment, but when the newcomers moved and groups formed in certain geographic areas of the country, problems of resource availability and local fears arose. In later years the federal government made efforts to resettle certain ethnic groups in "cluster" settlements, such as the Cambodian cluster projects. However, the already established ethnic communities continued to attract individuals as well as smaller cluster groups, sometimes through rumors of employment, welfare, or better living situations.

This internal refugee migration is really part of the American immigration pattern of ethnic community development and is well documented in history. Given our free boundaries, people make their own life decisions; they move and form their own communities. Consequently, although placed in all states, almost 50 percent of the refugees now live in California. Apart from its warm weather, California is a state, the refugees say, hospitable to Asian people, as well as having one of the most generous welfare systems in the country.

Part of the transfer process is accommodation. The refugees talk about their "harmony-oriented" minds and their ability to participate without actual conversion to a new culture. They are more apt to adopt new practical rather than moral or spiritual values. However, despite their capacity to adapt themselves to new circumstances, they have experienced various difficulties in the process of adjustment to American life. Most of these difficulties stem from the sudden change of environment and the large gap between cultures.

In coping with the new cultural environment, one refugee may react quite differently from another, depending on his or her own escape experiences, expectations, perception of the new culture, and ability to adjust to it. As a result, acculturation can be achieved quickly, slowly, or not at all. Le Xuan Khoa states that there are three possible scenarios or patterns of behavior in the Vietnamese refugee adjustment process: the old-line pattern, the assimilation pattern, and the bicultural pattern. The old-line pattern occurs when people cling to their old values and traditions and refuse to acquire new ones; the assimilation pattern occurs when people want to integrate so badly that they are prepared to turn their backs on traditional values. And in the bicultural pattern, people exhibit the ability to preserve traditional values while acquiring new values and practices that are necessary for a transition to life in America. Most Laotians and Cambodians interviewed agree that the above scenarios are applicable to their groups as well.

There are the inevitable breakdowns. The inability to transfer to a new community has manifested itself in what are often referred to as mental health problems. In general the attitude of this group of refugees is characterized by fear, rejection, ridicule, and stress. These concerns are most often found in Cambodians who have no family remaining to communicate with in Cambodia. Regrets, depression, and guilt weigh heavily on the refugee's mind.

In Vietnamese, Cambodian, and Laotian, the term "mental health" cannot be translated. These problems are seen as essentially private issues, talking about them indicates a lack of discretion and taste. Because hardships and suffering are considered as givens that are part of everyone's life, there is no point in complaining. To do so is a sign of weakness that denotes a lack of character. If in the end help is sought, it should be from a close relative, never a stranger. "For a Cambodian to talk with a psychiatrist about such personal problems," said former professor and judge Phat Mau, "is unthinkable, it just does not happen. That is strictly a Western thing to do."

In the transfer to the United States, misunderstandings and ethnic conflicts with the local population are inevitable. What were called "community tensions" in the early stages of the resettlement program seem to have abated, at least in the most outward forms. These tensions surface when a particular community or ethnic group dislike having refugees in their neighborhood. Disputes arise because of fear and ignorance, usually with undertones of economic competition. Accommodation has been made on both sides—this, too, is part of American immigration history. The following are conversations with refugees about their transfer to the United States.

QUAN NGUYEN
North Dakota to California

Quan Nguyen is a very small man who has very thick eyeglasses and continually smokes unfiltered cigarettes. This is the second time I have spoken with him in two years. He loves history and we talk at length about the French Revolution, and he goes on for some time about Talleyrand. His French is like poetry and he is very proud of his proficiency and vocabulary. He has a remarkable, broad smile throughout most of our talk.

I arrived in early October [1975] from Fort Indiantown Gap, Pennsylvania, to New Town, North Dakota. I was sponsored by the local Lutheran church. I could only stay there until early January and then I left for California because it became so cold I thought I would die.

Funny, but I still remember so much about the history there. There is much history in Mountrail County where I lived. This is history that I knew nothing about. The American explorers Lewis and Clark traveled there. Lake Sakakawea was an important place for the Indian tribes and President [Theodore] Roosevelt very much liked to go hunting in this part of the country. New Town is not very far from the Canadian border. There was a lot of other history I learned while I lived there. It's funny, but I still remember it.

The Almstadt family that sponsored me were very nice to me. They were very generous with their time and money, but for me the shock of North Dakota was too great. I kept thinking of Vietnam. I was a lieutenant in the Vietnamese army before I left. I had a good life, many girl friends, and although the last year was very difficult for everybody in Vietnam, I made the best of it.

What did you expect when you came to the United States?

I arrived in the United States, I guess, with a lot of grand expectations. I expected the U.S. government to take care of me for some period of time. I don't know—maybe for a year or two. There are still many bitter feelings I have about the United States withdrawal and I expected it to be easier, now that I look back at the whole situation. I remember meeting my sponsors for the first time. You know, I had no English and we both just smiled a lot. I remember how I had to get used to the way Americans touch you, something we never did. The Almstadts' house was very big, and for a while I stayed in a room near the kitchen. During the day, I helped work on the cattle farm and that was interesting, but there wasn't much for me to do after I finished work. The work was good for me and I think to work with my hands was something useful. But I couldn't feel comfortable with my new life. Everything seemed to get more complicated and some days I didn't even want to get out of my bed.

What was the most difficult thing for you?

The most difficult thing for me was the language. Even when you hear it all of the time and look at it, I was not at a level to take it and to understand it. I suppose you could say that I was in a state of shock, that I couldn't learn English even if I wanted to, but I know that is a bad excuse. When you feel bad about yourself, even the little things complicate your life. My sponsors knew that I was having a difficult time. There was nothing they could do.

They couldn't realize what I had gone through in the past or how it was for me now. They smiled a lot and kept wanting me to go to church. So finally I went to church, but that was even worse because then the English seemed even worse, more difficult to understand.

I remember that my sponsors promised to take me to meet another refugee. They said he was a bachelor like me and that he lived near Williston, which, they showed me on the map, was not so far away. I tried to remember if he was in Indiantown camp with me. Did I know him in the army? I had not met anyone when I was there that was going to North Dakota; maybe, I thought, North Carolina? So I had an entire week to think about meeting a fellow countryman. It had been almost a month since I saw a fellow Vietnamese. I talked with a friend from New York by telephone, but that is very expensive and my sponsor, I know, was always a little nervous about the cost of that. I did not know the distance from New York to North Dakota, or how to get there or anything. It was just easy to talk—there was always so much to say.

So, on Saturday, my sponsors drove me to Williston. This trip had all been arranged. I hated to take them away from their work, but they did this. I still couldn't imagine who this person could be; maybe fate would have it he was a separated friend or relative. I did a lot of dreaming. I even started imagining faces that I had seen in the camp and maybe guessing who this person might be.

The first moment I saw Mau, I knew he was a Cambodian. Here he was a Cambodian and me a Vietnamese. They thought we could talk—probably because they think we look the same. Well, we just stared at each other. We smiled, but later that night I cried.

What made you finally decide to leave?

The weather was probably the thing that made me decide to leave. By early December, every day was cold and snowy and I never wore so many clothes. It was so cold. I felt that I was trapped by the weight of all the clothes and the colder it became, the more clothes you were supposed to wear. It was terrible. I got sick with fever.

In New Town, there were gray days when the sun would never appear. Long days and I never saw this; it was very depressing. And all the time the snow came; it was terrible for me. My friend from New York had left his sponsors and moved to Orange County in California, where he had an uncle. He telephoned me very often and would talk about a lot of things, but mostly I was interested in the other Vietnamese: what they were doing and gossip like that. We talked about money. My friend told me about the welfare system in California. How you can get money from the government and how there are Vietnamese doctors there to help you when you get sick. It was good news and the snow made it sound better. I don't know—it seemed that the colder it got, the more I wanted to leave.

There were other Vietnamese, I learned, that lived in Fargo, and I got to meet them and they felt lost like me, and the weather was too cold and there was no Vietnamese community. We all missed the food, the language. I tried North Dakota, but I could not live there. After Christmas, I asked my sponsor for money to take a bus to California, to my friend in Orange County. What else could I do? I am sure that they were unhappy. They wanted very much for me to be like them, but it was not possible. I think they never understood and I think I hurt them. They all came to see me at the bus station to say good-bye. I won't forget that night because it snowed and snowed. After almost six months in California, I stopped talking with my sponsors, but every year we send each other Christmas cards.

CHOEUM RIM
Greensboro, North Carolina

It is a very hot afternoon and Choeum Rim is drenched with sweat as we begin to talk. I notice a discernible American Southern accent in some of his words. He is a man of medium height with enormous hands. There is a sparkle in his eye as he mops his brow, and the air-conditioned room begins to cool him down. He later told me his car had broken down and he had walked some distance to keep our appointment.

We lived for some time in Powelton Village in West Philadelphia. We had moved there two years before from Michigan where the cold made my family sick all the time. Many people were attacked and hurt—you know, mugged— in Philadelphia. Many people were hit in the head and a lot of people were afraid to go outside of their apartments. I also know some old people who never left their apartments for some weeks, even months. My wife became more afraid all of the time and my children came home from school having been in fights and were hurt many times. I know that they did not start the violence. I had a friend who lived in Greensboro and we decided to move to Greensboro. I hope this is the last time we have to move.

This is a very small community here, maybe three hundred Cambodian people total. It is much better than in Philadelphia, and my children are very happy here. The older ones seem to talk better, and sleep better at night. The government people like it better because only a small group of people use welfare. For these government people, if we are not on welfare, then they think we are happy. Many times this is not true. I know people who make good money, own a house and a car, and do not use welfare, but they are not happy.

We have a very strong MAA [Mutual Assistance Association] here. They try to help newcomers. They meet the new people and spend time with them. If you have a problem, you can go to them. This was not possible in Philadelphia. I did not know where the MAA groups were in Philadelphia, you see. The city was too big, too many people, and too many problems. It was easier to stay to yourself. Here the MAA tries to stop people from using welfare, although the welfare here is not like in Philadelphia; here you get very little money.

What do you do now?

I work in a factory that makes furniture. I am a wood-polish person. It is good. That is a person who gets to see the finished product. It is not a difficult job and the money is okay for this kind of work. Most of the people I work with are Cambodian. It's better to go to work with my own people. It is a good group of people; there are many Cambodians and two black people and white people in the shop where I work. We get along. We make jokes and it is okay. It is not true to say that we do not learn English or speak English; we do.

For me to work like I do is a better life. I enjoy the carpenter's job. I can see my own work become finished and see it become a beautiful object. It's not so important that you do not own it. To be able to create something that people can use is very important. I do not mind the long hours because to work with my hands clears my head. To feel the wood with my hands is like being an artist. This was not the work I did in Cambodia; there I was a tradesperson and worked in my uncle's store. It was not such a special job, but it was family and my job was for my lifetime.

What my wife and I feel the most is the kindness of the people we have met here. We see it in the community and in the sponsors and the way they help the refugees. They are different from the sponsors I knew about before. I could not say how, but they are different. I like this town. Greensboro is not too big and it doesn't get too cold. My family does not get sick.

Some American friends talk about the history of this part of the country, the South. I hear about this great battle that happened over a hundred years ago and how the North and the South fought many battles. It is like the battle between the north and the south in Vietnam in 1954. I still do not understand the reasons for the American Civil War. There were no Communists then, and I cannot understand why they wanted to have separate countries.

When we were living in Philadelphia, we used to go to New Jersey to pick blueberries. That was the only time we left the city. We made good money picking at blueberry farms while we were using welfare. My wife also works in a restaurant in the kitchen. She never worked out of the house before so this is a new experience for her. I do not mind that she works, we need the money she makes. Most men I know do not like the idea of the woman outside the home.

What do you enjoy doing the most now?

What we really enjoy the most here are the county fairs and events like that. At these fairs, they show farm animals and have fun contests. There was nothing like that in Philadelphia. I think I see the Americans enjoying themselves very much at these fairs. When I see the Americans this way, they become very special to me. I think they like themselves the most when they do these things. That is very important, to do something that makes you like yourself. In my little time in America, I have seen too many people do things they do not like; you can see it on their faces. I like the other faces.

WOMEN'S VOICES

We are the *noi-tuong* [home ministers]
of our families.
For centuries our women have participated in the decisions

that influence all that is important
to us as families
and as a society.

Even when our laws permitted our husbands
to have second wives,
they first had to receive
our approval.
So when you talk in the West
of the importance of the place
of women in a marriage,
we have much experience.

Ti Mai, Vietnamese, Santa Ana, California

MY LINH SOLAND
Lawyer and Client

We met through a mutual lawyer friend, and we talk in English about her life and her work before we begin our interview. Her office is on one of those quaint side streets in Alexandria, a second-floor office which is surprisingly decorated in Early American and cluttered with legal memorabilia. The familiar manila legal folders are stacked neatly into two piles on her desk. She is dressed in a smart three-piece dark business suit, having just returned from court.

I began my legal practice in Saigon in 1963 with my father. We were the first daughter-and-father lawyer team in the country. Most of our work was civil cases but we did criminal cases, too. You must remember that I came from a society in which the legal structure broke down with the political structure. I came from a society that slowly became unhealthy. We could feel it, especially the lawyers. The last five years were really difficult, but there was nothing we could do. It was a slow disintegration of law and order. If you don't have respect for the law, there is no society—well, this is how I felt.

I first felt it with the police. It was the police who seemed to depict the change and corruptness that came to be accepted as the way of life. There were no civil rights, no law and order. Everything broke down. If you were from a privileged class, you had privileges. For others, the police could arrest you and take you away without any charge, just like that. Nothing was safe. You had a friend one day, and then she would disappear the next and you could not find her. There would be no trace. She would be gone.

Tell me about your law practice here.

There are about 20,000 Vietnamese in northern Virginia. I would say the majority of my clients are Vietnamese. They need a great deal of legal assistance in different areas. I would guess that most of my work is in the area of family law, such as domestic violence, spouse and child abuse.

Let me tell you that you made me think about a case I had some months ago. There was this bilingual social worker who would call me for legal advice. Well, one week, she called me on a Monday and then every other day, sometimes every day. She asked me for advice about a woman who was abused by her husband. Each telephone call became more intense, more personal in nature. So finally I said to her, "This is your story, isn't it?" I heard a pause and then I asked her to come and talk to me in person. She did, and we eventually solved some of her problems.

The attorney-and-client relationship is really a process of trial and error and it must be based on trust or it will not work. Well, I try to build up that trust. To begin with, I don't really know Vietnamese perceptions of the legal profession—in Vietnam or here. I would think that most of the time it is negative. So you are trying to overcome that obstacle and you try to establish some trust. I am most effective and get the most satisfaction from helping women clients about my age or older. We can identify. I am a mother, a divorced woman, a professional. One of those issues touches them.

Most of the time, I am in Family Court with protective orders for abused wives. This is a complex social situation. You see, we are supposed to defend our clients' rights, but so often this defense is not understood by the community and I offend the community's mores. I am accused of promoting divorce, of urging separation, of destroying the family unit. Why? Because I get a court protective order for a wife who gets beaten every night by a drunk husband who can't adjust to life here.

Let me tell you, there is so much hypocrisy in the Vietnamese community. Look at this drawer of hate letters I get. You see, they don't understand the system, legal or social. I had a case last year in which I had to expose a love affair between my client's wife and a Buddhist monk. Well, you would have thought I was instrumental in some terrible act of destroying the fabric of Vietnamese society here. "A monk," they said. "He is a holy man; why make it public?" It is not good enough to tell her she broke the law. Here the monk was the exception, never mind that my client was hurt. You see, the woman is always wrong.

You know, I have to spend a great deal of time explaining to my clients how courts and judges work here. For example, I represented a woman who was a rape victim. When she was asked questions in the court, she would look at the defendants and smile. Then look at the judge and smile. I mean a big smile, almost a laugh. Why? Because it is her way of saying in public to the defendants, "You have harmed me, my spirit, but I will survive. I will not be driven into the ground." So, I had to explain to her and to this judge the differences. Usually they have not figured out this reaction.

Do the Vietnamese have a different concept of law and justice now that they are here?

Yes. I think they are still learning it. They are learning it is not like Vietnam. They see that money buys good legal help. And not all lawyers are good ones. I think contracts scare them. That is why when they first came here no one got directly involved in business. They avoided that for some time, but as they get more comfortable, they are getting used to contracts and partnership agreements. But look, there is still the thought that you can buy whatever you want, like it was in Vietnam. They hear about loopholes and exceptions to exceptions. They always want to write their senators and congressmen. One bad thing is that they don't like to report their income for taxes. They say they never paid taxes in Vietnam, so why should they pay taxes here? I am afraid this will catch up with them.

You mentioned your father. Tell me about your family.

I was one of eight girls. Can you imagine? My poor father! So, to compensate for having no sons in the family, he made sure that all of us became professional working women. All M.D.s, professors, and lawyers. All very different and yet related. I had a very rich childhood and went into an arranged marriage to an M.D. You see, my mother wanted the M.D., not me.

After Vietnam, we were resettled in Montreal and I got an M.L.S. (Master of Library Science) degree and put my husband through retraining so that eventually he got his license to practice medicine. Then I got my law degree at the University of Montreal and began to practice law. This was my second law degree. Well, the marriage fell apart for lots of reasons. We got a divorce and I got the kids. My mother will never understand that, never. Then I met a visiting scholar from George Washington University, Richard, and fell in love. We married and I moved to Virginia. Then I enrolled at George Washington University Law School and now have my third law degree. I am a member of the Virginia bar.

What aspect of legal practice here do you like the best?

It may be my professional insecurity, but I do not like litigation. I am not confident with the fine-line differences in the legal language. Before the bench, I get real nervous. But I am sure that all attorneys dislike some aspects of the practice. I'm also struck with my own cultural hang-ups about myself as a woman lawyer. Roles we live in life do not leave you, I believe. For example, I am at present the only member of the forty-member Vietnamese Bar Association who has successfully passed the bar in Virginia. The only woman lawyer, and what position do they give me in the organization? I am the secretary. Some of these things I remain quiet about. My husband and children support me; that is enough.

The best aspects of the American legal system are the appeals process, access to the courts, and especially the court of equity. This concept of equity never existed in Vietnam. We had the Napoleonic Code where everything is written, and if it is not written, it basically does not exist. You know, too, that under the Code you are guilty until proven innocent. In the U.S., to be innocent until proven guilty is like a spiritual release. It gives you self-respect.

The worst part of the system is the cost. It's very expensive. If you are poor, you have a big problem. There is a quality difference in legal representation. I do not accept all of this rush to litigation. It is sue, sue, sue. Everyone wants to solve a problem, right or wrong, before the court by suing. This tort litigation is ridiculous.

In what areas do the Vietnamese run into trouble with the law?

I see usually four areas. First, family breakdown and the resulting problems of spouse and child abuse. It is very common. Then there is divorce and separation. Second, youth problems, like petty crime, are common. Juvenile delinquency that results from parental communication breakdown. Third, as I already mentioned, tax problems, especially IRS. And finally, doctors and dentists have problems with abuse of Medicaid forms, but this is not so much. I also see a lot of immigration cases.

How could the courts be more sensitive to refugees?

Much of it has to do with how often they see these people. How frequently are they seen in the courtroom? The more you see them, the more you ask questions and learn about their life-style. So much has to do with having an understanding judge. You really cannot teach that in a classroom or legal training seminar.

I think the biggest problem is with translators. You know, at its worst, justice translated can be justice denied. So much can be lost in the translation, even by a very good translator. So many American legal concepts do not exist in Vietnamese law. It is difficult to get an accurate translation when people are under pressure of not knowing the system and then the language. That is the biggest obstacle, but I don't know how the courts can get over that one.

XOUA THAO
The Sleeping People

He never looks me in the eye, and speaks so low that he has to be asked to repeat his responses. There are very long pauses between Xoua Thoa's answers. At one point the interview stops for half an hour. There is a reluctance to talk with me about the subject.

Nan Pang was a good friend of mine. Nan Pang had lived in Seattle for more than six years before he died from the big sleep one afternoon. Few Laotians want to talk about it—it is a bad omen. We call these the sleeping people.

I knew Pang because he was a lieutenant in the army in Laos like me. We were in what was called the secret army in the 1960s. We both came from far outside Vientiane, the capital, and we knew each other quite well before we had left our village. I remember that his older brother and my older brother were about the same age and did a lot of things together, and that our families shared just about the same possessions in life. We were what you would call lower-middle-class.

For us the army was a career we could have in no other way. It was a big risk but we both succeeded. We could find no other way the kind of respect we did in Laos. We left the village and went to military training taught by the Americans. I was sent to the Vietnamese/Laos border and Pang went to the Thai border for a while. That was the last time I saw him until we saw each other in the Nong Khai refugee camp in Thailand.

We are what is called highland people, or Hmong tribespeople. We are very different from the lowland people mostly because they are Buddhist and we believe in spirits, but there are other reasons. They say that there are about five million Hmong all over the world today; most are in China. I don't know where they got those figures. I do know that since the days of the French—this would be back to the Luang Prabang, the royal capital days—we were tough fighters against the Communists. In the region of Moos Plains, it is a fact that for every one of our Hmong friends who died fighting the Pathet Lao for the CIA there would have been a CIA man dead. You see, we are known for our bravery and the Americans used this knowledge.

Did you see Pang often in Seattle?

I saw Pang very often—we both lived in Seattle. He worked first as a janitor and then as a security guard for a large storage company near the airport. It was heavy and hard work, but I think he liked it. It was security inspection of packages and crates. The hours were very long, moving heavy things all of the time. If there is one thing that I remember about Pang, it was his strength. For a highlander, he was big and very powerful. He liked calisthenics and kept himself in good physical condition. But even with all of this strength he could move so quickly, like a dancer. He liked very much American boxing—that kind of contact sport, much work with your feet. We went together several times to boxing events at the university with other friends. So this is how I remember Pang—it was a complete shock when I heard he had died.

There is nothing to the story about his last day. He had been working in the garden all morning, took a shower and rested on his bed and never woke up. His wife and children said that they never heard any noise, no cries or anything. It was just that one moment he was alive, and the next moment he was dead. Just like that, no reason.

I have read that after all these years the government health people still cannot explain the causes for any of these deaths and there have been over one hundred since we came. People just die. We call them the "sleeping people," and the fear of the Hmong people is that if we talk about it, then we get it, too—sleep and never wake up. The medical people say that maybe the reason is stress, that there is trauma that these people have gone through and that something happens to their system here. It dies. But we do not believe this. So many guesses and magic. The shamans in one community spend a lot of time dealing with spirits that have caused the deaths, maybe that is the reason.

Tell me about the shamans.

You see, to the shaman, many—maybe all—of the things in life are explained by good and bad spirits. Each shaman can give his own interpretation. These shamans are trusted by the people because they are in the community and because they give answers and advice that remind people of life at home. They don't cost as much money as doctors here in Seattle. Also, people think that they are in contact with life back in Laos. That is their real power: they can communicate with the families that are back in Laos.

In this case, the shaman looks at the way that the Hmong's traditional pattern of life has been disturbed and changed. You see, property is very important to us. In America, we are away from our traditional property where we believe our ancestors' spirits live and protect us. We are unable to practice our religion, and the shaman says that because of this change we have lost the protection of our ancestors and we are very vulnerable.

There are changing ideas about these deaths. Five years ago, what I have said was believed to be true, but today, with over one hundred deaths, many people blame it on the yellow rain that the Communists brought on Laos. They say it was this slow poison that has killed them, that made them into the sleeping people. Part of this is because even Christian Hmong people have died, too. But few people will talk with you about this, and if you try to talk with them, they will not answer. To talk about it is dangerous—you could become one of the next, the sleeping people.

NGUYEN HUNG DUNG

Seadrift, Texas

*He offers to take me for a ride in his new Thunderbird. We drive around
these small, unzoned Texas towns until dark.*

After I got out of the refugee camp with my wife and family, I came to Dallas.
We were sponsored by a Methodist church. They were very fine people. It
was an interesting time, but I could not get work in Dallas, and there was
nothing I knew how to do but to fish like my father and my grandfather. We
came from Phan Thiet in South Vietnam, and before the Communists took
over, we had a very good business. There were many fishermen in the camp
in California, and we talked about starting to fish here, but all we knew was
that you have to have a big boat and you need a lot of money to buy that big
boat.

What was your first job?

The church gave me a job as janitor for the church, but I could not be a janitor for long. There was nothing for me to do in that job. All I knew was the
sea and fishing. There, in Dallas, I was like a fish with no water. You see,
in Vietnam, to be a fisherman is one of the oldest and respected professions
and it is a very special profession. I know my family wanted the same for me.

I had a friend in Victoria, Texas, who moved to Port Luvaca. He was also
a fisherman and he had a very large family—seven or eight children. All the
time he talked about fishing along the Gulf Coast; there they have good
shrimp fishing and this was the kind of fishing we did in Vietnam. The more
he talked about returning to fishing, the less I could go on with my life in
Dallas as it was.

My two boys began school late in 1979 and soon became like the other
American children in many ways. It was easier for them to learn the language
and the ways. For my wife it was difficult; she often worked with me in the
church. We moved to Seadrift later that year when my friend moved there
from Port Luvaca.

In Seadrift, another Vietnamese man had bought a very old used boat for
eight thousand dollars. The plan was to help him repair it and then to use

it fishing for the shrimp. The boat was in terrible condition. In Vietnam, we probably would have destroyed it, but it was the boat we needed to be able to start all over again. It needed so many repairs, and for the price it was not a good deal. We spent many weeks trying to find parts and supplies. Most of this we did ourselves and we really got no help from anyone.

I would not say the people were not friendly, but, as some said, they never saw Vietnamese before. All they were used to was Mexicans—sometimes they spoke to us in Spanish! There were other problems: the owner had borrowed all the money he could and raising more to repair the boat was almost impossible. For the first time, my wife went to work in a factory and this was a big change for us. At one point I stopped working on the boat and took a job in a small luggage factory near our home. This is when the owner had no more money for making repairs.

When did the problems begin?

The problems began with the other American fishermen late in the year. We knew from the beginning that they did not want us there. I never understood their way of making less of us when they were in a crowd and now I undertand better, but that took many years. We worked very hard for long hours—much longer hours than the Americans would work—and I think they were jealous. The weather was so hot, much hotter than we had in Vietnam; but still we worked the waters at least sixteen hours a day. The other fishermen complained that we were too close to shore and other things. They said that we were not in Asia, and here, in America, we were to fish by rules. "What rules?" we asked.

Later, we learned the rules better, but this was a complete surprise to us. In Vietnam, you take your boat out and you put your nets overboard and fish. Here, it is different. So, at least we bought a small American flag and put it on the boat, but I think that made them even more angry.

It was not until other boats in the next year came with other Vietnamese, that the trouble started. A white man was accidentally killed by a Vietnamese man with a gun. The Vietnamese man said he started it; I do not know. One of our boats for no reason burned one night and there could be no reason unless someone set it on fire. We had some difficulty getting fuel and materials to make repairs; also, we had problems selling the fish at the market.

The waters to the north of Seadrift are good for shrimp. Now we know about size and distance rules for the fishing. In Vietnam, you take everything from the sea and being a good fisherman depends upon your ability. The other American fishermen said we stole from them and that we would destroy the shrimp industry. They said that there were many problems we caused when we came. It took me two years to save enough money to buy my own boat for $10,000.

What happened to the Vietnamese in the community?

My children were always in fights in school. They were beaten and called names. I know they were injured many times, both inside and out. The places the Vietnamese lived in were vandalized, and one night the KKK burned a cross in our neighbor's yard. Everyone was scared and some stopped fishing for a short time and talked about moving to Galveston or to New Orleans. Then people from Washington and the governor's office talked to us about the problems. Many newspaper people came and I am told they even made a movie about us. I just continued to work and did not stop.

They did not want us to come to Seadrift, but this was our work in Vietnam and it is our work here. We are good fishermen and work hard. I am now an American. If you are a fisherman, then you must fish. I suppose the fear for the Americans was when more Vietnamese continued to come. They said what we did was not American—they said no American works that hard, and with all our family working together was not the way it was done here. Well, why not? We were always told America was a country where you worked hard. I never was a day on welfare. But these American fishermen were afraid we would take all of the shrimp before they got out of bed.

This was five or six years ago. Things are much better now. We have a good fishermen's association led by Colonel Nam. Now, we build our own boats and go out further for the shrimp. The Vietnamese own over 100 boats here, and 130 in Galveston and over 200 in New Orleans. None of us wanted to be janitors—if you are a fisherman, you fish.

SAELEE SIO LAI
High School in San Antonio

She is a quiet teenager with long dark hair swept over her shoulder. She wears braces on her teeth, but has a full, friendly smile. She is wearing

shocking pink nail polish and speaks with her hands. There is a burst of en-
ergy with Saelee the moment she enters the room.

To belong here, you need to understand the way people do things and the
differences there are in doing things. This has been a hard lesson for me. Laotians do not compete as the Vietnamese. We are different. We look very careful and look for a long time at things. I think people in San Antonio think
I do things in a strange way, but maybe they do not take so long to think about
the differences.

The Laotians never touch, and for us a kiss on the face or slap on the back
is very rude. I also had to learn to wave my hand. In Laos, waving to call a
person is a sign of contempt, and to wave to someone waving palm outward
in the American fashion is rude. If we have to wave, we put the palm down-
ward with a little motion to our fingers. Texans do not understand this. It is
also considered rude to sit with your feet pointed straight out at another person
or to put your feet on furniture pointing at someone. Unlike the Christians,
we believe the body has thirty-two souls. So these are some of the things I
have had to learn and relearn here in America. Some of the Laotian customs
I can use in my own way and some I must forget.

I remember the first day of school, the teacher looked me in the eyes—the
eyes! I was frightened. She looked at me in my eyes! Well, you only look at
people when you are angry, when they do something wrong. Even after some
American told me this, I could not believe it. No one had ever done that to
me before except my parents before I was going to be punished.

To me, adjusting and starting over in San Antonio has been a matter of
coping with all the different meanings of things that are confusing and different. When you learn something a certain way, it is difficult to change and
do it some other way.

Being in high school here means understanding the way my American
friends do things. For me, a big part of living here is just to catch up on so
many things that have already happened and I know nothing about. I learned
these things late; like the way you have friends and form small clubs of
friends—you can't just be friends with everyone, you need two or three friends
and then you exchange with other small groups.

For us here, it's not possible to date boys, especially American boys. My
parents go crazy. Well, I suppose, for any boys. There is no compromise in
my family on this subject. You date and that means you marry. No compromise. All my friends have these weekend dates and talk about them all week.

All I can talk about is TV or homework, what else? They do not want to hear about Lao culture. We study Texas history because Texas just had its 150th birthday. Well, who cares about the 3,000-year history of Laos? Nobody wants to hear about Prince Souvanna Phouma, but they like stories about Sam Houston.

To become part of the San Antonio community is to continue to listen and learn. My parents are separated from me in many ways. They depend on me because they do not speak good English, so I am going in two directions: I celebrate Soukhuan [Well-Wishing] with my family. Last week it was Boun Bang Foy [Rocket Festival]. My plans are to go to San Antonio College next year. I don't know yet what I want to study.

LOST ELEPHANT

I remember our Mekong and Tonle Sap rivers
and the Cardamon Mountains
which made my Cambodia so beautiful.
My father came from the Mois Plateau.
As a farmer I think about the monsoons
which would begin about now in
November and end in May.
I miss the cool winter
and the hot summer.

Here in Michigan there is too much cold,
too much snow. As a child I remember
the excitement of seeing my first elephant,
but today they do not come close to the village.
Men have killed them for their strength,
not their beauty. Now they live in museums
for schoolchildren to come to visit
and to tease.

As a Cambodian refugee
I am such an exotic animal
and I live in this community

where they look at me like I were that elephant
who is not able to travel
his familiar Cambodian forests.

Cambodian high school student, age sixteen, Philadelphia

LE RIEU TAI
Second Thoughts

*This is my third interview with Le Rieu Tai. He is sitting in an oversized
chair, chain-smoking Camel cigarettes and sipping tea. He is most comfortable speaking in French but uses English when he talks about the American
refugee program or government. To start, he asks me several questions—then
there is a very long pause. He becomes pensive and a melancholy mood prevails. Toward the end of our talk, he is moved to tears and abruptly stops.*

I knew before I left Vietnam that I would have a difficult time in the United
States. I had absolutely no illusions about what life would be like here because I had worked with so many Americans and I had friends who had come
to the United States to visit, work, and go to school. My intuition was correct.
It has been a very, very difficult time for me, and in hindsight, I might have
put up a greater fight to have been allowed to stay in Vietnam. They would
always have had need of a surgeon. But my children and my wife get very
upset when they hear me say this.

Tell me about your life in Vietnam.

I came from a privileged family in Hanoi. Ours was a conservative ancient
family; we were traditionalists—I suppose you might call us royalists. We had
a special life and so many of my family had been to France and had contributed much to the arts and to the community. I am proud to say that. It was
a life in which we had everything that we needed. In the streets of Saigon,
I felt respect. People recognized me; they would not talk to me directly, but
they would nod and recognize me; I was known as a good surgeon and medi-

cal doctor. All that, of course, has changed. Now, people don't care who you are; they are too busy with their lives to stop and to acknowledge you; some of this goes for the young Vietnamese, I must say. I don't even know who my neighbor is in this building. That is one of the hardest parts of being here: no one would care or miss you. This has been a shock—the move here—I do not think I have adjusted to the transfer. I am a bird in a small cage and the cage gets smaller each year.

After the fall of Dienbienphu, Vietnam became a place of uncertainty and nobody could be trusted, nobody would trust you. Even the cousin of my wife had planned against my life! I remember almost giving a letter of introduction to the new government that stated, in essence, that I was an antisocial revolutionary and so ordered me to be killed. From my own family! Can you believe it? Fortunately, my Vietnamese intuition was working. I read the letter before anything could happen, but the idea in all of this is that you could trust no one. And from that experience I will never trust again—surely I would have been killed.

So, it is that fear and distrust which we have lived with for so many decades and which our children grew up with. You need to understand this fear concept because it is a big part of our character here today in America. You see, since 1954, many of us have lived several lives already. We have tried to change the system or work with the system, but we have been cheated and sold out. This can happen to you only so many times and then you become bitter, cynical, and you stop trying.

Have lessons been learned?

I don't know. I ask myself, what has America learned about Vietnam? I can't answer that. I get so upset. Look at Central America now. I do not know. What angers me the most is the way they talk about the war. People who were never there, who know nothing about the country or the history. I get upset when they call Vietnam a dirty war. Why a dirty war? You were defending our lives and our country. To me it was not a dirty war but a noble cause. I want to tell them—look, remember we are here as refugees, following the errors of the American military in Vietnam. There was nothing dirty about any of it, it was war. But I am too Asian, too polite, I say nothing.

I have three sons and five daughters. We arrived in Fort Chaffee, Arkansas, in May 1975 and I went immediately into a state of total disbelief and shock. I was drowsy and all the time in a dream. I had no reaction to any of it; it just happened. On the boat to Guam, our suitcases were stolen and all the money in gold we had went, everything. My wife had packed it and not told me what was inside. I failed to watch it carefully and it was gone—stolen. All that we had was gone. Yes, I think at times it was all a mistake for me to come, but my family would not leave me behind.

I gave up the idea of ever practicing medicine, but I have not come to peace with this decision. I tried but I will never pass the exams. I am too old and too emotionally rocky to concentrate. I look often at my hands and think of the skill I had and how it was just taken away. All that was dear to me in my country is now a memory. How do you counsel someone like me? How do you tell me to start all over again? My children are my consolation. Oh, for my children it will be good, but I just wait and wait. I have stopped working three years ago as a counselor; it was me who needed the counseling. I stopped work because the money from the project was cut so I was out of a job. So I sit at home and think and drink a lot of tea and watch and listen to my wife, who has become very religious with the temple and Buddha.

When I became a United States citizen, I thought I would be able psychologically to renounce my past. But this has not happened. In Vietnam, I had a chauffeur and maids; now, I do not even own a car and I clean my humble apartment myself—it is all too much to explain. Lately, I have thought a great deal about the people left behind. My sister is one of the persons forced to live in a new economic zone, and we have not heard from her. So many friends have not been heard from, and our fear is that the United States will soon forget completely about Vietnam. But people are still fleeing and starving because of the Communists; a kilo of rice costs more than five dollars.

I expected to have a difficult time when I came to America, and I was correct. My only consolation is that I was a good physician in Vietnam—I saved many lives and helped people. These are some of the things I have been thinking about lately. It helps balance the decision I made to come.

CHAPTER 5

Photo: Ph. Theard/UNHCR

ESTABLISHING
ROOTS

There are a variety of ways to measure how well an immigrant or refugee is adapting to a new community: becoming economically independent, learning the language, understanding the culture, and eventually participating in the political process. The experience of adapting to a new society is a process unique for each person. The degree of adaptation, of "making it," is affected by individual needs and the possibility of participation in the new society. But exactly how do refugees themselves measure success? Much of what they talk about concerns a gradual process of establishing roots over time. This chapter explores the process that many refugees call "making me real American."

The refugees emphasize that the most important adaptation measures for them are employment and language training. They argue that, while related needs like medical care and obstacles like mental health issues continue to affect the degree to which someone can support himself or is capable of be-

---

◁ FACING PAGE
This young woman from Vietnam works in a laboratory in San Diego, California. For many refugees finding a suitable job or acquiring new skills is one of the most difficult aspects of resettlement.

109

coming a part of a new community, they are not primary needs. "To become part of America is simple—you get a job and learn good English," said Fresno farmer Ge Lor. "It's just two basic things: work and language; the rest will follow."

Getting oneself adapted economically is dependent upon several factors, such as the refugee's educational and work background, household size and composition, and the state of the general economy. There are also other related issues. For example, the characteristically large and extended refugee family can create a housing dilemma. Often misunderstandings between landlords and local housing authorities have generated or helped reinforce unfair stereotypes about values and life-styles of the refugees. This carries over into the local community's understanding and general acceptance of the people themselves.

An integration theory used by social workers and others who work with immigrants and refugees seems to determine that the longer a person is in a new community, the more able that person is to become a functional part of it. Time is seen as the great healer, smoother, and builder. But along with every other generalization are the exceptions. Often the refugee with the camp stay experience arrives with or later develops some adjustment problem that may take a considerable period of time to overcome, if he overcomes it at all. "You know you are dealing with all of these different personalities from so many different experiences. Generalizations of these people will only get you in trouble," said Le Rieu Tai. "For example, I am a Vietnamese. I have no idea what a Cambodian does or the way he thinks."

It is generally thought that employment opportunities increase with time in the country—the longer one is in the United States, the greater one's chances are for full participation in the labor force. This has often been described by those interviewed as not necessarily true. Rather late in the resettlement program, it was realized that the refugee population contained a sizable portion of vulnerable groups: widows—who are often heads of households—the elderly, and unaccompanied foster children under the age of fourteen. Because these children may have spent a considerable number of years in a camp waiting to come to the United States, they are often years behind their peers in education and training. These groups need extra time and special consideration.

Another important consideration in understanding these refugees is that there are very distinct racial, ethnic, and class characteristics among them that go unnoticed to the Western eye. Ethnic Chinese/Vietnamese (those whose ancestry is from China), for example, are viewed in a very different way from "pure" Vietnamese among their own countrymen. The highland Hmong from Laos are seen differently than the lowland Laotians, and often the Cambodians will discuss the influences of Chinese or other Asian, or "non-pure" Khmer, people. To Westerners, these may seem to be points of subtle distinction, but to the refugee they are a former source of identity fundamental to the community structure; therefore they affect adaptation here.

Do Van Chi, a former Vietnamese academic now living in New Jersey, explains that to understand the refugees you might try to understand their cultures in a village community structure. "You need to see it in an anthropological view." Outside the West, and especially the United States, the notion of seeing life in a global perspective is unthinkable. A basic shared value of these Southeast Asian groups is that one thinks primarily of promoting and protecting one's immediate family unit and then maybe the local community. Do Van Chi continues: "First I am concerned with my family—what you call extended family, which includes cousins and uncles, and then I might be concerned about neighbors; usually not. This is the way it is. We protect our own family first—all the rest is of a secondary concern."

What has become clear from these interviews is that the Southeast Asian refugees are quickly learning the new system, including how to participate in the political process of coalition building. It is beginning to be seen in the over four hundred Mutual Assistance Associations, ethnic self-help organizations which have developed around the country. "We have these refugee associations so that we can better organize ourselves. We have got to learn the American political system, but that will take time," said Washingtonian Pho Ba Long. "I suppose when you get to the bottom of it, the Vietnamese and the American politician have a great deal in common. But it is a new way to act for us, to walk in a new way. We do not want to appear naive or silly. We are still learning. I think some day our vote will swing elections."

Some of those interviewed commented that one should take into consideration the "exterior picture" and set of values acquired by these populations from the U.S. military during the war years. Americans presented an image of a life-style and values that many refugees are either still looking for or rejecting. "We always thought this representational democracy would eliminate the worst features of the Vietnamese political system. We thought this one-vote idea brought about the good life. But I see so many poor people in America who do not vote and are not represented in this system. You really need to live here to understand all of this. Much of it is not attractive," said Ninh Van Nguyen, now living in California.

The refugees arrived to find a new society with different values and ideas. They were sponsored by secular and religious voluntary agencies whose networks around the country had resettled over two million refugees since the end of World War II. For the refugee, the very concept of volunteerism was foreign. "The idea of a stranger helping a stranger was so bizarre, so foreign to me. I thought surely there must be an economic gain for them in this. I was wrong," said one refugee in Boston, commenting on the sponsorship process. Also, sponsors varied in motivation, cross-cultural skills, and resource supply. For example, some refugees benefited from having a very generous sponsoring church which provided them with a car and an apartment, while others may have received only information about how to buy a car or rent an apartment. This disparity often caused misunderstandings for both sponsor and sponsoree.

The use of welfare remains one of the key issues troubling the resettlement program. Few sponsors and fewer refugees understood the pitfalls of the American welfare system as they have come to know it. Essentially what exists are fifty separate state-administered public assistance systems federally funded for a period of eighteen months of total reimbursement to states for refugees. Often, however, the refugee's needs exceed eighteen months (it was originally established at thirty-six months but reduced) and the refugee then became dependent upon state funds. Each state is unique and each system determines eligibility and benefit levels and these change over time. By the end of 1989, for example, over 41 percent of refugees in the country for two years or less were receiving some form of cash assistance. Refugee welfare utilization rates also vary from state to state and differ by ethnic group and length of time in the country.

In part to address this welfare concern, the Department of Health and Human Services (HHS) funded a rather extensive national program of refugee assistance and self-help demonstration projects to encourage employment. The policy goal for the program has always been self-sufficiency in as short a time period as possible. These HHS projects, however, have met with varied and limited success.

Certainly no other issue has angered federal and state law and policymakers and the general public as has the issue of welfare. It remains an emotionally charged subject and a great deal of present reaction has historic roots in the concept of welfare abuse which, by interpretation of the immigration statute, ultimately is capable of denying someone citizenship. This "public charge" concept dates historically from the turn of this century.

Using welfare also invites what one refugee called "mythical notions." It negates and tarnishes the American myth of the homeless immigrant who arrives with nothing and becomes a bank president in his lifetime. It is a sentimental Horatio Alger scenario that captures the spirit of hard work and American values. "In America, you have this idea of success," said a woman from Cambodia. "To come without a penny and to have money and power in a few years. For a very, very few it is possible. All things, including luck, must be on your side, but for the majority, it is a storybook adventure. It is not real. Sure, we make a living, but we pay a very dear price in the end. Nobody ever talks about peace of mind or things like that. It is just to have a flashy car and to own a big business. Well, for most, this is not possible," said Sirathra Som. "Nothing less."

Welfare use, however, requires a much closer understanding of the system, which currently provides a "package" consisting of cash assistance, medical assistance, and food stamps. Often a request for medical assistance is addressed by federal regulations that require an applicant to be informed of his right to cash assistance. Too often the job-training programs available in the local community are only open to persons receiving cash assistance. The other side of the welfare story, however, are the increased reports of fraud by the refugees themselves by not reporting income earned while receiving welfare—what one refugee termed the "working off the books" situation.

The process of learning English elicited a great deal of discussion. From the interviewees' perspective, the quality of English language training received is seriously questioned. The method of instruction, usually ESL, varies greatly in the way it is taught. Too often, respondents report that the classes are not relevant to their needs, are poorly taught, and are held at hours that are not conducive to learning. And the debate remains over whether or not a refugee should learn English first or get a job first; it is said that ideally they should occur together at the same time.

Once in the United States, refugees continue to move. The patterns of refugee residency affect the way a newcomer establishes himself. This has proven to be an extremely mobile group. If the distance to a fellow countryman is too far or the weather or economic conditions are not good, the refugee might move. "Why not move to where we feel comfortable with our own people? This is a free country," said Cambodian Sam Song. What has happened, then, is a geographic redistribution of Southeast Asian refugees to selected areas of the country. This, again, is not so different from other groups in the country, native or immigrant. "We went to San Diego because there was a job there and it was good weather. It makes good sense, does it not?" said Laotian Ge Lor.

The greatest unmet need refugees report is access to health care. Apart from the cost and the availability of insurance, many refugees arrived with special health problems, such as inactive tuberculosis, tropical amebic infections, and other disorders not often seen by health-care workers in the country. Many refugees have never had access to Western medicine, and they complain that they were never given a description of the procedures being performed on them. Extensive and unexplained drawing of blood, for example, often causes refugees to refrain from returning for follow-up treatment. "Who would ever think that this rich and powerful country would treat its people so bad? There are so many medical people and hospitals here, and to use them one must be rich and very privileged. It is not right," said Vietnamese Van Tran.

Once they have met their basic needs for survival and such secondary needs as home ownership and career direction, the refugees have begun to question their role in the larger society and to confront the problems facing them as a minority group. The quiet racism and discrimination that once went unperceived because of the refugees' inability to detect inequitable treatment are now surfacing in the form of prejudicial responses and reactions. This is forcing the refugee as a new American to deal with his American situation and to come to terms with himself in his new country. In the following conversations concerning the process of establishing roots in America, the discussion focuses on the issues of needs, employment, and obstacles.

The Needs

S. P. BIP
The Elderly

He is sixty-nine years old but looks older. He has very bad posture, probably due to arthritis, and has difficulty hearing my questions. A French speaker, he talks a little about life in Santa Rosa, California. He arrived with a friend who was later identified as his cousin. The cousin shakes my hand and leaves. Later, he returns and sits quietly, waiting for our talk to end.

I was the director of a small machine factory outside Phnom Penh before the Communists took over. I arrived in the U.S. when I was sixty-seven in 1979. For me that is very old. I think I was too old to come here.

When the so-called liberation of my country took place, everybody in the capital was expelled to the countryside in five directions: those who took the Pochentong Road and national routes 5 and 6 went to work in the north; people who took the Takhman Road, the national route number 1, and the road that follows the Bassac River went to work in the southeast. We were on that road. I lost everything. I lost everything that I had owned, that is all I can remember. I was in Camp Sakeo before I came to this country.

The St. Francis Church on 47th Street took care of my family. I remember Miss Betty Allen and Father Hilferty and the teacher, a nun, Maureen Winifred. They were very good to my children. But not many good things happened to me. We live in Stoneleigh Court in West Philadelphia, and the black people do not want us to live here. In Bristol, Levittown, they threw a bomb at some fellow Cambodians.

I am an old man to live through all these things. I am too old for all of these things. I want to be able to go to the pagoda and to walk in my gardens. This will not be possible ever again. Three of my children do not live here and I do not see them every day. They talk to me about things I do not understand, and I talk to them about things they have little interest in. I went with my wife to study English, but it was too difficult for me. The teacher talks too fast and I cannot understand her. In my class is a woman from Romania who speaks French. For the first time last week we spoke. It was exciting for me, although I cannot speak French as good as she does. She is the first person here that smiles a kind smile at me.

We live in a small apartment that is always crowded with fellow Cambodians who have no place to stay or are visiting from other cities. I would like to be able to return to Cambodia someday, but I know that would not be possible. I think that the Khmer Rouge destroyed it completely.

VIETNAMESE OLD WOMAN

My children forget
that I am head of home in America
as I was in Vietnam.

My children do not obey
my requests
and think I am without the new wisdom
they have learned in America.
I have the old wisdom.

My children forget
the teaching of our ways,
of what their father once taught them,
of life in Vietnam.
Too much television, too much music.
They tell me always,
I am in America.
My children change
and I do not change.
My children forget
me.

Vietnamese Woman, Dallas, Texas

TI LY and HUOR KIM TANN
Urban Widows

Their Bronx apartment building is in a neighborhood that could be taken as a scene from a New York City crime movie. The signs of urban blight and poverty are harshly evident everywhere. The front door to the building is missing, the elevator broken. Behind a series of door locks is a clean but barren apartment. On the wall above a large filing cabinet is a framed picture of President John F. Kennedy, which is next to a Chinese calendar for the Year of the Dog. Both women converse in Khmer.

Ti Ly: I was born in the province of Battambang, in the city of Sisophon, in Cambodia. I went to school for two years, and then my marriage was arranged for me. Even if I wanted to continue school I could not, because Cambodian tradition has it that your time is for your husband, and when the Communists took over, all of the schools were closed. The Communist rulers forced everyone in the city to go to the countryside and to be farmers. I was eighteen years old then, and I worked in the rice field and took care of cows. My husband had to dig ditches for the farm irrigation. It was very hard work. We received very little rice after the day's work, and we were always hungry; I was certain we would die because we had so little food.

In the time before Pol Pot was expelled by the Vietnamese soldiers, he was in control of Cambodia almost four years. It is said that in that period of time he killed half of all Cambodian people. Most people died because they had no food or medicine. Most of my relatives died and so many of my husband's family, too. They were killed like animals. Why? Because they were city people or because they had some education.

How did you escape?

In late 1979 we escaped to Thailand and stayed in the Nong Chan refugee camp for four months. Then the Thai government sent all the refugees in that camp back to Cambodia because they did not want us. There were many bombs on the way, ground mines, and a lot of people died. After I got back to Cambodia, I lived there for only three months. If we stayed longer we would have died, so we fled Cambodia a second time.

We lived in Khao I Dang camp for fifteen months, in Mairut Camp about three months, in Chanbori Camp about four months, and in Galang Camp for four months. In the last month, my husband died from trouble with breathing. So I had to come to this country alone. We never had any children because he was sick. I came to New York and have been here in the Bronx.

Huor Kim Tann: I grew up in the capital, Phnom Penh. I went to school for three years and was married and had three children. In 1975, the war ended and we thought there would be peace, but it was worse than we could ever dream. From 1975, life was miserable and unhealthy. The Communists controlled everyone who lived in the cities and provinces. My husband and I were forced to leave. We walked four days with the children. It was very difficult, and all we had was a bag of clothing.

We decided to escape. The main roads were filled with Vietnamese troops and there were so many ground mines along the way. The road was narrow, like a sidewalk. It was crowded with people trying to rush forward. They stepped on the mines and were killed; my husband was one of those people. The people I was with helped me with the children, and we had to leave him and go on or we would have been killed. I knew my life had ended with him there.

I remember that along the way there were many dead bodies of people killed by mines and robbers. We could not go back so we walked for two days. We kept moving step by step and with the children it was very difficult. After some time, we saw the Khmer Rouge soldiers, but they did not want us; they were on their way to attack the Vietnamese troops. After one day, we got to the camp of the Khmer National Liberty Army and then to Thailand and the U.S. Now I am here.

T.L.: St. Rita's Church in the Bronx is a place many Cambodians meet. Most Cambodians live in the Fordham Road area. For all the time I have been here I have not learned English very well. [*She points to her lips and shakes her head.*]

Have you studied English, ESL?

Three times I tried ESL. No good. Many bad things happened to me here in America. They took my money and many times they tried to rape me. This has happened to many Cambodian women I know. It is very dangerous at night. My world is this apartment, you see. The social workers tell me about learning English—better English so that I can get a job. They tell me I am too young, that I need to work. I do not listen to them, so for these years I take welfare and food stamps and stay at home. My friends tell me that I am still pretty and I have sometimes boyfriends—although it is difficult to be a widow with no children because married Cambodian women cannot control their husbands around widow ladies and they get very jealous. Sometimes my boyfriends bring me presents when they come to visit.

H.K.T.: My youngest baby died of measles in the refugee camp in Thailand. Now my two children are in school in grades four and five. They have many problems and other children fight with them sometimes. Often the teachers want to see me, and I must go with a friend who speaks English—my English is not good. Because of the children, I have not been able to work; mostly staying at home and visiting some friends.

It is not possible for me to learn good English and at the same time get a job. They keep telling me to learn English—but all of the neighbors speak Spanish. [*She laughs.*] I think I should learn Spanish. Ti Ly has been a good friend, and before her, I was very much alone here. It was not good to live that way.

Many widow women live together because the rent is high, and for protection. Ti Ly and I are like sisters now. Sometimes we visit friends together and always we travel together when we go shopping. Sometimes we go with some other Cambodian women who live in this building. Almost all families here are now Cambodian—five years ago, only two families were Cambodian.

T.L.: I never really knew about life here before I came. I did not expect anything but peace. But after so many years here in the Bronx, I would like to do something different.

LE VAN AN
High School Dropout

He looks like any high school "punk" type from any big city. He has a distinctive, tough air as he enters the room. It could be an '80s version of James Dean's Rebel without a Cause. *Behind the image appears, after we have spent some time together, a young teenager who wants to be accepted by a peer group. There is something very likable about him. He offers me a cigarette.*

I sit in this classroom and listen to the noise about the American Civil War and about civics. Who cares? For me, the reality is the streets and money and getting a good-paying job. What do these people know about war, and history, about life? I lived through the war.

I live in the Mission District in San Francisco. I came to the U.S. about eight years ago when my parents paid for my way out of the country. The boat landed in Malaysia.

My father was in prison for two years before I left Vietnam. They spent all their money on getting me out. They kept me back from going to school, sort of preparing me for leaving—not wanting others to know and not letting me make friends or get familiar with the school officials. All the time I knew I was going to leave, going to never see my familiar streets again. I was told that my parents would follow, which never happened.

Why were you placed in California?

I had an uncle in Fresno. They called us "unaccompanied minors," and the first two years here were okay, but things got bad in my uncle's family—I did not get on with his wife and his daughter. So eventually I split and came to the Mission. I ran into some trouble. Then I went through several foster-care mills, group homes, and then my first log cabin, which is a miniprison for young people. It was all the same and I got bored with it. My uncle gave up on me a long time ago—said CYA [California Youth Authority] would know what to do with me now that I was in America. What crap! He just wanted to get me off his back. For me, I just wanted my same room and some quiet for longer than two weeks before I was moved.

Tell me about the gangs.

I got involved with a Chinese gang four years ago. They recruit us Vietnamese as runners, which means we do a lot of the small car crimes, you know, the small stuff. They know how far we can go with the police. They know that we won't get thrown in jail because we are youth. Some of the small stuff were easy drugs—lots of marijuana and pills. What they're doing is building up the networks not only here but in southern California. Knowing Chinese was the part that got me in.

I'd like a good-paying job and a place of my own, but I can't see that happening right now. I do a lot of walking and thinking on those streets and I think about Vietnam and home.

HO XUAN TAM
Dreams of Stanford

He is wearing a three-piece blue business suit. There is a great deal of self-confidence in the way he presents himself.

I would like to study math at Stanford University when I finish high school next year. I have been in the United States seven years this fall. Sometimes, I wish I could just skip my senior year and go to Stanford; I've learned enough—I'm bored and I've learned all I am going to learn from high school.

My mother and father were very educated people from Saigon, and there was always pressure to study. I can remember my father helping me with my studies when I was first in this country; he had difficulty with the language, but somehow he always understood my assignments. It was always a big ritual after dinner to study with him; I know he looked forward to it. The higher math I had was difficult for him, but he kept at it until trig, and then he said I could complete that assignment without his assistance. My mother played hardly any place in this homework help.

My father was a famous lawyer in Vietnam; he had a great love for books. He always told me that a book was like a beautiful bird—the more you read of it the more beautiful it becomes. He was very, very proud when my older sister got a scholarship to study premed last year at Stanford. It was as if he got the scholarship. So this is pretty much what I'm going to do—go to Stanford.

We have always lived in the Tenderloin section in San Francisco, and I go to Galileo High School—which isn't so bad. Most of the students are okay, but your friends are always from your people—your own nationality.

Tell me about your friends.

I have two Vietnamese friends. It is difficult to break into any new group, people stick to themselves. My one Vietnamese friend knows a few Chinese, but it's more that they are polite to her rather than they are friends.

Scholastically, Galileo is not the best high school in San Francisco. Most Asians do pretty well in school, and there is always some jealousy by the black and Spanish students, but I don't care. If they are jealous, I can't do anything about it. I work hard, they can too. Besides, the Vietnamese are supposed to raise the math and science scores in all of the San Francisco schools, so we help improve the system for everybody.

I think one of the big problems in the school is all this wasted time in lunch and study halls, and most of the teachers are not so good. They just keep repeating what they've already said. Me, I'd change the whole system and speed it up—let you get out of there earlier.

To get a full scholarship to Stanford is very difficult. They want to see somebody with everything going for them. I don't think my guidance counselor at Galileo understands how important this is to me. All he talks about are the second and third choices of schools. I want the best and he doesn't know my father. In some ways, I'm following in my sister's shadow. So everyone thinks I will do the same. I wish my parents could see that.

Do you attend school sports events?

No, and I don't go to school dances; there are more important things to do. I want to be able to get a higher SAT score than my sister had. It's not impossible, but it's not very realistic because I'm still weak in my verbal scores. I need to practice more. For me, math is the purest of all sciences. It is the most powerful language, and you can learn to speak it even if your English is not perfect.

HENG MUI
Citizenship

She has very expressive eyes, and has brought me a collection of photographs of herself, mostly from her life in this country.

I became a citizen last year; I am now an American. I do not especially feel like an American, but I don't know if there is any special way I should feel. There are lots of stereotypes about how Americans look and how they act; I don't fall into any of those categories.

For some refugees, becoming an American is not an easy thing to do. It means you give up that final thing that is yours, your nationality. To take away your nationality is to deprive you of an important piece of your identity. We have lost so much, so many of us arrived with nothing. To give up our nationality is just too much to ask. I know people who are not ready to do this; it's too painful, too embarrassing.

I remember when my sister suddenly died in France, and I went to the immigration office and applied for a travel document. When the woman at the desk asked me to write my nationality, which was question three, I wrote South Vietnam. When she saw the application, she took a pencil and put two lines through the word Vietnam and wrote "stateless." Those two pencil lines scratched through my heart. In a few minutes she took away my nationality. There was nothing I could do.

When I took my oath, I thought, "Oh my God! Everything is gone!" But after it happened, I never thought about it. The most painful part was just thinking about it. There is something exciting about holding my new blue passport and knowing that I will vote next year for the president.

PHYLLIS and TOAN NGUYEN
Bridging Two Cultures

I first met Phyllis and Toan in Houston where she was a social worker and he was in his last year of dental school. They both have a great sense of humor, including practical jokes I observed they played on each other. They seem to understand each other's background and culture and are very comfortable talking about their own likes and dislikes. Doing the right thing in an ethically tough or questionable situation is very important to them. They have survived together, as they say, in spite of their families. They are both very much involved with their church work.

Phyllis: I was not what my mother-in-law expected when she thought of a daughter-in-law. I guess I never will be, but that doesn't worry me now. She had an image of how I should be. You know, it's that Pearl Buck type daughter-in-law image, which is the traditional, subservient, and above all else obedient daughter-in-law. But I think it's the same with any mother-in-law and daughter-in-law relationship—there are the good times and the bad times. I like talking about the good ones.

My in-laws live in Midland, Texas, which is a safe distance. I think it's real important that married people respect their mates first and not parents; that's a real twist from the Vietnamese relationships. Mind you, there is a great deal of room for misunderstandings in all of these issues. I don't mean to criticize or be unfair, but that's just the way it is.

I spent two years in Vietnam, 1972 to 1974. There were a lot of political changes going on in the country—right under my nose—and I missed most of them. I was a journeyman for the Southern Baptist Convention; which meant I was a support person to the Baptist mission. Vietnam was not my choice; I really wanted to go to Africa or Israel. But it proved to be a great choice and I fell in love with Vietnamese culture and the Vietnamese people.

There was no way that I could get enough of the language, the traditions. There I was, this small-town Texas Baptist girl headed for all of these new experiences with Asian culture. It was a great thing. My eyes couldn't get bigger.

Toan: I am an example of that very ambitious Vietnamese who wants to get ahead here. You see, I always have to prove myself. I do very well in the educational systems here. I like the way you can study and are able to excel. You either know the answer or you do not. I like that, that exactness.

I got my mechanical engineering degree from the university of Texas and worked for a year for Atlantic Richfield. It was a good job and good money; but I got bored so I applied to dental school; in part because my dentist made it sound so good and encouraged me, and I thought it would be a good job. Well, I graduated top in my class. But I was restless and after two years I wanted something more. I was very good at surgery [*he shows me his hands*] and I wanted a more challenging outlet, you know, something more creative. I want to be a plastic surgeon so here I am in my first year of medical school in Lubbock.

Did your families agree to the marriage?

Phyllis: Both of our families were opposed from the start to our marriage—and I mean dead opposed. We met at the University of Texas and were married in 1978. Toan has seven brothers and sisters. They all have Vietnamese spouses. So for us the families were the difficult hurdle.

I don't think my mom ever really accepted the marriage. Although she was what you call a "concerned Christian," I was her daughter and there are limitations to these things. Anyway, she died six months after we were married. My father accepts Toan and they get along very well. The kids help the situation—we have two boys, Jesse, who is six, and Mark, who is four. The kids bring us together. A large part of it is seeing we are happy, but the fact that Toan is a professional, ambitious, and successful person helps.

What does education mean to Vietnamese?

Education is God. That is how the Vietnamese look at it. You want to talk about success stories, well, Toan's family is a perfect example. Every one of his brothers and sisters is a professional. The youngest brother is trying to find himself right now, but he'll work it out. I have enormous respect for my father-in-law. He was very wealthy in Vietnam, a high-placed minister in the government, and then he lost everything and now he is a machinist. He had to learn how to work. I'm serious—it's a different kind of work style.

The main difference between the American and Vietnamese families is, I guess, the discipline aspect. The father's role is to monitor and control and help the kids keep focus. It's that focus that always impresses me. It's real direction, no deviation. You just look straight ahead. For example, Toan's father was aware of all the kids' university exam schedules and would call the kids before the test and after it to find out the results. Talk about pressure! And what's more, they were expecting his calls.

Have you experienced racism?

Toan: Racism—sure, I've experienced it, but I don't like talking about it. You sense it—it has never been direct. It's sort of a feeling. You know the stereotypes, so when they push me to the wall, I show them my degrees. Sure, I am a minority person but this is what I really am and this is what I really do. It's a weapon, a defense; I know that, so what? As a minority person with your degrees, you get power in this country. You better your position in society. I never think of myself in terms of being a minority.

As a D.D.S., you are kind of a second-class citizen; the M.D.s run the hospital. There are only two hundred D.D.S./M.D.s in this country. It's a prestigious combination and I will soon have it.

I've gotten a lot of teasing mostly when other Vietnamese get angry about me having an American wife. I don't think it's really malicious or evil. They joke and tell me I have betrayed Vietnamese culture, that my wife is a capitalist. Can you believe it—who could be better capitalists than the Vietnamese?

What makes a successful marriage between people from two different cultures?

Phyllis: For me, the success key to my intercultural marriage is having lived there on his soil. You have to know the society—that speaks directly to the way the person will react with you in your marriage. If I didn't have that, I'd be in deep trouble. I have seen other couples in that trouble. You've got to know the likes and dislikes of these people, how they play and work—all that sort of stuff.

Toan: I understand American reactions to Vietnam. First, no one really understands the war and the loss of the war; second, no one really understands the culture and history of Vietnam. A lot of people came here and they can't adapt like I did. An American wife helps. But for me the language is the most important thing—you've simply got to get the language. You know, I know many Vietnamese people who deal only with Vietnamese; like they are still in Vietnam. These people left with preconceived notions and aren't about to change. They like to ghettoize and I don't like it at all.

Let me say that there is also a negative aspect to this Vietnamese-American community and that is the way some do business; many people cheat on their taxes, and a lot of dentists cheat on insurance forms. It happens. Why not? In Vietnam, it was part of the system and it was the way you did business. Getting away with something was the way it was. Okay, these are just a few, but they are the greedy ones who make a bad name for all of us. They want to beat a system they do not yet know. Boy, I get angry.

Phyllis: I suppose there is cultural snobbishness by some of the Vietnamese. They get Americanized to a degree and then they stop. They want to keep their identity. I understand a lot of this, but most Americans would be really critical of this, like: "Who do they think they are?" Some of it is a survival technique. They want the enclaves just to hear the language, to remind them that not all is lost, and they strive real hard to hold on to something. But for some it is just too much and they refuse to participate.

You know, I lost the thrill of Vietnamese culture when I married. The fascination went out the door. I don't know why, it just went. We never speak Vietnamese and I don't want to. Funny, isn't it? It is like something in the past that I accomplished and now I can't go back. I speak English with Toan's family. All of their English is getting better, except his mother's—who refuses to learn it and uses an interpreter. She may always need one, but that's okay.

How is your marriage different here than it would be in Vietnam?

Toan: What America gives us as husband and wife is more freedom from the family—I mean the in-laws. The wife in Vietnam is more submissive, the mother-in-law more powerful. Parents control more there. For me, all of the events in my life were planned. You see, I am very much involved with my church here. God planned all of this for me. I really believe that. Funny, in Vietnam you don't believe in many things. I mean you know all about war, bombs, and death; you get used to anything. But here, your life is organized and you can believe in a future. You see that's what America is all about—the future.

Employment

SOKHOA GIOI
Domestic Work

She is a diminutive person wearing a black turtleneck sweater and pearls. Her conversation is punctuated by French expressions when she is excited. We are sitting in a room with oil paintings of birds and flowers that she has painted. There are certain things she doesn't want to discuss, and I feel her past is frozen. Somehow you can tell she came from a wealthy family.

I was a schoolteacher in Cambodia. I taught grade four for eight years, then the war came and my husband and two children and I went to Thailand. Here in Washington, D.C., I clean people's homes. I am a maid.

At first, my husband would not let me leave the house and the children, but I put the children in a Cambodian day-care center where there were other children with mothers who work like me. We very much needed the money because very often my husband does not work and it is easier for a woman to get a job than it is for a man. My husband was a teacher when he was in Cambodia.

I have worked for this one woman for almost one year, and she still keeps talking to me about Vietnam and Vietnamese boat people. I know that she does not know I am Cambodian, not Vietnamese. I like to work better for men. The American woman demands too much for the money she pays me and the more I do, that much more she will want done.

In Cambodia, I had two servants. I remember them very well; they were older women and they worked for us for many years. I knew their families. Here, no one cares about me except to say that I come on Tuesday and Friday. I don't know if ever I would be able to teach again. I just keep working and trying to help the family maybe buy a house in Maryland.

There is nothing more for me to say. I just go to work and come home on the Metro to then work for my family. No, I try not to think about what my life was before Pol Pot, before we left Cambodia.

MONG PANG
A Soldier without a Country

He is wearing green, institutional work clothes, probably from Sears; a red checked bandana is tied around his neck. He is graying at the temples, bespectacled, probably five feet tall. We sit on a bench, talking in English, and drink coffee.

I am a janitor for the Baptist church in Atlanta near Ponce de Leon. This is the job that I have had since I came to the U.S. and to Atlanta in December 1980. I don't think about this fact too much. It is a job for us and we do not live on welfare.

Sometimes when the work gets too much because they have a wedding or some celebration, my wife Duong helps. She never worked for another person before she came here, and she does not mind too much. I have four children. The oldest has just finished high school and wants to study computers. We all live in the same house that was given to us by the church here. The rent is good and it is close so I can walk to work. It is a simple house and often many of our friends are there. You see, Laotians do not mind many people in a house. The Americans do not like this. Here, everyone has his own room; this is not so with Laotian culture.

When I was in Laos I was in the army. I was a colonel in the north and worked for some years with the Americans. I never got to know the Americans but I worked with them and some seemed nice. They drank too much beer . . .

It was a good life in Laos and I miss my country very much. I want to go back if the Communists get out. I look to that day all of the time. We left so quickly. We just locked the door and left. We don't know about our possessions or our house. I hope it is still there. I think about relatives and friends. Every time the news talks about the war and the Thai/Laos border problems, I worry about my brother left there. I am sure others do the same. I fought very hard for my country, and now all of that is gone and it will not come back. It is very sad, very sad.

There is nothing I wish to do here. Why should I? I do not have my heart here. My family soon will become U.S. citizens and they have new lives here. All of that is good and they start new lives. I will be happy for them.

When I first started this work, the tears went into the toilet, I was so sad. There is not much else I can do here in America. What do they do with a soldier who has no country? What could they educate me to be? I don't know. All of these years that I clean the church, I just do it. No one bothers me—I am my own boss. They are good to me, these Christian people. They gave me my first station wagon and they always invited me to church, but I just went to hear the music. I like the organ. Every Christmas they give us food and money.

LAO HOSPITALITY

Come and take rice.
That is the Lao greeting of welcome.
Take rice with Pa Dek and we will talk.
I remember Vientiane and my family that for so long
I know nothing about.
I live here in Fresno with other lowland people,
but I dream of my city that as a child
I knew from darkness to light.
I miss the familiar streets that were always filled
with the people that my family knew for many, many
generations. Now, all that is only dust
and my dreams become distant.
I work on a farm here in Fresno. It is very hard work.
There are many here who live like I do—with memories
and the dust of their dreams is what we work with
in the fields each day. Dust that fills the fields
with all of our secrets and memories of a life
we no longer will know.
Now come and take rice.

Laotian farmer, Fresno, California
[translated from French]

DR. G. CHAN
Medical Needs in the Bronx

We are sitting in the corner of a very crowded living room with piles of cloth-
ing, books, and boxes pushed to the center of the room. Dr. Chan explains
that his cousins are on an extended stay with his family. He speaks in
French and English. He is a round-faced man, quite short, and wears a sur-
gical shirt and blue jeans.

On the coffee table are medical textbooks with a variety of colored markers
inserted throughout. It's a very muggy day and we are drinking iced tea. He
is distracted by the doorbell and what turns out to be a neighbor's request for
medical advice for a sick sister.

We came out of Cambodia after four miserable years of life when all reason
had stopped. After six years, I am still trying to get a residency to practice
medicine here in America. To take on the AMA is like confronting God. I
am forty-five years old. If I do not succeed by the end of this year, I will
change to another profession.

I planned to come to the U.S. in 1974 when I got a scholarship to study
family planning, but I did not have the money to pay for the airplane ticket.
This was the year after I graduated from the faculty of medicine in the capital.
I remember thinking that it probably would not be so difficult to obtain a license to practice medicine in the United States. I was quite wrong. The main
problem is that they changed requirements and I have to take a Flex exam.
But the further requirement is that I need to provide the original diploma and
a transcript of my university work. Who can produce these things, the way
we left? I left without these things because it was impossible to obtain them.
Really, impossible to do and still be alive today. Surely, people must understand this?

Tell me about the medical profession in Cambodia.

When I left Cambodia there were five hundred medical doctors in all of the
country. Today, fifty survive, and of those, thirty-five escaped. So that means
fifteen M.D.s are in Cambodia today. Can you imagine? They were the first
to be executed. The Chinese have this saying that to get rid of grass you must
remove it by the roots. I believe the Khmer Rouge thought that we were the

roots. You see, the fear was that we were educated and could not be trusted to think only about medicine. That one day, perhaps, we would ask political questions and become involved in political activities, therefore we were a threat and were to be eliminated. Destroyed. [*Long pause*]

The Khmer Rouge believed that everything that was old was bad. That is, everything before Pol Pot was bad. Everything that was new was good. This was the logic the Khmer Rouge had. They were simple peasants who now had the guns. They had control. All of my colleagues and my fellow students are gone now. It is difficult to describe, and for me it is still impossible to comprehend.

You know, there are six thousand Cambodian refugees in the New York area and not one Cambodian medical doctor is able to help them. I think I understand that the hospitals have a responsibility to the graduates of U.S. medical schools. I believe the availability of residencies matches today the number of U.S. medical graduates. So there is little room for graduates from foreign schools.

It is as if the U.S. officials opened the gates in this country and let you into the courtyard. But nobody will now open the front door, and that is the door that counts. The way I see it is that the U.S. government brought us to this country and we deserve more than we are getting under the circumstances. All I am asking for is a chance to qualify to sit for the Flex exam, that's all.

What are the health-care needs of the Cambodians here?

The situation of health care in the Cambodian community here is complicated. First, almost a third of the population are widows. Most are simple country people who have never come into contact with modern medicine. The second issue is cultural sensitivity. There are no people in the clinics and hospitals who know how to ask a question beyond the obvious or to interpret a yes answer to mean a no answer. Take, for example, a woman who goes to the emergency room and tells about abdominal pain. She maybe will hide where the pain comes from to avoid any gynecological exam. This is especially true if it is a male doctor. Then she has a serious perforation problem. Then what do you do?

A lot of misconceptions and myths are involved here, too. The birth-control pill, for example. Somehow it is thought to cause cancer and now no one will use it. I mean no one. I do not know who started this rumor or how it spread, but everybody I talk to seems to believe it. I say, then why not use condoms? But they smile, turn red, and give excuses. They tell me they don't know how to ask for them and where to get them. This is a very personal subject and usually only a woman medical doctor or nurse can even ask the question, let alone give instructions on using it. Forget the IUD—that is too complicated.

What you have then are more and more people going to Chinatown for medical treatment. Or what they think is medical treatment. You see, in Cambodia, when you went to the doctor, you always got a shot and some tablets. Always. This is not so here, and people think they are not being treated properly.

In Chinatown they give you B-12 shots and maybe sugar pills, but to them that is treatment—you see, that is what medical care is supposed to be. Now this costs money, it is not covered by Medicaid, Medicare, or welfare. People give up food money to do this. The other thing Cambodian people cannot accept is the way blood is drawn and used. One, two, or maybe three vials and they ask—for what? Are these vampires? Do they sell it? They take all this blood and do not give shots or tablets. Something is wrong here.

Do you feel you have been unfairly treated?

If you mean by the medical profession—yes I do. Yes, there is discrimination between the way the AMA treats Cambodians compared to the Vietnamese medical doctors. They recognize many more affidavits and transcripts and in general make it easier to let Vietnamese people sit for the Flex exam. There are reasons for all of this. Most Vietnamese escaped with their documents and diplomas. It was a different departure for the Cambodians. Plus the Vietnamese know the system here so much better and they are more aggressive. I asked a Vietnamese medical doctor here to help me and all he could say was that he did not know who or what I was. I suppose I do not blame him. We did have one Cambodian dentist qualify for his exam but that was because he knew someone in the White House and a lot of pressure was put in the right place to help him. That is how it works.

What do you do now?

I came close two years ago to the possibility of a residency at Montefiore Hospital, but they ran out of money and had only six open and told me they had to give them to the American medical school graduates. Now I am a social worker in upstate New York for only two days a week—it is all I can get. Not very much money, but my wife works. I still buy my medical books. I write letters and I hope. If I do not succeed by the end of the year, I will give up. I have several Cambodian medical doctor friends who have already given up. They became social workers and work for the post office. I hope that is not what happens to me; my people really need me here. It's painful for me to see my people who have suffered such psychological and physical pain. They come here to the United States and still have pain. How do you say no to a worried mother who is your next-door neighbor here when her baby at night is sick and she knocks at your door? Do I say I cannot help her? Why, because it is the law? But she knows I am a medical doctor, I probably treated one of her family members in Cambodia or the camps. What does she do? She goes to the emergency room where no one speaks English. Maybe, if I fail to become a doctor, I will apply to be a teacher somewhere.

PAULINE and PHILIP VAN THO
Transferring Status

They are a very elegant couple. In their own way, they complement each other. I would imagine that they could do well in Washington, D.C., or Hollywood. They make you comfortable without asking too many questions or lecturing you on what they know. They are gracious and very attractively dressed. The interview progresses in French and English.

This is the fourth interview I have had with Pauline. She is warm and personable. There is an external Pauline that makes her a spokesperson and leader; she has the ability to listen carefully. The internal Pauline is still trying to come to grips with her loss of status, power, and place in a society in which she held a prominent role. Her husband is extremely supportive and totally engaged in his work.

Philip: I was head of the dental school in Saigon before it fell to the Communists. This was a very important position. I had all of the good things in life from it. I liked teaching and administration very much. Then the end came, and in two hours we lost everything. It was a nightmare. It was with the American ambassador Graham Martin's help we got out. Then when I got to the

United States, I was in shock for almost two years. I almost slept through two years of my life.

But I was lucky and I made the professional transition with my work. Many years before, I got my D.D.S. at Northwestern and my graduate work was at Yale. I knew the American dental system. I have been a professor of dental surgery at the University of Houston now for ten years. For me the job status is there, but all that I worked for before is gone. You never really get over that. You work hard and acquire things, then they are taken away.

Pauline: I was a congresswoman and the first woman senator in South Vietnam. I am still angry. They say time changes things—not me. I am angry at the way the Americans just pulled out. One day we are fighting together, and then the next, without warning, they leave. To me, it's like someone coming to your home and convincing you that you must have a very expensive wall-to-wall carpet. It is free and it is installed free. You and your family learn to live with it and enjoy it, and it soon becomes part of your life. You don't even notice it, you take its comfort for granted. Then one day they enter your house without knocking and pull it up, take it away, and you are left with the dirty floor. Well, the Americans took it all away and we were left with nothing. If we did not go with them, we would be dead. I always wanted to know how the page could be turned so fast, without notice. I never said good-bye to my father. That is what hurts the most; I keep thinking about him.

Here in Houston, I have worked for ten years for Catholic Charities as the refugee resettlement director. Ten years—it feels like a long, long time. I get a lot of satisfaction from the job and certainly know the politics of Texas refugee work, but it's always the same troubleshooting situation, like chasing a fire truck. Lots of shocks and complaints to deal with every day. A few days ago, the emergency ward of a hospital called me to translate. A Vietnamese girl had swallowed Drano, attempting suicide. My God, it goes on! It's all of the ups and downs. How can you compare it with the jobs I had in Vietnam? It's like two different persons, two different lives.

Philip: I was also in the government in several administrations as secretary of health, secretary of education, and secretary of cultural affairs. So I know politics, too. I am a good judge of character. I know that there is an ever-so-present silent discrimination that goes with my teaching work. But what could change that? I have been through too much to fight that one. I suppose I just let it go over me, but I know it is there.

Pauline: We are special types, Philip and I. And others like us. We were both educated in France and the United States. We knew the American community and all of the U.S. presidents and American ambassadors. We were well connected and comfortable. We had money and all of that, but it was not our raison d'être. We loved Vietnam and it was taken away so quickly. We believed it would be worked out, that the south would not fall to the Communists.

I want to get another job and leave Catholic Charities for some other kind of work, but I don't know what. It's taken me so much time to learn the system here and to learn the unwritten laws, that was the most important. So I guess I'll stay where I am, but I am suffering from burnout—you know what I mean by burnout?

LAOTIAN MEMORIES

It is May in Laos and the rainy season has begun.
I miss the rice planting.
The holiday, Bounpha Vet celebration, I think of today.
On that day we celebrated the many lives of Buddha
before he found enlightenment.

I, too, see the many lives I must go through.
Life now has been so much movement. Noise.
Moving, moving, always moving.
My next life, maybe, will be more peaceful.
I am very old.

Laotian woman, over eighty, Philadelphia
[translated from Laotian]

VERN SAECHAO
Working at K-Mart

He is still wearing his K-Mart smock as we talk in English, over a cup of coffee in the restaurant. He has a yellow pad and draws doodles. He appears nervous or just shy.

In Laos, I worked very close with USAID in Vientiane from 1967 to 1971. I got a very good understanding of the American mind and way of thinking. They treated me very good. Here in the United States, I have worked in a clothing department store for six years now. The job is okay, but it's not much of a challenging job.

Even before the Pathet Lao seized power, we knew that Laos would fall to the Communists. To look back now, the Communists were more cruel in Laos than they were in Vietnam. More people went to reeducation camps in Laos. When the border trade between Thailand and Laos stopped, the food supply began to stop. It was just a short period of time that you could see the difference in the markets. There were no imports. Simple foods became impossible to get—even rice was difficult to get. I tried to stay out of sight and waited to see what would happen.

To me it was clear that I would go eventually to a reeducation camp where everyone else was being sent. Many people I knew went there; then there were many people that just disappeared and were never heard from again. This was the most difficult time for me because of all the rumors that we heard. We didn't know whom to believe. The stories of the people who disappeared, who were sent to the camps and tortured. So many families were separated, children lost. Then at the same time there were terrible floods that destroyed many crops and killed animals and people. The Mekong rose and flooded so many homes.

When did you decide to leave?

It was right after the Lao New Year's in 1979 that we decided to leave. I had no choice. I had not worked for many years and could not work. I would be sent away and probably killed. The plan was to get into Thailand. One night, my wife and our two young boys and I left with a group of thirty others. We crossed on bamboo floats across the Mekong. To me, that evening had the brightest moon ever. It was just like the sun. That is my memory of crossing the river, bright moon and the cold water. We were arrested by the Thai police when they found us the next morning and eventually put into Nong Khai camp. We stayed almost one year before a Methodist church in the United States, in Ohio, sponsored us.

The church people were kind to us, but they never understood us. How could they? Sometimes they confused us with the Vietnamese boat people.

They always asked us questions about Vietnam. They didn't understand a lot of things about us, but that was no problem. Everything was new and different. I made many mistakes then. Simple things like maybe wanting to agree with our sponsors even sometimes when I did not understand what they wanted. They always wanted us to go to church with them. We tried this, but it was not important to us. I remember telling them one day about the Laotian belief in Phi, which are the spirits that live with us. You see, we believe that each person has thirty-two souls. After I tried to explain this to my sponsor, he stopped insisting that we go to church with them. I suppose he thought we would not become Christian so he gave up.

When the steel mills closed in Youngstown, the economy went bad. We always heard talks of the unemployment. Many people lost their jobs and many had not worked for some years. Some stranger once asked me why we foreign people came here and took jobs from Americans. I just told him that I didn't know anything about the steel company, and that Americans would not want the job I have, anyway. I don't think he believed me. These first months in Youngstown were difficult. They were what a Laotian calls a test of *piap*—of honor and pride.

Is your family adjusted to life here?

I think my sons are well adjusted now. They like baseball and sports. I try to always remind them how important it is to study and learn—to get good grades and go to a good university. But this is something that their friends do not seem to have an interest in doing. Most of the children have no interest in education. Their families are laborers, what you call blue-collar working people, and I guess it's not important to them. It's what I call very anti-intellectual here. People don't want to think too much.

My wife works now at the same department store as I do. It's not very interesting for me, but perhaps one day they will make me the assistant floor manager. That is three dollars more per hour. I know other refugees who have moved to California and Texas for better jobs. Maybe they make more money, but the cost of everything else is so high. I don't think that is such a good idea. Every Sunday we take a picnic to Mill Creek Park. After everything that has happened to us, it is a peaceful time. If we move, there is no promise we could have such things that we have now. Ohio is not too bad.

KIEU CHINH
Movie Actress

She enters the room almost on her toes and we sit on pillows before a coffee table tastefully cluttered with movie memorabilia. I would imagine her to be in her late forties or early fifties, but looking a good ten years younger than that. I am struck by her natural charm and beauty. Her twentyish-year-old son is introduced and departs. We are interrupted several times by calls from her agent. The windows in the room are stained glass which flood the room with warm colors and remind me of being in a church chapel. We talk at length in French and English about the current American cinema and life in Los Angeles.

As an actress, I have lost something very special by coming here. I have lost my identity as an artist. That is a very difficult thing to explain. It is something that is internal. You don't know what it is but it makes you respond—to bring out what is inside of you that makes you different from other people who do not make a career from acting or from calling themselves artists. My life and career are so different now. I have had to start over from zero. All over. I was hoping to build a career here. After all, Hollywood is known all over the world. You see, I had an audience and could be on the screen; my audience was Vietnamese; but now, that is all gone and it will never return. It is all destroyed and somehow part of me is destroyed with it.

Did you expect your transfer to the United States to be easier?

Silly, but I thought I would be able to transfer my career from Vietnam to the U.S. without any great shock. Well, there are few things that I could have been so wrong about! It is a shock still. I know plenty of Vietnamese artists here: poets, writers, film people. I would say we are all in a similar situation. We have been uprooted and we are not growing and becoming successful like we would like to be. We want to resume that which we know and are familiar with—but at the same time we know that this cannot be. America is with us now and we must adjust and change, if change is possible. For some, it is not possible. I have a very dear friend who was a poet in Vietnam. He lives here in Los Angeles now. He is a fine human being and he loves to write. Here he has not written a thing—nothing. What a tragedy! He said that no one has time for poetry here, no one cares about writing and literature. They only care about money, making more money, and surviving in this new society. He means Vietnamese, too.

My career in the United States has been up and down. I have been in a *MASH* episode and every year I do get some parts. I have been in over twenty parts here in the States. I have starred in over thirty films in Vietnam, the Philippines, and Singapore. I had a wonderful life in Vietnam, but that is all history.

Tell me about growing up in Vietnam.

I was born in Hanoi and left in 1954 as a refugee after the fall of Dienbienphu for Saigon. Most of my family still remains in Hanoi. I forgot what some of them might look like.

Three years after I came to Saigon—I was seventeen—I was offered a part in the American film *The Quiet American*, which starred Michael Redgrave. Before I could accept the offer, I had to get the approval of my mother-in-law; being an actress was not considered a good profession, it was not an honorable profession in Vietnam then. Unfortunately, the role called for a woman who was not a prostitute but did have a few love scenes. Well, you can imagine the difficulty in just trying to explain the part to her; this was not acceptable to her, and no protests could be made.

A year later, another role was offered to me in which I would play the part of a Buddhist nun. This was presented to my mother-in-law and she said okay, but not until a great deal of time went by. She said she did not like the idea of me as an actress, but since the part to be played was respectable, and the fact that the filmmaker was a friend of mine—but more important, she knew my friend's mother very well—this made it acceptable. Permission was granted. My big hit in the late 1960s was *A Yankee in Vietnam*, with Marshall Thompson. This was a war picture in which a wounded G.I. is rescued by my family, we fall in love, and he eventually must leave.

What has been the most difficult obstacle to overcome?

I know that my career has been hindered by the way I pronounce English; I have tried so hard, but it is those little sounds that always blow it. I used to practice for hours in front of the bathroom mirror. I also think that the work dynamics here are forcing me to look at myself in a very different way. I never auditioned for a part in Vietnam. I was a star. They came to me with the scripts. Now, I go to them and I hope for something, hope that I might fit somebody's image of an Asian woman. I measure every word in audition, I try to speak slow. I can't tell you how many times I've auditioned and I could hear the *th* or the *r* slip and immediately I knew I was out, that I had lost the part.

What American filmmakers want is an Oriental with perfect English. Well, not all of us can be like Connie Chung. I also think that there are special parts for some women, or maybe it doesn't matter. An Oriental part could be played by any Asian woman, but I feel some parts should be given to Vietnamese—especially when the story deals with our life and history.

For some time now, I have been under a big misapprehension about Americans' willingness to look more seriously at the war and U.S./Vietnamese relations after the films *Apocalypse Now, Coming Home,* and *The Deer Hunter,* but to my surprise, the wounds are still healing. I thought it would be like after World War II and all those U.S./Japanese films like *Teahouse of the August Moon.* There are so many themes to be explored: love stories and stories about both our peoples. After fifteen years in Vietnam and so many millions of Americans affected by the events of Vietnam, I thought the questions would be there to be answered. Not yet. But I believe they will come. This was a very painful time; it will take time. Look how long it took to get the Vietnamese War Memorial in Washington.

What else have you done in this country?

I worked for ten years for Catholic Charities after I first arrived. I worked with the refugees like myself and I got a great deal of satisfaction from that. I came into contact with so many people and so many problems. As a film star, I was separated from so much of this. I have learned so much about human nature. I have since returned to the refugee camps in Thailand and the Philippines. I still see the suffering and it touches me very much, it goes right to the heart—to think of these women raped by pirates on the sea.

To be a refugee here means that you always think about those who remain. They are with you always. It enters every aspect of your life, whether you are aware of it or not. You can't eat a piece of good steak but think about those who haven't seen meat for months or are starving. You can't enjoy your home too much, thinking about those friends and family in concentration camps. It haunts you.

When I took my citizenship oath a few years ago, I was bitter. I asked my-self, what am I doing? Why am I doing this? But I knew why; my future was here and freedom was here, that's enough. I have been a refugee three times in my life, and I believe the United States will be the last stop for me—I hope. For me the United States has a high standard of excellence and freedom of expression for an artist; what more could we ask?

The United States has been good to me and my three children. I was di-vorced here, but life goes on. It's hard to deal with an artist, no matter what nationality. There is a Vietnamese proverb, "We do not open our shirt to show our backs." To talk about it is not part of our culture. It's hard to take a movie star to a new country and begin again. I'm still looking for my break into Hollywood society.

URBAN LIFE

They take us and put us in boxes to live.
Each family lives in the same kind of box.
Everything is controlled.
There are no neighbors to visit like back home
because our boxes are not all in the same building;
I must walk a great distance to find people I know.
So we talk on the telephone and imagine
what this person does and
how he lives in his box
and I tell him about life in my box.

Cambodian woman, Bronx, New York

NGUYEN NGOC LINH
On Making Business in Texas

We meet in a crowded Vietnamese restaurant and I strain to hear Nguyen Ngoc Linh's answers to my questions. We talk for three hours. It becomes easier as the noontime crowd disperses. He is a very large and energetic man who is able to talk about profit margins, risk management, and helping troubled teenagers find a job and find themselves—all at the same time. He appears tough and decisive.

My advantage here—my key to success—is that I know how Americans think and live. I was a university student and graduate student here. I graduated from New York University in 1952. Then I worked for the *New York Times* as a journalist. I never expected the U.S. government or anyone to give us a damned thing when we got here; I was just glad to get here. That's the truth.

Business in Houston is going through a rough time now, and it affects everyone. The price of oil is way down. This affects the Vietnamese very much. We were the last group in the last ten years, the last hired and the first fired; you know how that goes. I don't think we've bottomed out yet, and I don't think we will see the light at the end of the tunnel for some time. Remember that line? I personally think we've got some rough waters ahead. So the refugees respond in their own way.

I don't know that the Vietnamese are moving out in any large numbers. Take, for instance, the Hughes Tool Company; they hired a lot of Vietnamese. There were a thousand employees. Well, now everyone is out of a job, the whole place closed, gone. So a lot of the Vietnamese are moving to Dallas and up north. We are good barometers of the economy, with our ears to the ground. Many are moving to California, you know, to the Southern California "Little Saigon" communities. That is how I read the economy.

What did you do in Vietnam?

Many things. I was a publisher and a businessman in Saigon. I tried and succeeded at many businesses, I mean a lot—hundreds. I got a good sense for starting a business. I was trained in economics and business so I was pretty close to a lot of government decisions. My specialty was rural development.

You know, I met very few Americans who were culturally sensitive to working with Vietnamese and seemed to ask the right questions. But those few people who were sensitive were not the people that made decisions, not people in positions of power. By and large, the Americans never asked questions of Vietnamese, they just did whatever they thought was needed to get the job done.

What is your theory of being a success here?

I've got a theory that if you were successful in Vietnam, then you'd be successful here. This is assuming that you learn English and get a good grip on the emotional stages that a person goes through in coming here. I get really angry at capable men—some ten years in this country—still on welfare, and working off the books. This is a bad thing and it affects all of us and maybe the future refugees. But look, people are people—these are the same elements who in Vietnam would try to carry out their lives in the same way. Something for nothing. Come on, you've got the same thing here with other people. The real culprit is what California represents.

If California didn't make it so damn attractive to get the total welfare package, people wouldn't abuse the system. You see, there are lots of expectations. People developed some wild expectations sitting idle in those camps for years, wishing for things to get out of the United States. They had to dream about something, things to get them out of the miserable state they were in; they just made shopping lists. For many, welfare was on the list.

Tell me about your business in Houston.

I started in 1975 with four businesses in Houston, which took $20K down and I got a $100K loan. Taco, chili, hot dog and hamburger shops. You see, I like diversification. Not like a true Houstonian, only with this oil thing. I learned to grow with the businesses. I experimented, planned all of that, and learned whom I could trust as employees, whom I couldn't, I experimented. I learned the hard way that I needed Vietnamese. I taught them many things. I got two good years out of them until they got enough English and stability to move from their $3.50 to $7.50 per hour jobs, but that was two good years. Can't say that about most types I tried.

I don't like what has been happening to the American family. It's reflected in the business world. You see, it's a demographic change in part. People marry late, have kids late, the mother works full-time and the kids leave home early. There is little time to talk, to be together with those kinds of schedules, rush, rush. The parents never encourage the kids to stay at home. It's all of this pushing from the nest. Well, it's costing society here and I see it in the workplace. Kids don't want to work or don't have the patience to stay with anything too long. It's become a disposable economy. Throwing the fast-food papers away is like the interest in anything: quick and short, then get rid of it. Use and dispose. Well, for this you pay a price.

My wife and my son manage two of the businesses. My wife has a Ph.D. in chemistry. She takes the systematic approach; my son is the organizer and designer. It's a good team. I am a publisher of the Vietnamese paper *Today*, which is the largest Vietnamese paper in the country. I also run an employment agency called Sixteen–Twenty-five, which helps youth get jobs. I've learned a lot about the Vietnamese work ethic and mentality here, and I am still learning.

I believe in work first and then learn English. Do any work, but work, that's what is important. Self-pride. Picking up paper on the street, I don't care what it is. It's pride. Sure, I know there is shock coming here. You tell a Vietnamese to take out the trash and you will see the look of total disbelief, total! So they learn, we all learn.

You see, the 1975 group were the best educated and had all the privileges. We knew Americans and thought we knew the system. Well, we learned to work it—milk it. It took time but the Chinese/Vietnamese learns the system. It's unfair to place a peasant boat person or a Cambodian in the same category as the '75 group. They never had the advantages we had.

Every ethnic mom-and-pop store in this country at some time cheats on sales tax. Don't let anyone kid you. Who runs the register is real important. It comes down to the fact that it's just too damned expensive to be totally honest. I make $2 million a year gross on the businesses now and I do the same amount of paperwork as if I was making five hundred million. It's a fact. Too much paperwork, and regulations. People say that Reagan has been good for the American small businessman. Well, I don't see it.

Now, I've seen the Harvard M.B.A.s, and by and large they don't impress me. Sure they know theory, but that's just it—theory. Give me someone who is streetwise and knows the business from the floor up. Breathes it and lives it—and don't forget that if you are Asian you have got to be twice as good. The white men are keeping the scorecard. You just have to be that much better.

The big problem with Vietnamese is that in the business world, they are too Asian in the way they think and work. I keep telling them they have got to learn the American culture, the American family structure. Learn to talk about sports, all Americans revert to sports. One real important thing I keep telling my son is to be able to go out and drink with the boys. It's very important. The Vietnamese does his job and goes home, stop. He is always prompt at work and does a good job and he will stay late. But come promotion time, the boss remembers John or Bob from the bar last night. He knows how they think and he is comfortable with them. So I keep telling Vietnamese to make themselves available for small talk. No easy thing to do. It is a trust factor for Americans. That is the way it works. American business is a tough, tough thing for Vietnamese to understand. But I tell you one thing, the '75 group has learned their lesson on that one.

Overcoming Obstacles

HOUMPHENG PHENGSOMPHONE
Community Needs

We break after our initial greetings and introductions for an unexpected lunchtime banquet with the entire family. They touch you with their generosity and warmth. The younger members translate from Lao into English for the older ones and therefore conversation seems to flow along. The room becomes very crowded, card tables are set up as new people arrive. Some twenty-five people are eventually seated.

What we need more than anything in Hartford is a building so that the Lao people can come together. You see, we are a small community of maybe seven hundred people. Most Lao live in West Hartford. We need a temple and a monk, too. I think a monk would help a lot of the older people. But all of this is very difficult to get because it costs so much money.

The problem for the older person, over forty-five to fifty, is that they are so alienated from the rest of the community, and I think they just do not have a good touch with reality about how to change their lives here. One thing is for certain, and that is that if these people had a choice, they would not come to America; but then, you could say that about all of us. We would still be in Laos. None of us wanted to leave. But you see, we had no choice, there was no option for us. We would have to leave or be put in prison or be killed. This confronts us all the time now.

I think everyone here has problems in adjusting at first; it is only natural. I know I did. It is just a degree of pain. So you look around in a beautiful country like this and you say, how can I be depressed when everything is so clean and beautiful and there is peace? But you are depressed and you cannot forget any of that.

What do these people need?

People with these mental-health problems just need someone to care for them, someone to listen, to talk with, and to give them attention. They need warmth, love, and care for the inside, that's all. I think if we had a mental-health facility here in Hartford, that would help all of us. These people can come and go and feel that they belong.

I hear a lot about the former soldiers' attitude toward their life here. They are probably the most difficult people to resettle. They do not learn English very well. The soldier sits and watches television all day, doesn't understand the language, but just watches the pictures move and the faces change on the screen. I ask them why they sit all day long watching a screen with language they do not understand, and they tell me that at least these are other real people that are in their lives and, for the most part, they have nothing else to do, so they watch television all day.

These are the same people who are afraid to pick up the telephone and answer it because they might have to speak English. They are also afraid to go out on the streets because they might have to use English and they will have to confront strangers that they think will not be friendly toward them. I tell them that this does not happen in Hartford like it would in a big city, but they are afraid and none of what I say they believe.

What about the highland people?

There are about one hundred highland Lao [Hmong] people in the area. They have their own associations, and we don't see too much of them. You know, I consider them Laotians, but our experiences in Laos are so different. We really have no contact here as we had no contact in Laos.

This is a rich community, Hartford. Look around you and you can see all of these big houses and the expensive cars. But there are poor people here, it is just that you don't see them. There is a lot of emphasis on money here, I think too much emphasis. But that is the way America is. There are jobs for the Lao out there, most are in the tool factories and on the assembly lines. Usually they start out at $4.50 or $5 an hour and they get better. But you see, the Lao, they work hard; sometimes they work seven days a week, and the wife also works. They save this money and it usually is not in a bank; we Lao never trusted the banks. People think we are very rich because we pay cash for everything, but this is not so.

I think the children are doing very well. Not so many go on to university like the Vietnamese, but they are doing well. We see some Lao punk-type teenagers around, but these are just exceptions, most do not behave that way.

Do you think the Lao here get equal treatment with the Cambodians and the Vietnamese in the area of services from the state and federal government?

You mean we are getting less, we Lao? Well, of course this answer will change from each person you ask, depending upon which group he is from. But in Hartford, it is my opinion that we get the same. But you know, the Vietnamese are a much larger community and they are better organized. This means a big difference. Certainly there are some feelings about the Vietnamese from the Laotians, especially by the army people; this seems only natural to me.

What do the army people say?

If you are really listening, they are talking about why we are in the United States, and they say it is because of Vietnamese. The war in Southeast Asia was because of the Vietnamese, so there are some bad feelings about these things, but this is what I hear from the military people. They also blame them because the Vietnamese invaded Cambodia and Laos.

We have a Lao Association of Connecticut that tries to help all of the Lao people. Sure, we are not all equal. There are class and education differences that will not dissolve, but in general, people try to be friendly and work out a relationship that helps everyone.

The Lao people in Hartford are still struggling in many ways. It costs a lot of money to live here. But I am glad we are here. I think it is better in a smaller community; if you have too many people, you just get too many problems, that is the way I look at it. I am satisfied here and I have no desire to move to California. People still move here to get work and they know it is a good place to live. They have been coming recently from Colorado.

When I want to think, I drive to the seashore. I need the time to relax. My wife does not like the sun or the salt water. So it is the time when I am alone to think.

NO PAGODA

My boy will soon be seven too and I have no pagoda
in Kansas City to take him. No monks here.
No reading of *satra*, *satra chbab*, and the *satra tes*.
How will he learn properly of the life of Buddha?
How will he work in the pagoda to become *samaners*?
We have no pagoda.
How will my son gain wisdom to be a *bikku*
in the way of Buddhism?
Our duty as parents we fail—then his duty as son he fails.
He will not give us wisdom for making us proud.
No Dhamma, no peace.

No pagoda here in Kansas.
Very dark days.

Cambodian father, Kansas City, Missouri
[*translated from Khmer*]

PHUONG NGOC TRUONG
Reaching Real Freedom

*He is known as a refugee dealmaker, which means he is savvy with the state,
federal, and private voluntary agency officials in being able to get monies for
his program. We meet across a desk and he is very official, dressed in a
houndstooth sports coat, white shirt, and red tie. He orders coffee through his
intercom. He told me he has been thinking a lot about the meaning of freedom both in Vietnam and in the United States.*

I was trained as a journalist in Paris and worked two years in restaurants to
pay for my education. I fled Vietnam via Cambodia in early 1965. I was a
student leader and my father was in a high position in the Diem government.
I left Vietnam in just enough time. I came to the United States to work for

the Voice of America and then as a language instructor for the Department of Defense. I trained many of the military people before they went to Vietnam.

I knew their mentality, the way they solved problems. And I knew the difference between the career people and the recruits; that was a very wide difference. Most of the people I taught would have preferred to be learning French, I am sure. Nobody—or very few—wanted to get their feet wet in the rice paddies of South Vietnam. The military approach was pragmatic—always pragmatic—but there was no emotional commitment to the cause. They didn't care if Vietnam won or lost. But all of that is obvious now, isn't it?

Tell me about the evacuation.

I knew the end was near early in 1975 when I was invited to meetings with General Lansdale and other VIP people. At that time the United States started to quietly ship home large computers and other sensitive equipment. If you ask me, it was a lousy evacuation plan, and I am bitter about how it was organized and carried out. I still to this day cannot help but think that some of it was planned that way. The way it was executed just added confusion, or created more confusion, and to forget so many people who were faithful to the Embassy is simply inexcusable. All those people waiting for the last helicopter, the last helicopter that never came. Peace with honor. Well, that never happened for the Vietnamese or the Americans. No peace, no honor.

When did you know the war was lost?

When President Thieu cried publicly, I think the population then knew what was going to happen. Here was this Asian leader reading that letter from President Nixon and he wept in public. He wept bitterly for all those people who would never be able to leave Vietnam.

Being here in the U.S. was painful in a different way. Night after night, the way the evening news covered the final weeks of Vietnam, days—it was very depressing. I watched helplessly from my living room. I still see Walter Cronkite's face. I was viewing the destruction of my homeland and my culture as if I were watching some soap opera. What are the words that say what I feel? I still use them: bitter, angry, disappointed. I did not know that America would wash its hands of Vietnam like that, and its hearts, too. The very men I had taught and been with for all that time training, this is what would happen when they got to Vietnam. Now the refugees just remind them of all of those past events. This was all too much for them to take.

What happened then?

I decided to quit my job and help my people. The same people that ten years before I had run away from—but now they were my people, my family in some way I cannot explain. The time was right to do this. I went to Harrisburg, Pennsylvania, and began to help a coalition group of religious people resettle refugees in the Harrisburg area. Fort Indiantown Gap was not far away and a lot of the people would try to stay in the area.

What I remember about the church people was how naive they were and their humble way of trying to understand. They admitted they knew little about Vietnamese people or culture and that they knew little about how the refugee resettlement process might work. Well, these were people that I had not known existed in America. All those years of working for the military gave us an impression of the American that is self-confident and at all costs never admits a mistake. What a surprise I had! These church people were honest— although I have since learned that not all church people are honest either. But these church people genuinely wanted to help, and that's what I found exciting and refreshing about the general American spirit of helping and volunteering to help, or as they say in Harrisburg, "pitching in."

Tell me about Harrisburg.

It is a small community. Now there is something unique about a rural community in America. I am not talking about Harrisburg, but the small areas that surround Harrisburg. These are special places that are not understood by most foreigners. The people there are friendly but they must be approached in a special way. You need an introduction, and you have to deal with the way they warm up to you when they are ready. Timing and patience are important. There is a willingness to help, but there is a process you must understand and respect. What is surprising, and it should not be, is that the values of the small community in America are shared in many ways by the Vietnamese: family, closeness, thrift, and hard work.

Harrisburg first impressed me with all of the churches. There seemed to be a church on every block. It was a good first introduction. The people who live there have rural American values, which means they work hard for what they get. Harrisburg worked as a refugee resettlement area because a group of influential community people wanted it to work. They pushed the issue of refugee resettlement, and there was enough support and enough resources to make it work. It's not a big city, Harrisburg, but it's not country either. It's in between, and that's why I think it's good for refugees who come from rural areas to live here. It's a good way to be introduced to a new life.

What happens in a living situation like I am describing is that when people want to do something, they do it. But often they don't ask the right questions or they don't ask *any* questions. Well, that's okay at first. That energy is so crucial, but later on it causes some problems. For example, there is little time to try to understand cultural differences between the refugee groups. What surprises me here is that people do not ask—they just do, or assume, which causes trouble sometimes. The people mean well; they just have this focused approach to getting things done. You know that concept is very Asian. They do it, and maybe if it doesn't go smoothly they will ask questions. But fortunately most of the time they do okay and things get done and people get on with their lives. But sometimes it's a big mistake.

What about welfare?

I suppose with refugees there is nothing that makes Americans more furious than welfare, especially the people who are very removed from the lives of the people who use welfare. It is a class division in this country. Americans value success and success means making money, not receiving it. Use welfare and it says to the American people he is not going to try. They give up. Sure, there is a lot of hidden racism in the whole system. Remember, the majority of people who use cash assistance are not white.

So they think if the Vietnamese use welfare, they are really minority type people, not honorary white people. You are like the rest of them and you know whom I speak of when I say "them"—I mean black people. The quick response is stop cheating us, get a job and go to work. I have seen little room for compromise on this subject, even the argument that medical assistance is needed and what about people who only use medical and not cash assistance. Welfare is welfare, they say.

The success of Harrisburg is that refugees built it up themselves. It was close to a camp and it had a need for labor and a willingness to accept people. It's been a good thing because it's limited. It's a reasonable size, but it's still possible to walk down a street and hear Vietnamese. That is very important. That makes it real for you. Many refugees will one day move out of Harrisburg, but a lot still move in, too. I think the Chamber of Commerce likes it because it's good for business. A lot of new businesses get started by Vietnamese. It's a strange mix to see the Amish Dutch and the Vietnamese on the streets of downtown Harrisburg.

What else have you been thinking of?

What I have thought of the most in the past twenty-one years I have been here in this country is when and how the refugees will be truly empowered to design and take control of their own future. After two decades here you do a lot of reflecting. That is an advantage I have over the others. There were a handful of us here before the fall. Most of the refugees are still trying to cope and function. My life is different and I see it a different way. I see American society from a different perspective than the '75 refugees do. I want more than to just survive. I want more real freedom. That means equal treatment not based on skin color or racial features. Talk to the people you are trying to help and get to know them—that's what has surprised me in the resettlement program. Few people have really gotten to know the people. It's a little like the colonialist experience. The decisions are still made in the capital, Washington, D.C., and dictated to the provinces.

So I ask, when does our turn come? I think as the years add up for the refugee here, they will ask the same question. And don't give us tokens—those French cadre–like government employees as substitutes for representatives of people. I've met some Vietnamese government workers who are more Anglo than Anglo, you know what I mean. Oh, I'm sure our time will come, it is only a matter of time. I've seen a lot of good here in Harrisburg. It's been good to me, this town. But sometimes you have to ask for more because you want more.

GE LOR
Learning American Farming

He has enormous hands and a big smile. He tries very hard to make me comfortable in his modest house decorated with Early American furniture. He speaks in Lao.

We were highland people in Laos. I had worked for an American company and left Laos for Thailand in 1979. After one year of living in Kansas, my family—a wife and two sons—moved to Fresno, California. We moved mostly because there were no other Laotian [Hmong] people in Kansas. When we arrived, we met other Laotian people from Providence and Minnesota. They came to California for the same reasons. There are now about 23,000 Laotians in Fresno County.

The one thing that we could do that everyone else was doing in Fresno was farming. But this was a different kind of farming. We are talking about hi-tech farming, not the hand-tool farming we were used to in Laos. It's not so simple as turning the soil and planting seeds. Farming here is very modern, and to compete, we had to learn about these new techniques.

I was part of a program that helped train thirty-five new farmers in hi-tech farming skills in 1981. The program lasted almost one year. It was about all aspects of farming from technical fieldwork to using pesticides. The program was from the federal government, and we were supposed to eventually teach other refugees about farming.

Our idea was to get involved in planting cash crops that we could work on as a community. It would be crops that the large farmers didn't want to grow. For many Laotians, farming is a good job because it doesn't require English and all of the family can work on it at the same time. Laotians have large families so this could be a good thing for business. Other ideas were that it meant the families could be together, not separated, and that it was good to work in the sunshine.

What did you learn?

What I learned most was the technical-mechanical things about farming as a big business. How to rent and lease land, to hope for some venture capital to buy land. How to guess when and what crops might bring a profit. I never thought of farming as such a serious business. What I learned was more business than agriculture.

We had the idea of forming Laotian cooperative gardening that would be able to use the Laotian people in cash-crop ventures that would be long-term profitable for the people—not just to supplement incomes, but that would be their main source of income. We made many mistakes. What we learned was that there is a lot of competition in the United States, especially from Mexico, for bringing in these crops. You must really understand marketing and distribution ideas about getting your fruits and vegetables out when they are ready.

Tell me about the farm cooperative effort.

Well, in 1982, with the land leased because we had no venture capital available through any of the banks, about twenty of us started a cooperative farm that would, we hoped, bring in about a hundred families total. But this never worked. We were very new at this and we had no marketing experience or knowledge of selling things and we did not see our competition. What happened was our first crop was cherry tomatoes. They had brought in a good price the year before. They are a good crop to grow and we looked at all of those aspects. The market price for tomatoes is usually top price, but what we did not know was that all other farmers would plant cherry tomatoes. What happened was that the market was flooded and by then Mexico was sending tomatoes at even a lower price. Most important, these tomatoes all came ripe at once and we had not planned for the transportation of them. To rent vehicles at that time was almost impossible. We had no way to move them and they were rotting in the fields. It was a disaster.

What did you learn?

From that disaster we learned a great amount of information. We are looking for our place in the agriculture business. For example, the Koreans have the poultry business and the Japanese have oranges—we are looking to the small gardens for the Laotians.

I hope the Laotian people make it as farmers. I am part of a cooperative now that is hoping for a government contract for vegetables and fruits for Merced Air Force Base and possibly a base in Texas. This would be a big deal—$4 million contract a year and would employ one hundred refugees, but this is not yet a firm offer. We have the workers but what we need is the ability to buy and improve the transport system. We need a Laotian trucking association with coolers. Then we need heavy farm equipment. I think it will come in time but it takes so long.

We have our successful program here. Not far from here is a family cooperative of twenty acres. They own the land now. The father has three sons and all of them are married with children. They all live at the farm, so about twenty people work on the farm and the expenses are low. They have a very good business this year in eggplant—very few people grew eggplant and the prices were very high. In their third year, they are going to buy machinery and a big refrigerated truck to ship the produce.

NO HUSBAND

I know the suffering of Cambodia has been great.
I know many people die and will never be the same in Cambodia.
Women and children perish and never will we find them.

My world was my husband and he is dead.
They brought me to this new place and the life is hard.
Many wives without husbands say the same,
but I am not many wives.
I am me and only one husband is gone now seven years.
Life is always the lonely life without him.
I tell my children about him, but they cannot see him
like father, only like ghost.

I must forget my husband's life and go on with my life,
but it is very, very difficult.
I still suffer and he is in my dreams.

Cambodian woman, Dallas
[translated from Khmer]

DUONG CHAN
Refugee Women's Needs

*She appears to be a very tense and complex person who has been forced to
come to grips with a variety of emotional and psychological layers in her life.
And now she is asked to help others cope with loss and pain. She has become
a liberated woman by default, and at the same time a spokesperson for others. There is no subject matter, it appears, that she is unable or unwilling to
talk about. You immediately respect her courage and strength and, more im-
portantly, her ability to laugh and joke.*

Please understand that your life as a Cambodian is divided into two periods:
life before and life after Pol Pot. Most of us try to forget the first period. I will
share with you the second period.

Tell me about your work.

I work as the director of a Cambodian women's self-help project in New York City. The program is designed to help Khmer women adjust better to life in the United States. I like my job, but I guess it would be honest to say that I relieve my grief by helping others. It sometimes lessens my pain. I deal with many women every day who have so many problems. Every day it's something new. I deal with many women who can't cope with their lives.

The most obvious problem I see is violence—I mean family violence, wife and child abuse. Now we are talking about something that is unique for Khmer people. Yes, the woman has not been liberated and she is a second-class person, but the physical harm done to her here in the United States is unlike that in Cambodia. I have seen women with terrible wounds on their faces and arms, teeth missing, and much more. For me, it's even harder to understand when the children, I mean small children, are harmed. All of this is a combination of grief and guilt and somehow there is depression that makes these people violent. This is usually not their nature.

Khmer women want very much to survive in this country, but they need confidence in themselves and some positive experiences. Often I do not see either of these needs being met. I believe that even the poor, uneducated women—women who cannot read or write in Khmer language—want to become self-sufficient, but because of their own personal history, the chance of success is very small.

The widow also causes problems in the Khmer community. Sometimes she cannot avoid it. She is a single woman and is always suspect of stealing the husband of another.

The Khmer men are always treating women as inferior. Now, in the U.S., he can have his pick of so many if he wants. He just controls the situation and both women are helpless. So wives are very jealous of their husbands and are not kind to widows. Often it is the widow who needs help. It's very difficult to manage children and an apartment alone. Things happen. There is also a problem with prostitution when the widows try to earn money. Well, it's not easy for these women and then there is always the fear of robbery or rape.

So many times I hear of women who are robbed right outside of the bank as they cash their checks. People wait for them. Now, most women separate the money in the bank and put only ten dollars in their purse. They call it "robber money." The rest of the money they hide on their body somewhere.

Most of the women have learned not to go to the bank or shopping alone. So you have a group of five or six women who travel together. Many have been raped, too. The problem with rape is that the women are so ashamed that they do not report it and then nobody knows about it. When it is reported and the police do come, I know, they try to be helpful.

So you have got 3,000 to 4,000 women who are very vulnerable. Perhaps the majority are women who lost part or all of their family in Cambodia. Most of them came to the United States in 1980–1982, especially when they had the Khmer cluster resettlement program that put people in the Bronx. I don't know if the Bronx was such a good resettlement place but they live in four locations: 193rd Street, Andrews Avenue, Bronx Park East, and Taylor Avenue.

What is the biggest problem you see at work for women?

The biggest problem for every woman is the language. English for us is very, very difficult. I know women here for five years who still do not speak any English. I try to tell them why not learn one new word a day or a week, but no. They refuse and say it is too difficult at their age and they will never use it. I know a woman who has tried ESL classes three times and every time she never learns even one word, not one! It's true. When I ask her why, she says that when she sits at a desk she panics and can only think of her dead husband. What can I say? Really, what could anyone do?

This is shock and I think she needs to have something more than English in her life right now. Then, there is another woman who has tried several times to learn English but refuses—she says she lives in the Bronx and they speak Spanish in her neighborhood and that they should teach her Spanish. You see, what all of this does is very much affect the woman's self-esteem. The real goal of the work I do is to restore some self-confidence and self-dignity to these women.

Without the language, these women get separated from their children. The children go to school. They learn the language and then they fall away from the mother. They think she is stupid. They also know that the money comes from welfare, that the state supports them. This puts mother in an even lower estimation by them. So then you get many discipline problems. This was not known in Khmer society before coming here. If there is one thing special to their family it was total respect for the parent. This is changing here.

For some women, there is such a separation from all that they are familiar with, that they know. There is little hope of regaining a normal life again. I give you an example: Mrs. A. telephoned me and asked me to go to her daughter's school because she got a note from the teacher about her bad grades. I promised to meet her the next day and go with her, but an emergency happened and I really had to go to Montefiore Hospital to translate. It was an accident, an emergency. I telephoned Mrs. A. and told her. She started to scream. She did not believe that I would not come. She became irrational and I really didn't know how to deal with her. She said to me she had ten children in Cambodia and eight were killed before her eyes—that she had only two children left and how could I be so cruel as to do this to her only daughter. I simply could not communicate with her. She would not listen. Well, this is how some women react to their loss. They stop functioning at times, then they stop functioning completely.

Now, don't forget that there are success stories. Mrs. B worked with her husband cleaning offices at night for five years. She earns good money and now speaks good English. She learned secretarial skills from a state program and now has a very good job at a law firm. She makes much more money than her husband. I suppose you can say that the traditional roles have changed. But the husband has learned to adjust along with the situation, why not?

I arrived in New York City on August 24, 1980, at JFK at ten P.M. Oh, it was a beautiful flight, the lights, the buildings. It was magic! The next morning, we woke up in Long Island and it was all changed. The magic was gone. Life for me is always changing. After Pol Pot, what could be the same? For these women, most will do well. They need time.

MARY PHUONG
On Being Single

We meet across a truck-stop restaurant table. She is wearing a rock band T-shirt and is extremely shy throughout our talk.

I live in Florida and like it very much. I will tell you a little about my background. My parents were Catholics from the north, near Hanoi, who fled to the south when Vietnam was separated in 1954. I wanted to become a Catho-

lic sister but things changed. I was, I guess, too worldly. I like too many material things. But I broke tradition when I decided not to enter the convent. I
was told to find a husband but I taught school and lived with my parents. My
father died of cancer during the Tet Offensive in 1968. My mother died only
two days before the evacuation. I was told she could leave with me. It was
so difficult to leave. My aunts made me feel guilty. They thought I should
not leave but stay and settle the family affairs. It was a very difficult decision,
but I soon realized there were no more family affairs. I was the family and
I had left.

Tell me what it's like being single.

To be a single person, an unmarried woman, is difficult anywhere. But it is
a little bit easier here in the United States. Maybe there is less pity, less ridicule. Most of my friends here are single women, widows. But they still feel
sorry for me. I was lonely when I first came. I am okay now. I have my job
in a day-care center, my own apartment, and I have some friends. In many
ways this is a better life for me here. I really didn't know what to expect when
I left Vietnam to come here. It all happened too fast. I had English and I was
independent; that's a very big advantage for starting out. To go back to live
is not an option for me. Maybe not even to visit; I am here now.

   I like Gainesville. I don't regret not living in California. Too many people,
too many politics. I am studying part-time at the University of Florida, right
now at a liberal arts course. Everybody thinks I should study computers, elec-
tronics, or math. Well, there are some Vietnamese who think about
humanistic-type things. You don't have to be a monk or a nun. I like history
very much and I have no pressure. Last semester I had a course in philosophy.
For me it was a new world: Hume, Descartes, and Voltaire. My parents
would be so proud because if there is one thing that Vietnamese love, it is
knowledge and learning. If you told me ten years ago I would be studying philosophy in Florida, I would have told you I could just as well be living on
the moon.

   Most of my friends are foreign students. I have only two Vietnamese
friends. It's funny to be a minority person all the time here. I mean in a larger
city, people wouldn't turn their heads and stare. Some think they do it without me noticing, but I do. They look at me from side views. At first I thought
maybe I was paranoid, but I don't think so. If you are Asian in Gainesville,
they automatically assume you are related to the university. They don't even

ask you if you are a student, they ask what subjects you are studying. Americans make a lot of assumptions; I think it is part of their character.

I have a friend in Wacahoota—funny name, isn't it? It's west of here near Levy Lake. He was a dentist in Vietnam and now works in a pharmaceutical supply company. He is a very good widower friend. Sometimes a group of us go to Cedar Key which is a very nice drive to the Gulf Coast. It's a nice trip on Sunday when we are not working. We take a picnic. It's a joke with us— like we are doing the great American middle-class trip.

The last time we were there, we were approached by three young boys who thought we were Chinese. There were a few names called, the usual. We said we were Vietnamese and then they started talking about the war and about how we Vietnamese had lost the war. Well, what can you do? Correct their history? Argue with them? No. How do you respond to such things? They call them "crackers" or "rednecks" here. I suppose this is the most unpleasant part of life here. But I have no guarantee that this is something I would not confront in Los Angeles or Texas. Maybe the Americans here are more simple, more honest. They just say what they feel and don't hide things. This is something that will not go away, and we always say we just have to learn to cope, always to cope. Other than this, I like my job and life in Gainesville.

CHAPTER 6

Photo: John Tenhula

THE

FUTURE

The interviews in this book reinforce the notion that the refugees see themselves as individual ethnic groups confronting the realities of America, trying to use their traditional and acquired talents to develop survival skills. "We are, above all else, survivors," said Vietnamese Pho Ba Long in Washington, D.C. Once the impact of the shock and transfer are over, the process of establishing new roots and starting anew begins. For some, especially children, it has been an easier process to accomplish than for others. In this respect, this group is no different from countless other immigrant or refugee groups coming to the United States. Sang Seunsom, former education minister of Laos, described the future through his children: "You have anything you want here. You must work hard, and I mean you work very hard, but it is here. That is the future for the refugee in America. I have ten children and, except for the two oldest, they are like all other American children. They like baseball and sports, ham-

---

◁FACING PAGE
At the Jubilee Refugee Camp in Hong Kong,
children greet the author, who interviewed them
eleven years later for this book.

burgers not rice. They have been made over into the American way. America is the future for them. They are intelligent and hard-working and they are honest. They are the future for America."

"I see the future for Cambodians as a big mirror," said one woman in Boston. "The mirror has been shattered and the pieces are scattered, and we carefully, slowly put them back together. It will always be a cracked mirror, because our lives were nearly crushed to dust. I was to survive, most were killed. We survived to carry on our culture and traditions. What else is left? What else can we do?" Ma Chan continued. "The question about when I will stop seeing myself as a refugee is a good one. For the future, I will always be a refugee, always. I will always be lost, maybe some days more or less lost, but lost. You see, I came from an ancient Khmer society. It is my two children who really see the future; ask them this question. They will see beyond this period. When they smile, they will smile from their hearts. I know this. That, too, is my future, to see them smile."

Ethnic community development—how the new refugee groups organize and prosper in the United States—is complicated to measure in terms of adjustment. The ethnic support structures traditionally serve as a kind of intermediary between the new arrival and general American society. They help refugees share expectations and community interests so that they can reach out beyond the community to institutions that will affect their future. The Mutual Assistance Associations (MAAs), a loose-knit community of ethnic self-help organizations, play an important role in assisting refugees toward both social and economic adjustment. They can also be a possible source of social and emotional support at a time when many refugees are confused about the future.

In Orange County, California, Le Duc Tran said that the rivalry between the ethnic associations is "based on prearrival political organization and very complicated. We take our politics in America from Vietnam. It's just a new cover to the book. Everyone has some interest. You belong to a certain MAA, maybe because you came from a certain class in Vietnam or political interest. So you brought those interests here, that's all. Everyone argues in Southern California in the refugee communities about who will be the first Vietnamese-American congressman to go to Washington. That's what I see, that the refugee is going to use the doors open or he will force them open." The majority of the refugees are deeply concerned about the conditions in the country from which they fled. This is related to family and friends that remain and the hope of bringing them eventually to the United States.

"What I am afraid of is that the United States will close its doors to my people. I have two sisters in Vietnam that I hope will get to Thailand and then the United States. I don't know if this is possible, because the questions they ask are very difficult. My sisters' names were on the ODP [Orderly Departure Program] list, but the Communist government never let them leave," said Mary Trang in Boston.

Adaptation is a process that occurs in a different way for each refugee. A former high-ranking military person will have needs different from those of a rural farmer. "But we are all tough or we would not be here. What we need to get rid of is this refugee pity. You know—pity the poor refugee because he is homeless," said Pho Ba Long in Washington, D.C. "The future is with the resources we brought and the resources we found here and learned to use. Don't tell me 'can't'—for me it doesn't exist. We are from a capitalist society, we Vietnamese, always wanting better and able to work harder to get it. Well now, for many this is the big chance, the best chance of their time on this earth," Long concluded.

For refugees who arrived in 1975 and have been able to transfer skills and prosper, there are larger issues now confronting them concerning their place in their new society. "As a minority person—we never used that term 'minority' in Vietnam—you begin to see your life differently," said Le Tran Ha in Columbus, Ohio. "Things you never thought would be important are now important. There is a lot of racism against people from Asia, and there is racism between the minority groups. This is new. You don't know the rules and everything seems clear, but it is not. We look at the Chinese experience in this country and say, well, that's history; but then we say, well, why not again? It may come back. You know some people will never accept you. Well," he concluded, "these are some of the things you begin to worry about the longer you stay in this country."

Finally, for some, maybe a small percentage, the American dream will never be realized or even partly attained. Some come and just can't make it in the United States, or don't want to make it—mostly due to the separation or loss of family and friends. "I want to go back to Laos. I am a simple farmer and my life is there, it is not here. I saw my two children drown, and my life in the refugee camp was hell. I came because of my friend, who was also a soldier, but I would go back if I could," said Phnom Vallampang of Fresno, California.

The following are interviews with refugees commenting about their future in the United States.

SICHAN SIV
Cambodia at the United Nations

He is a very tall, elegant man who is smartly dressed. As we pass through the U.N. corridors, he is greeted by and greets a wide variety of people. You get the distinct impression he should be teaching international law, not lobbying for the Cambodian causes he so dearly believes in. His grasp of history is extensive.

The political events since Cambodia was overtaken by the Khmer Rouge and after the Vietnamese invasion are difficult to understand. I do not think they are made easier at the United Nations. You see, what you have at the U.N. is a triumvirate of power among three organizations: the Khmer People's National Liberation Front [KPNLF], Prince Sihanouk's party, and the Khmer Rouge. The future of Cambodia has to be sorted out among these groups. It is the future we are concerned about but not without understanding what happened at the time the country fell to the Communists. Our future as well as our past are intertwined.

Describe the history of the representational issues at the U.N. since 1979.

When the Khmer Rouge invaded, there were a number of pro-Soviet governments that supported Pol Pot and the Khmer Rouge, but when the Vietnamese came in 1979, they quickly switched allegiances to Heng Samrin, the Vietnamese and Soviet person. The political issue is that China and the U.S. back any government that is not backed by the Soviet Union. This has meant support for Pol Pot at the U.N., and it has really become a political issue.

The issues are representation and resolution of the dispute as seen for the last eight years, and there has been no easy answer. Representation means who will sit as the legitimate representative of the Cambodian people at the U.N. After the Vietnamese invaded the country, there was what we call in legal terms no superior claimant to be recognized. Or, in other words, no higher claim for the seat was recognized. The invasion violated the U.N. Charter which states that there should be noninterference of states and a peaceful settlement of disputes. In the credentials committee, the U.S.S.R. keeps referring to the "so-called Democratic Kampuchea" as a band of outcasts, driven from their country for their violation of the Charter. So if Heng

Samrin pushed out Pol Pot, the U.S. was to see Pol Pot as the legitimate representative to the U.N.—certainly they would not support the Soviet candidate.

The resolution goes back to November 1979 and is supported today—the vote was last week on the issue and it was one hundred fifteen in favor of it and twenty-two against. The votes against were all from Soviet bloc states.

The resolution calls for the withdrawal of all foreign armies from Cambodia, to restore and preserve independence and sovereignty, and a commitment by all states to noninterference and nonintervention in the internal affairs of Cambodia. Then it calls for free elections and self-determination. This is what the Cambodian people want for their future—self-determination and free elections. You know there are many Cambodians who want to return to their country when conditions change.

I have talked with many people in this country who feel that their lives are just in limbo. They want desperately to return to their country. I know how they feel. You see a refugee from Cambodia has left his heart there, that's what many say to me. They say they want to go home, that their future is only in Cambodia.

Describe the political efforts of your organization at the United Nations.

The KPNLF was founded in 1979; Sihanouk's organization was founded in 1981. Our goals are the same but some of our methods of getting to those goals are different. We oppose the Vietnamese occupation of Cambodia and we oppose the return to power of a genocidal regime. We also oppose the return of a corrupt government. Above anything else, our final objective is to rid Cambodia of the Vietnamese and to bring about free elections.

So it is our pressure that is needed at the U.N. That, for us, is the future. We keep that 1979 resolution alive, and we want to continue to promote the U.N. Charter guarantee on noninterference. To do this, we need to constantly call to world public attention the illegality of such actions by the Vietnamese invaders.

How do you explain your organization's sitting at the same U.N. table with the Khmer Rouge?

To the West, I know this seems strange. Here we have represented a group that caused so much destruction against humanity. I still cannot believe what they did to my country. There is no way to describe it. I lost my family and friends.

Well, beyond the personal and emotional issues, all we do is emphasize that continued occupation of Cambodia by the Vietnamese is a greater—yes, greater danger in the long term than what has already happened to our country under Pol Pot. We think of their potential mischief and power. We need all the strength we can on this issue, so there are three organizations at the mission to the U.N. that try very hard to gather this international strength to fight the Vietnamese occupation and oust them. It's sort of like the situation in South Africa today. Some days it is very hard to put personal animosities above it all, to keep that goal and objective out in front.

Can this issue be resolved?

Yes. Withdrawal of the Vietnamese army. That is the only future for us. We have a plan. It's a two-phase withdrawal with an eight-point peace proposal that calls for an interim government and elections. Heng Samrin is included in this proposal. But the Vietnamese have already rejected it. They said it was a Chinese fabrication.

Where is Pol Pot now?

Officially he retired and is supposed to be living in the countryside somewhere. He is supposed to be very sick. Keep in mind that you cannot separate Pol Pot the person from the Khmer Rouge. They are one and the same. He is only a figure but he is still the organization; remove him and you remove the organization. We all want to get on with our lives.

PHO BA LONG
Bringing Former Talent to Life ·

He is the ultimate salesman and optimist for his people. He'll not take no for an answer and "acts like a cheerleader even in the rain," as he was described by a fellow Vietnamese. Pho Ba Long is a very small man, slight of build, with heavy Coke bottle–like glasses. He has a constant smile and unlike almost all other Southeast Asians I've met, he touches you—pokes you with his finger when he talks. When I left our talk, he gave me several pats on the back, telling me to "take it easy." He is a gentle man, a kind of grandfather type you never forget.

I was minister of labor in South Vietnam. I came to the United States in April 1975 with my wife and six children and hoped for the best. I had no illusions about life being at all similar to what I left. I knew the U.S. pretty well; I had studied at Harvard University.

The future is in the hands of the newcomers—I often avoid calling them refugees, but I will call them refugees here with you. What I am involved in here is a program called the Vietnamese Entrepreneur Training Program. This is at Georgetown University, and I am the director. This is a four-month bilingual training program that teaches students bookkeeping, finance, and marketing. To graduate, it requires a written business proposal employing all of these functional tools. The direction is toward small business management. We encourage former entrepreneurs and new students to get back to business. What we want is to develop people's skills to go into business and to succeed. We don't get hung up about English. Soon enough the student realizes he's got to improve his English. This is a psychological push he does for himself.

What do you think about English language training?

You know this whole question of English is hard to address. Sure, I know English is needed, but I say not all people are the same. Give some who perhaps are shy or have been through trauma extra time. But don't shut them out because they can't speak good English. Here, the Georgetown program gives them the chance to show other skills. It's a big boost.

You see, when confronted with a language problem, the average Vietnamese reacts one of two ways. First, he keeps quiet. Silence. He is humiliated. And second, he has this haughty silence. He doesn't care and wants revenge. Both reactions are a terrible waste of time and energy.

Sometimes with the older people, it's almost impossible to make the bridge here. Past age fifty, it's difficult to learn again. But I say, why not try—at least use your business knowledge and skills with your family, such as bookkeeping; that's always needed.

You know, there is functional English and there is good English. I think everyone should be functional, but to speak good English, well, that takes a long time, a lifetime—I know.

It's a little like the Korean greengrocer. It's a family deal and the one at the cash register speaks the good English. Who needs to speak good English working in the back, stacking bananas and grapes? Besides, how many different phrases do you need in a situation like that? "How much is this?" or "Do you have . . . ?" Really, there aren't so many different phrases you need to know.

Why are the Vietnamese known as good businesspeople?

The success of the Vietnamese small business is because it is a family business. That structure is a checks-and-balance. The family model controls the front- and back-door theft. You work harder. You care and try harder when it is your own business. Here in Virginia we have this 7–Eleven phenomenon. So many Vietnamese want to own a 7–Eleven. Eight years ago it cost you $30,000 to get a franchise and today it is $80,000. People want them and somehow they are pooling their resources to make the down payments for the bank loans. Another important thing is that the Vietnamese people prefer to hire their own—no management or language problems that can't be worked out.

About the refugee's first job, you know I think a lot of problems occur between the refugee and sponsor because of the refugee's first job. So the sponsor says you take the janitor's job and in a few years you will be manager of the company. It's part of the sponsor's American dream. Well, all it is is a dream. How often does that happen? It's a myth. For the refugee, there was no labor market mobility in Vietnam. You tell a military general to be a janitor and you get some reactions real quick from him! I say work it out where, with a little more time and investment, a more suitable job is found. Just a little more time.

You know, the '75 refugees fell right into the U.S. middle-class value system. They were made for it. Those who came later were a little different; they not only suffered because of the trauma of exit but also because they were less prepared to deal with the U.S. middle-class value structure. The class of '75 learned the rules of the economic game quicker because we were better educated and better exposed to what was going to happen to us here. We were more savvy; it helps.

How do you describe the future?

With optimism. For the '75 refugee, we established a network that is getting more intertwined into the greater American business community. It's breaking into new industries. More people are owning their own businesses and helping others understand the ways of the business world. I am optimistic, what more can I say? Don't I sound optimistic?

LAOTIAN TALE

In ancient times, an heir-apparent handsome prince
fell in love with a lord's daughter.
The king feared for his son's safety,
but disobeying his father he secretly married her.

The princess plotted to murder her husband.
He was hit by a poison dart,
but the poison was not strong enough to kill.
It was a curse as the prince got well,
then sick again and fell into a coma.
It was a cycle. Just as it seems that he is at last down,
it brings him back.
Suffering now is his lot,
hope never completely realized.
The curse always prevents him from being crowned.
So it is today in Laos.
Hope and then death strike.
It is a cycle.

Laotian folktale as recalled by a woman of over seventy, Seattle, Washington
[translated from Lao]

TEENAGER IN MEMPHIS

Biology and math make me feel good.
I hold them close like I would my mother
when I was a young girl.

Too much disaster is found in current events,
I keep a distance—like the black plague is
near or an ugly boy.
I am sad to hear of the journey to America,
but glad that I am the future.

Cambodian girl, age fifteen, Memphis

PHAT and SOPHAL MAU
Reuniting Families

This is our fourth interview, and we talk in French and English. Phat has a keen sense of humor and smiles a lot. Sophal Mau is an extremely shy young man. He follows all of our conversation but answers only when his father cues him. His eyes never leave the floor.

I was a supreme court judge in Cambodia and a law professor. I wrote the Civil Code and trained all of the lawyers that are now in power in Cambodia. I was never interested in politics. I didn't care about politics and I think my students knew this. I was out of the country when it fell to the Khmer Rouge. I really believe that one of my former students helped facilitate my son's return because he remembered me. I would like to thank him for that.

Tell me about your son Sophal.

I never saw my son. He was born in Cambodia after I was assigned to the Cambodian Mission to the United Nations. After my wife had given birth to Sophal, she joined me in the U.S. with the two older children, Sontary and Sopha. My assignment was supposed to be short-term and we thought it best to leave Sophal with his grandparents. You know, grandparents in Cambodia have this special care for grandchildren—it's their honor to care for the grandchild; it is not seen as a burden in any way. We thought it would only be a short-term assignment, maybe two years at the very most.

I was in Geneva as chief of the Cambodian delegation to the Law of the

Sea Conference when I learned from other contacts that the U.S. would evacuate the Embassy in two days. This I could not believe. To do this meant the U.S. would give up everything and leave Vietnam eventually, too. But my information was accurate. I telephoned my wife in New York that evening and she was able to telephone her mother in the capital. Her mother would not believe her. She said the Americans were still there and that the city was calm. She did not want to leave Cambodia; where would she go and how would she get there? she asked. Well, it was too late. The Americans left the next day and all communication stopped. The airport was closed and the communication with the rest of the world was cut off. They were trapped. These were very difficult, dark days.

When Pol Pot took over the government, my contacts told me that my father-in-law, Chaum Sokhum, was arrested. He was secretary of national education and was also minister of justice and at one time minister of industry under the Sihanouk and Lon Nol governments. So my in-laws and son were evacuated to the countryside like everyone else in Phnom Penh. By then, Sophal was two years old. One day, the Khmer Rouge came and took my mother-in-law by force to the nearby forest and shot her and threw her body in the river. My boy was hiding and was adopted by a local peasant family.

Father Lee—that's whom my son still talks about, the old man who became his father. It was this Father Lee and his family that saved his life. I am sure of this. My son was like their own son and he lived as a peasant's son, taking care of the cattle and gathering fruit. The Khmer Rouge looked for him but no one gave away his location.

Sophal Mau: I remember Father Lee and other people who were my family there. I never went to school in Stung Treng. I only took care of the cows. I thought Father Lee was my family. Now I have two families.

How did you discover where your son was?

I had a job after the United Nations with Lutheran Immigration in New York. I went almost every day to JFK airport to receive the refugees. I speak French, Vietnamese, Chinese, and Cambodian, so I met so many Cambodians. I asked all that I could about my son. About where they had come from and whether they had seen or heard about him. Nothing. There was nothing. And I did this for several years. So many of these refugees were in border camps and I thought they would know something. I began a campaign of writing letters to people in the U.S. and France. I began to follow every lead I could. Most often it was a big waste of time.

We knew we could identify Sophal because he had a three-quarter-inch, rectangular-shaped, very pale brown birthmark just above his left eye. That mark could not be confused, and we had a photo of the boy. So we looked for ten years. I traveled all over the place for him. I tracked down evidence that I thought would lead to something, any clue was not to be rejected. What I started was my inquiry in the grapevine of the Cambodian community in the U.S. and Europe.

Then, in the spring of 1980 during a trip to see my father, Khanh Huynh, in Paris, I got my first break. My father told me to contact another Cambodian refugee in Paris who had heard of the search for Sophal. This refugee woman knew a woman in Phnom Penh who had been a friend of the elderly relatives with whom Sophal had lived in the village of Stung Treng. The only clue the refugee woman could give was that this woman was the sister of a well-known former government official. So I quickly contacted my wife's aunt, Sinath, in Phnom Penh to ask her to track down this woman. Two days later, my father died. But being Buddhist, we believe that my father's spirit then entered into the search.

On March 25, 1983, I got a cable from Ho Chi Minh City from another relative who said that my son had been found by Sinath and that a letter would follow. The trip took Sinath three days by bus, boat, and horse, but she found him. It took a great deal to convince him to leave, and much more to convince his father Lee and the family.

He had become their son, and I feel for the loss they had to go through. I owe them much and I know one day I will be able to return their kindness; I know this will happen. Well, they eventually all went to Phnom Penh. This was the first time for them to see a movie. There was no electricity in the village. My son still talks about the first film he saw. Now he loves cartoons in America.

None of this would have turned out as it did if Congressman Stephen Solarz was not going on a fact-finding trip to Phnom Penh. You see, he met with the foreign minister and his last agenda item was a humanitarian request for our family reunification. Sophal was permitted to leave on February 28, 1983. There was so much red tape, you cannot believe it. It took one year, but eventually we got him a visa and got him to Bangkok. He was accompanied by a representative of a church relief agency that was working in Phnom Penh.

How did Sophal recognize you?

When I first saw him at the airport in Bangkok, I wore a brown shirt—the same brown shirt that was in the color photo that had been given to him. I wanted something to be familiar.

Sophal was the only child—the only person—to get out of Cambodia to the U.S. this way. No other person has left the country as an immigrant. A lot of Cambodian parents have contacted me for help. My story gives them hope, but it is so difficult to do nothing for them. I tell them not to give up hope. Never give up hope. The Cambodian government does not even acknowledge these requests now. I do not know why the Central Committee responded favorably to my request. I still believe it was the kindness of a former law student who remembered me. I may never know his name.

DO VAN CHI
Newark Race Relations

We walk through the Newark neighborhood that he talks about and occasionally he stops to point out a friend or point of interest. We sit on a park bench and drink soda.

The hardest part for me was the unknown. We left a war zone in Saigon. We came to America and the Catholic Church resettled us from a refugee camp in Indiantown Gap, Pennsylvania. We went to New Jersey. I had never heard of Newark. I thought a mistake was made and the social worker meant New York. But Newark was correct. It has been a good life here. There are some problems, but it is good here.

I never saw a black person in Vietnam other than the U.S. GIs, and, to me, the uniform makes them look alike. The GIs were all the same. They carried guns and they were there to help the South Vietnamese. My father would say that the GIs came to save us from Communists; now we know that it was a mistake to say that.

What do black people think of the Vietnamese?

I know that they hate us. For me, it is difficult to explain. It is the little things that always tell you the most. Yes, if they burn your house, rob you, or cause you physical harm, you know there is hate. But it is not always so obvious to us. There are little things that happen every day that tell me. I see it in their eyes, the way they look at us Vietnamese. When we walk down the street their eyes follow us—like from the corner of their eyes. It makes me feel small.

There are many GIs from Vietnam that live now in Newark. Many, too, that were hurt or killed in Vietnam, or their friends or family were hurt. They know us when they see us on the street. They remember what it was like during their time in Saigon, in the war. "Mama-San"—that is what they call my wife when we walk down the street. There are worse names, too, like "yellow dog" or "gook" and other names. These are not nice words and there is hate in them. But for us, we try not to hear them. We do not call them "niggers."

How do you describe your life in Newark?

You have to be very careful living in Newark. Once you learn the system, it's okay then. Newark off Clinton Avenue is dangerous for us. Late at night to come home can be a hazard. I work for a cleaning company that cleans large offices at night. I have done this for three years. The money now is pretty good. When I leave for work, my wife locks the doors. She won't let anybody whom she does not know in the door. We have been robbed two times. The last time they came down from the ceiling and stole our television and the bed. Then the second time they took our clothes. Can you believe it, our clothes? Look at me and my clothes. Why would anyone want to take them? I am a very short man. Americans are very tall.

I have learned a little about the history of this country and about slavery and Mr. Abraham Lincoln and how he freed the slaves. Black people here—some are nice to me, but I do not trust them. Behind the smile they do not trust me. They think we are all yellow people who take from them. Take their homes, their jobs, and that we take what the government would have given to them if we had not come. You can see this, especially in the welfare line. They look at you like they know what you do: "Why are you here when we know you work and have all of your money?" They think we all save our money under our beds. So, the hate and the distrust, it is there. They are jealous.

To get by in Newark, we must learn to live with them. My friends talk about how they teach their children to walk fast past black people. Do not stop. Do not talk Vietnamese. Do not look up. And to cross the street, if there should be any problems, well, just cross the street. Always avoid possible violence, avoid contact.

It is sad, yes? Here we are teaching more fear, more hate to our children. What will they teach their children? More fear, more hate. It goes round and round. But we must protect ourselves. Our children will not live here forever on Clinton Avenue, not even maybe Newark, I hope.

Do you feel you are a part of a community?

Community? Well, we are a people who belong to a community. We are here and we want to be tougher. It is easier that way. Our people, our culture and language. If we forget this, we are truly lost—then we will be refugees forever. For me, the Vietnamese community in Newark is like a big family. Some members you like more than others, but you get along with everyone. We have two or three leaders and we have people who want to be leaders. But there are differences among us. Much has to do with the way each family was situated before they left Vietnam. Was he rich, was he political? You do not forget the values and the differences. We bring them and keep them. In some ways, the Americans gave us a lot of our values: money, to own things and to work hard to get things.

So it is not so strange that we want what most Americans want, is it? Peace, a good life. Money, why not? We are much alike on these things. There are many things I think I know about the blacks that maybe are only half-truths. There are many things I see that I cannot understand at all. Like why so many children without fathers? In the past when they have called me names or laughed at me, I guess I laughed at them so they would forget me and not notice me. Like I would go away. Leave their street, their city. But that is not how it is now. We are here in Newark. We come as new Americans. The old Americans brought us here. We are here and that's just the way it will be. We are not going away; there is nowhere else for us to go, really.

NEW LIFE

Minnesota is a new life and place for me.
It brings surprises for my friends and me every day
Our parents looked for freedom for all of us

and we came to America;
Freedom for our hearts and our minds.

We walk now through shopping malls, not fields of oxen.
Without grandparents life is without history
of our days before we came,
Like reading a book in school but pages are missing.

We speak of home but know this is our home now,
America. Like rustling leaves I gather in the fall
in Minnesota, the winter brings spring
and the seasons remain but the forest
has unfamiliar trees and the harvest
is with different fruit.

Laotian girl, age fourteen, St. Paul, Minnesota

CHANGES

Today the daffodils and cherry blossoms
are in full bloom in the capital.
I hear again and again
the lyrics of a Vietnamese song:
"I'm looking for a spring in my youth but nothing,
not even a faded image is retained."
I feel like a Wandering Jew;
I am a Wandering Vietnamese.
I miss the heat of Saigon,
the trees around the pagoda grounds.
My dead are too far away to burn incense on their graves.
How many changes to live with, how many reactions:
depression, panic, homesickness, fear.
To hide all of this in the mind's closet
is to destroy the spirit that survived. The change is today.
The spring is today and images are now.

—*Trien Thi Nguyen, Washington, D.C.*

SIRATHRA SOM
The Donut Queen

We meet at one of her donut shops. She is wearing a very stylish black jump-suit, her hair pulled back tight, gold accessories, and very large sunglasses. Her new black BMW car is parked outside the window. She exudes an air of confidence and has a series of amusing anecdotes concerning cross-cultural experiences.

I was born in the capital, Phnom Penh, and led a very comfortable life. I can still see the school I went to as a child. I see the trees on the street and I think of the familiar things that made my life happy. I grew up a happy child with friends and school to keep me busy. My parents were educated but we were not what you would call rich. We never talked about money. Things just happened with my life, that's how I describe it—things just happened. That was the way with the war and leaving, it just happened.

What is the role of women in Cambodia?

The role of women in Cambodia is very defined. A woman is supposed to act in a certain way. Women are wives and mothers—those are the roles. We never questioned any of it. Not me, not my mother—we accepted it. If you grew up in a society where the rules are established and the community obeys them, then you just go along with it. You ask no questions—just go with it. I suppose it was expected. I would go to university and get an education, but more important, I would get married and have children. Those were my duties. I gave up university when I married. My marriage, of course, was arranged. I was young, and before we left the country I had two babies. I fit the traditional role of a good wife and mother and listener.

No one can forget the final days in Cambodia. It was only yesterday in my mind. Cambodia fell before Vietnam, and by early April we had to leave. My husband worked for the U.S. Agency for International Development, so we would be in a dangerous position if we stayed. No question about it, we would have been killed. I was twenty-two then. We left on April 7, 1975, and went to Camp Pendleton and were released to a sponsor in Texas three weeks later.

All of my family and my husband's family were killed, all of my friends. No one was left. It was like a plague of death and everyone is gone. The

Khmer Rouge killed everyone. All of my family were educated people—those were the ones that Pol Pot wanted most to destroy.

We arrived in California with nothing, nothing. Only the clothes we were wearing. I could not speak English and everybody looked threatening to me. Simple things seemed complicated. Colors were different, sounds were different. Each day was filled with more questions than answers.

Tell me about your first job.

My first job was at the Sheraton Hotel in San Francisco as a domestic, and I earned $2.50 an hour. I was lucky to get the job—there were a lot of people who wanted it. We lived in Oakland and the job was in San Francisco. To be without a car in California is like being a bird without wings. You can live but then you can't really live. So I commuted by bus with several transfers. I remember the first day when I had to transfer from the first bus to the second one and I got lost. I panicked. I could not speak and I used hand signals. A nice man took my hand and took me to the bus. He had a wonderful smile and it was that smile I will never forget.

I learned English but not in a classroom. That's too much wasted time, it's too tiring. If you want to learn, you listen to people on the street, listen to the radio and TV, but also you force yourself to speak. After I learned what I thought was English, although it wasn't so good, I registered for sixteen units of accounting at night school; but I had no time—work and family forced me to quit.

For me there was no question of whether I should work or stay at home. One of the first things you learn in America is that you need money. You can't be without money. There is no one then to help you. So we needed two incomes and I went to work. I know my husband did not like it, but it could not be helped. The journey here created problems for us and this work situation was one of them. I could work easier than he could and I began to do well and I supported the family. I became the breadwinner.

He had bad feelings about this, I understood this, but the feelings got worse. It's hard for me to talk about it. I understood his pain but there was nothing I could do about it to help him. Eventually, we were divorced. Divorced! This would be unheard-of in Cambodia where you are married once and that is it for life. But he could not make the changes here. The money was always a problem. Now he has a master's degree and works as a counselor in San Francisco. That part of my life is completed.

What do you think of American women?

I find that American women think too much about things which complicate their lives, and it seems strange to me. I suppose all women have been raised to follow, but you must take the chances while they are there. Too many American women also lack patience. They want everything so quickly and they want the impossible. No patience. Life is not that way, and it only leads to unhappiness. Our Buddhist tradition teaches us patience. Maybe it cannot be learned. When I got divorced, I felt sick; I lost twenty pounds. Silly? Well, I had three children to care for and I could not have the luxury of worrying and wasting time. So I accepted my situation and made peace.

Tell me how you started here in business.

Before the U.S., I had never worked. In 1976, I persuaded Winchell's Donuts to give me a manager franchise and to work off the $5,000 fee. Then I started a small Winchell's shop in Berkeley and was able to pay off the franchise fee in four months. I built up one business and sold it in five months. I doubled the money I had paid for it. In 1982, when I was visiting some friends in Stockton, I noticed a run-down Oriental food store being mismanaged, and the owners were glad to sell it. The Asia food store is doing very well today. The store is ideally located in a busy shopping center within a few blocks of a new housing subdivision full of Asian refugee farm workers.

I began with nothing and now I have something. For me, that's what is great about America. I know the Cambodian men say I am tough—so what? By American standards you need to be good at business to survive. So maybe I am tough. But it is very hard work. I am working every morning at four-thirty in one of my six donut stores. I want to buy that McDonald's hamburger store next door, that is my next investment.

Have you experienced discrimination in the United States?

I know about discrimination against Cambodians. It was not so long ago that hate groups wanted to burn down the section of Stockton where the Cambodians lived. The KKK was here, you know. I suppose we remind people of the war. But then, too, we get discrimination among our own refugee groups. Most people think we are Vietnamese, they only talk about Vietnamese refugees. Well, we are different. The Vietnamese get better training programs and other services. They are more forceful than Cambodians, but that is part of our history.

I have no problems as a working mother. I am remarried now. My three children are happy, and I spend time with them every day. I am at a point that if I want to take a few days off or take a vacation with them, I can do it. Just knowing you can do that is a good feeling. My kids are doing very well in school. They get rewards. For every A on the report card they get ten dollars. Anything less than an A, then they must do housework for me. It is my incentive system.

I care deeply about my fellow Cambodians here. I know their lives are miserable and painful. I have helped thirteen families start their own businesses around here. I share my experiences and the lessons I have learned. I get upset with refugees who live too long on welfare if they are able to work. I get upset with the welfare caseworkers, too, who encourage a lot of people to take cash assistance and to stay on welfare. They need their clients. I feel that anyone can achieve success here if they are smart and willing to work hard. I encourage people to start a business.

I have no regrets; how could I? I want to get my M.B.A. and I worry about the first time my twelve-year-old daughter brings home her first boyfriend. No, I have not seen *The Killing Fields* movie about Cambodia. I am not ready for that.

MEMORIAL VISIT

I showed up at the November 1982 dedication of the Vietnam War
Memorial in Washington. It was a warm, sunny day
and the warmth of the sunlight radiated off the black granite
as you walked past it. I remember seeing the little groups of
soldiers. They were friends reunited and many men were crying.
I felt my interior collapse with them.

There was this terrible silence at times;
it was like walking between people who stared at you but
I didn't have the courage to look them in the eyes,
to tell them, I, too, was a soldier.

I lost my brother and uncle and best friends,
don't look at me that way.
But I didn't know even if they were looking at me.
I could only respond like I was a stranger.

I thought I saw a familiar face
but then many faces looked familiar.
The green fatigues and caps brought back sounds and sights
I thought I would be able to forget.
I stared at my feet and walked back in the direction
I just came from. It was more painful
tracing the V-wing of the monument in this direction.
I was alone and needed to be with a fellow countryman.
I needed to be in a small group,
but when I saw some other Vietnamese
I was not able to talk with them.
I only said hello and continued to walk,
I guess I wanted to suffer alone.

At the farthest end of the monument
A woman was putting a small piece of paper
between the cracks of the stones.
A prayer, a wish, a message to the dead?
Was it her husband, her brother, a cousin, a friend?
Her little girl stood quietly holding a rose as
I turned away.

I got more courage as I was going to leave
and wanted to talk with an American soldier
but I couldn't.
I saw three men standing with a hand on each other's backs,
the one man was on a crutch.
I almost did it but I stopped.
I didn't want to disturb their silence.
I was an intruder.
I wanted to tell them about my sorrow,
But I could not,

I could not.
I was not part of the healing today,
I was only a visitor.

Hang Thu Tran, Washington, D.C.

SALOUTH SOMAN
Beyond the Killing Fields

He is a very friendly man who never seems to stop smiling. He is dressed in a three-piece suit, and although it is quite warm, never removes his jacket. He speaks to me in Khmer.

You know I had the courage last month to see the film about the life of Dith Pran on videocassette at a house of a friend of mine. For me this took a great deal of courage. I always said that I would never do it, never see it because there are too many painful memories for me. I had heard so much about it that I think I pretty much knew most of the film. You know the actors were not Cambodian, most were Thai or Vietnamese. But that is okay.

The memories of the escape and the terrible things that happened to all of us have permanently made scars on our souls for our entire lives. We are wounded and there is little we can do to respond to the pain except get through our days the best we can. For those with children it is easier. I lost my wife and two babies trying to escape. There is never a day I can forget this, never. But this is not to say that we do not try to forget about some of it.

We must be like Dith Pran. Dith Pran survived and he had a new life in America. He has a story that has become part of the refugees' hopes for the future. We cannot forget, but we must always try to forget. That for me is what Dith Pran is trying to teach us. Every day, every day again and again and again we try to get along here with our lives. So much of it is not pleasurable, even after many years here, we fight it. But that, for me, is what *The Killing Fields* is about: it is a story of survival at many levels.

I visit friends in Philadelphia and they tell me about the problems they have with their children and how they are disappointed with them. I am silent and inside of me I cry. I cry for my lost babies and my wife. I cry for the other family that I have lost and for my village that is gone. But I say nothing. I do not tell what is really in my heart, that they should be so happy that they have children and all of those things. You cannot say too much. But this is from *The Killing Fields,* too. We must learn to see the past as it was—the past—and move on with our lives as Americans. That is why we are here—to be Americans.

Conclusion

Trying to bring closure to the many conversations, meetings, travels, thoughts, and ideas that went into the research, editing, and writing of this book is not a simple matter. Oral history can haunt the researcher. You are sometimes left with a combination of short statements, a phrase, a word, or a very long monologue to transcribe and integrate into the book. The emotional impact of these interviews and stories hits you at a later time, often when you cannot ask that one last question. You must depend on the patience and interest of the translators. You must read the transcripts several times for accuracy and length.

Before concluding with a discussion of policy issues, that focuses on refugee admission, it seems appropriate to draw together some final thoughts and ideas the refugees shared with me on subjects as important as expectations, citizenship, the resettlement program, race relations, and the definition of the term "refugee" itself. Their personal comments on these topics, in many ways, remain the most telling conclusion to this book.

Expectations

When asked about their expectations of life in the United States before they arrived, the majority of the people interviewed said they had little idea of what life would be like in the United States. This included those from privileged backgrounds as well as those who had previously visited the country. "I was a bank president with good ties to IBM. It was IBM that eventually helped me after I had been in this country some months, but I expected nothing. I was lucky to get it," said Bui Duc Tin, New York City. "But then, maybe I had a cavalier attitude or a fatalist attitude. I mean, now that I say this, everybody has to have some sort of expectation. But I was resolved to end my career and not have any plans or expectations about the future. I had been rich so I suppose I had this Buddhist notion of fate. My fate in America was unknown, so I would not expect anything. I was wrong, and I am glad for it."

Moni Rat from Cambodia, a senior at Tulane University in New Orleans, had the following comments: "I guess I had an American dream in mind. Ever since I was a little child, I dreamed of going to a Western country to get an education and becoming a writer. Then I wanted to be a scientist; now I am finishing undergraduate work in biology and hope to get into Tulane Medical School next year. I think a lot about Einstein who was also a refugee and I also think about the author Joseph Conrad and about the way he writes about life and the relationship of nature to people. He says on paper so much of what I think in my mind."

Moni continued: "You see, my dream coming here was a child's dream come true. It is always the same. When you are young, you desperately wish for things that you know nothing about. I still have this idea of doing something great, and if I can do this, I know it will be in this country and nowhere else. I feel it. The reality of life in America is that you work very hard, harder if you are a newcomer. If it takes my classmates four hours to read the assignment, it will take me six; I am prepared for it. I know I must work harder. Yes, the reality is you work harder than you thought you would. The reality of life in America is that you work very hard."

Phon Shanomoney, Greensboro, North Carolina, commented as follows: "I spent so much time in the Thai camps and they were terrible. We were like prisoners. When I was taken by the U.S. program, all I could think about was not looking at the camp. It was some years and there was some time in the camp when I thought I might be able to go to France, but that never worked out. I wanted America. No, I did not expect to be given a car or a house, like some said would happen, by the welfare people and the sponsor, all I expected was to be able to work."

Le Rieu Tai, San Francisco: "I didn't know really what to expect but I thought for sure I would eventually be able to practice medicine here. Surely, I thought, they would need me to practice medicine—what with so many refugees and people who need help. I was wrong. No one helped me at all on this. This sense of need and the talents you possess requires the avenue of the possibility of a position. I learned that you cannot expect a job like in Vietnam, even if you are qualified. You must know the system and know someone in the power structure. You cannot function at the level of your former life. All is difficult and different. And you must expect things to be different. If you are my age, it is difficult to forget the way things once were and adjust to a new life. I certainly expected it to be easier."

Huot Huon Ly, Dallas: "We talked about a lot of things in the camp, what we would do in America and where we would go. I thought for sure that when I arrived they would buy me a car, a flashy car. . . . I was very surprised—shocked—they did not!"

Mai Pauteamy, Philadelphia: "What did I expect coming to America? Well, I don't know if I can answer this question. Maybe it is true to say I wanted first to see my sister who lived in Philadelphia and I wanted my children to have a future. There was no peace and no future for them in Cambodia. Pol Pot took away all of that and nothing more was left, nothing. This idea of expectation is very Western, maybe that's why I have a problem with giving you a good answer. In Cambodia I did not expect anything from life. My husband provided me and my children with everything. It is not the place of Cambodian women to have expectations. I know this is different in America but I did not know any of this before I came to America. Expectations? To see my sister and to have peace for my children, that is my answer."

Citizenship

Bui Van Binh in Dallas said: "The moment I raised my hand to give the oath, I thought of my father and I thought, what would he think about what I am doing with my life—changing my nationality? Would he say that I am renouncing my Vietnamese heritage? Would he forgive me?

"My father died in 1974 but he was a very powerful force in my life. He always taught me to be proud of Vietnam. I have thought he would have been happy with my decision, but there is still that lingering doubt in my mind. I guess that it will always be there. I think he would have to have understood the circumstances, the escape, and how we came to live here, all those sorts of details, to understand completely.

"Most of my American friends never asked me this question. I think it is because they really have no idea what it would be like to start again. You take your country, I tell them, for granted, like it will always be there and be there to give you the sense of security we Vietnamese never knew. But to come here and to want to become an American, well, that's a great deal of work and effort. For one thing, you've really got to know the history of this country. Not just memorizing the history, but you've got to know what you are answering for the exam. But now I am an American citizen, like you. I cannot worry about what my father would have said or anything like that. I have got to be a good American now and I've got other things to worry about."

Phat Mau, New York City, commented: "Probably no other event in the refugee's time here has such diverse meaning and impact as the oath of citizenship. I said to myself, now you can vote and travel anywhere. Now you are a real American!"

Cam Ba Dong, Sacramento, had this to say: "I will never forget it. When I raised my hand I felt cold. I felt my grandfather's and father's eyes. I would now renounce Vietnam. The land of my great-grandfather. Gone. It took only a few minutes and centuries of history went away. Like that! My father would not understand this. I had this image in my mind of Vietnam. A sort of déjà vu. I kept seeing a flash of Saigon, the street I lived on, and the faces before me were the faces I knew but could not remember by name. This is what I thought about as I was becoming an American citizen."

Sengbo Chao, Atlanta: "Well, I was so happy that day. I went down the main streets in Atlanta. Just riding around thinking about what I would do in only one hour. I thought about all the good things. Then after it was all over and I was riding back through those streets, I tried to imagine what it was that I was going to do that would be so special now that I was an American citizen. It was a better feeling before it happened."

Resettlement Program

Concerning the resettlement program in the United States, the refugees shared a wide spectrum of experiences, views, and recommendations. What the program did accomplish was to bring Southeast Asians into direct contact with Americans. Usually an accommodation was worked out and in some cases, lasting friendships were formed. Above all else, two ideas emerge clearly from the interviews: that no one planned the American resettlement program and that it offers something in terms of assistance and service that is distinctly American. That "something" is the local community help, enthusiasm bordering on the desire to do good, as well as a genuine motivation to do good. The refugees made the following comments about that program as they experienced it:

Van Tou-Fu, Los Angeles, observed: "I was twenty when I left Laos and came to California because I had a brother in Sacramento. A Baptist church sponsored me because they said they helped sponsor my brother. He was on welfare but worked sometimes, too. This made the sponsor mad. When I wanted to take a training program for auto repair, they told me that the training program was open only if I was on welfare. So I went on welfare to get the training and my sponsor got mad. If they want us to stop taking the money the government gives us, I do not understand why they make the system operate like it does. My brother does not understand, and he has been here for four years more than me."

Ma Vang, Philadelphia: "I was a widow in Cambodia and I had three years' education in my country, which is the same education most married women get in Cambodia. My husband and his brothers were killed by the Khmer Rouge and we escaped with my brother to Thailand before the Americans brought us to Minnesota. I have four children; the oldest is now twelve and the youngest is six. They have many problems and I stayed home to care for them after we arrived. I use welfare because I could not work because I never learned English. You know it is not so much money that they give you and if my sponsor would not help me now, I do not think my children would have good food to eat or good clothes to wear. They tell me I must get a job, but I never worked in Cambodia and I do not want to learn English here."

Doan Ngoc An, Memphis: "When we left the camp in 1975 and went to Memphis, a Baptist family sponsored us. The family was nice to my family and in the beginning they did nice things for us. Then about six months after we came, they always wanted us to go to church, and finally they came with the car and took us and I did not like it. I am a Buddhist and all the time they talked about Jesus and their religion and they never stopped this. In the end, they got angry and said things I did not understand because this was when I could not speak or understand English very well; it was seven years ago. They finally said they would not help us anymore. They told us I had made Jesus angry. Well, I told them I never met Jesus so how could I make him angry? This they did not understand. That was the last time they came to our house."

May Yang, Portland: "Many refugees in Oregon did not understand how it was the government could stop giving us money. It is very difficult for the refugee to get a good job and then we were told that the program had changed. It was something about how the money would come for eighteen months after we go on welfare and not for thirty-six months; so if we had to use welfare it was to be for only eighteen months. As a community leader, I tried to warn the sponsors that many people need to understand this better, but there was much confusion. There was an older, single man who stopped getting money and they said he hanged himself because he would no longer have any money for food."

Kao Hen, San Diego: "My sponsors were so angry when I told them I would go to California. They said that Chicago was a good place and I should stay there. My sponsors never understood why I left. . . . It is difficult when you are alone. You want the company of friends. Most people in the refugee resettlement program do not understand this. How could they? They worry about money, budgets, and welfare. This is what the government cares about. Who talks about your needs for friends, family or just being lonely and scared? Nobody cares about this."

Race Relations

Most of those interviewed were reluctant to discuss racial prejudice. The meaning of the concept of prejudice is often not understood, and perceptions of exactly what and how it is manifested vary greatly. The subject usually triggered responses that were not directly related to the question asked.

Pauline Van Tho, Houston, observed: "See the skyline out there? Houston is a pretty city but there is a lot of conservative thought out there. I would call a lot of them 'rednecks.' The majority do not understand us and they think we all take money and do not pay taxes. There is a lot of quiet discrimination in all of this. Well, that's okay, we have been through a lot tougher things in our lives. Now we have got to work the political process. That's what we need to learn, the political process here.

"There is an ABC [American-born Chinese] lawyer running for judge here in Houston, and I am trying to get the Vietnamese voters to back him. He is a very nice man and a good lawyer. I tell them it is important to get an Asian face in Texas local politics, but most do not have the time or money to help. Well, we need that and that will happen in the future. It may take some time, but I am sure it will happen."

Le Minh Chinh, New Orleans: "Look, I now know how Americans think. When they come into an American fast-food joint, they don't want to see an Oriental face taking their money. They want an Anglo face and that's it. I don't think this will change. So the hell with it! They don't need to know I own it. I will give them the faces they want to see. I came to this country because they brought me, they accepted me to be part of their society. For this I am grateful. But I do not really understand the hate between different peoples in the United States. I do not understand it at all. Aren't there enough riches here for everyone? I guess not. There is so much hate."

May Pham, New York City: "Most Cambodian women are afraid of the black man. He robs and rapes her. I am always afraid. We teach our children not to talk to black people. Never. I did not feel this way in Cambodia, and when I came to New York City, I did not want to believe this, but it happens to me now and I know it is true."

Ninh Van Nguyen, Carmichael, California: "We are aware of the way we are treated after we accomplish things that people say we are good at. There is a stereotype of the Asian kid who excels in math and is brilliant. Well, I say that kid can go only so far in the system as it now exists. The rewards have boundaries. How about an Asian being president of a big corporation? Oh look, I know these are things to worry about in the future, but nevertheless we are thinking about them."

On Being a Refugee

Attorney My Linh Soland said: "I never thought about being a refugee—as if I was in some special state of being or something comparable to that. Events just happened and they force you to be something, that's all. I don't think a person has many guarantees in life, no matter how optimistic his outlook is.

I think it's just that some are fortunate enough or strong enough to respond and that it works in their favor. I have found a great deal of comfort in Buddhist thought since I came to this country; perhaps that has helped me to get through these difficult periods.

"When I went first to Canada to live, I adjusted to an entirely new set of circumstances. I had three children and a husband being retrained as an M.D. I did not think of myself as a refugee then. I thought of myself as a survivor, nothing more. There were certain things I had to do to keep surviving, that's all. You go on with your life. For me, perhaps the escape and the initial first week of shock made me feel like a refugee, but after that I began to feel something different. It was sort of an in-between state. I guess that's when I stopped feeling myself to be a refugee."

Samphy Iep, Washington, D.C.: "In reply to the question about when a person stops being or thinking about himself as a refugee, the answers varied greatly, mostly due to the degree of accommodation and adaptation that had taken place with each person. I will never stop being a refugee, never. It is part of my story and my life. You live with it every day and when you get into a melancholia, it hurts you very much."

Nguyen Van Kim, Los Angeles: "I was three when I came here. My parents try to teach me their language, but why? I am an American now. All the rest of that is ancient history. That is for my parents to worry about. That's very dead history."

Le Tan Chinh, Hawthorne, California: "When I raised my hand to take the oath to become a citizen, I gave up my title of 'refugee.' Sure I think about refugees all of the time. That is my inner being, but my exterior, the surface I deal with to survive in this society, is that of a new American. I am proud to say I can vote Republican for the next president."

Mary Mai, New York: "Like anything else, this depends upon your background and experiences. Really, to me, being Vietnamese is a very special honor. I gave it up when I came here. Don't think the society here is compatible to be both. One wins out over the other in some ways and eventually you start doing things like Americans. Well, now do not misunderstand me; the things they do are good."

Dr. Ngo Minh Son, Arlington, Virginia: "I am too old to change, too set in my former ways. That is all there is. I became a citizen because I have a brother in Vietnam that I want to see before I die. I became a citizen only because I want to bring him here. I have no other reason. For me, I am a displaced lawyer from Vietnam and I will always be a refugee at heart and in spirit."

The newcomers' comments directly or indirectly reflect on the subject of refugee admission policy. Refugee experts see the United States today in a period of "compassion fatigue" when dealing with future commitment to the refugee program. Defining who is or is not a refugee appears to be getting more difficult; dealing with increased government rejection rates, for example, seems to anger all advocates. "The bottom line for any refugee or person seeking to be called a refugee," said Phat Mau, is "who gets in and who does not get in."

Policy Issues

Who gets in? How do you determine who gets in? What are the limits? The growing concern of not only those interviewed for this book but a diverse body of Americans born here continues to challenge our laws and our policymakers on these questions. And as the Roper polls have indicated for the past twenty-five years, no single issue can elicit such an immediate and heated response as immigration. When pressed, those polled are almost unanimous for urging humanitarian support for refugees but become confused about how that support should work. "We must give money, but can't they live somewhere else?" is a not-so-uncommon response to continued refugee resettlement in the United States.

The current argument over the subject of whether a person is an economic or political refugee continues with little clarification. Adherence to our refugee laws in light of continued pressure by so many for entrance shows no sign of lifting. In his testimony before the House Judiciary Committee, Subcommittee on Immigration, Refugees and International Law, on 12 September 1989, Roger Winter, Director of the United States Committee for Refugees, said, "While humanitarian in rhetoric, the United States refugee program is also highly political. It has historically mirrored the United States confrontation with the Soviet Union and other Communist countries. Foreign policy considerations have been the prime determinant of which refugees would be resettled in the United States. Despite the changing world scene, this is still the case."

Leonel Castillo, former immigration commissioner, often prefaced his speeches with the statement that the United States had become the "magic magnet for the unfortunate, the hungry and the homeless." Castillo went on to say that the new arrivals to American shores continue to bring with them determination, resilience and a willingness to fight to succeed that reinforce the spirit of what America means to so many: freedom and opportunity. The Southeast Asian refugee experience offers a good example of new opportunity; and the influence of these new Americans on communities around the country is already being felt in the professions they have joined and skills that they have acquired or regained. You can see it in the shops they have opened, for example, and in the art they are creating.

Our immigration policy has provided almost one million Southeast Asian refugees with an opportunity for a new life in the United States; and at the same time it gave American citizens a view of how we as a nation are responding to international and domestic changes that affect refugees. Americans have been forced to see the refugee issue not as a short-term emergency but as a long-standing global phenomenon with underlying political causes and with few practical solutions to address the needs of the almost fifteen million refugees that the United Nations estimates exist today.

In June 1989, the United Nations held a conference called by the High Commissioner for Refugees in Geneva to address the issue of solving the Southeast Asian refugee problem, a full decade after the first such conference was held for the same reason. However, this time it was clear that the world community had lost patience and, it would be safe to say, sympathy with this issue. The dramatic scenes of drowning boat people were no longer captured on documentary tape, even though they still occur. There is a growing frustration with those refugees who continue to escape from Vietnam, with those who languish in camps; an embarrassment that this exodus won't stop and that a solution to the problem has not yet been found. It sometimes seems that the world has grown tired and angry with those who use their best survival skills to show the West that they still exist, they still suffer, and they will not just go away.

The Southeast Asian host countries, burdened by a continued outflow, have vociferously said "Enough." There is continued talk among those governments of strict limits, ceilings, forced repatriation, and always of today's "compassion fatigue." This term may be best exemplified by Hong Kong's forced repatriation, in late December 1989, of fifty-two Vietnamese from a detention camp back to Vietnam—against the protests of the United Nations and Western governments except for Great Britain. And there were threats of more deportations to come.

Western countries make reference to each country's responsibility to take a "fair share" of refugees for resettlement, somehow based on resource and space availability. For the United States, the lesson of fair share in our generous admissions, since 1975, needs to be balanced by getting to the root causes of why these people continue to flee, and by addressing the geopolitical dynamics that continue to dictate this human misery. Several people interviewed continue to refer to the need for the United States to recognize the government of Vietnam and resume diplomatic relations. For others interviewed, the idea of diplomatic recognition seems totally unacceptable. "You must understand that many refugees are still waiting to return to Vietnam," said Le Xuan Khoa, Washington, D.C. "But the fact remains that the root cause of all the outflow has a great deal to do with Vietnam's economic isolation and human rights abuses."

From a domestic and legal perspective, the Southeast Asian refugees have helped influence and change federal immigration and social service policy and law. In terms of immigration policy, their plight was instrumental in forcing the United States to establish and codify its own refugee law, which subsequently became the Refugee Act of 1980. One can argue that the way we accept and treat refugees has influenced the policy we have established in looking at a broader picture that includes all nonresidents.

The Refugee Act of 1980 in itself remains a landmark legislative event that was a direct result of the Southeast Asian refugee exodus. This Act codifies by law for the first time a definition of "refugee" and establishes a coherent federal refugee policy. The Act also conforms in principle to the 1951 United Nations Covenant and 1967 Protocol Relating to the Status of Refugees, which Congress ratified in 1968. Prior to the Act, a series of ad hoc measures were used by Congress to permit refugees to enter the country during times of emergency, such as the Hungarian exodus in 1956 and that of the Cubans in 1962. The Act normalizes emergency administrative measures and provides an annual admission and funding process. Exactly how the United States wishes to adhere to the spirit and principles of those treaties (such as the treaty provisions that prohibit the forced return of any person who fears persecution) remains open for review. But it is an important foundation.

In a highly critical review of the implementation of the Refugee Act of 1980, the New York City–based Lawyers Committee for Human Rights reported in March 1990: "The decade since the enactment of the Refugee Act of 1980 has been largely a period of failure and neglect in implementation. Immigration enforcement priorities and foreign policy considerations have overwhelmed humanitarian responsibilities in refugee status determination. Planning and policymaking by the agencies have been reactive; the resources devoted to implementation have been inadequate. With increasing frequency the federal courts have had to intervene for the rights of refugees. The purpose of the Refugee Act has, in many respects, been frustrated."

Southeast Asian refugees have encouraged government policymakers to make a closer examination of public assistance programs, especially those administered by the states. This kind of scrutiny of existing programs gives a broader public a clearer understanding of what is involved in welfare use, abuse, and reform. Increasingly, federal and state officials are being asked tough questions about the appropriate use of cash assistance and eligibility requirements that affect all Americans' eligibility for welfare programs.

Also important are the lessons learned about a wider American perception of government's seemingly preferential treatment of these refugees over others (Haitians, for example), about their perceptions of who the refugees are and what, by law, they are entitled to receive. Refugees interviewed believe that the notion prevails in the greater population today that refugees are privileged over the domestic poor and disadvantaged, that they get a better deal. "I've heard it said we are guaranteed a monthly check until we die!" said Pho Ba Long, Washington, D.C. "The truth is that we don't receive any more for any longer than any other American."

Commenting on his perceptions of welfare, Le Huan Ho, in Philadelphia, gave his own description of the welfare system: "The federal government in Washington has this big bureaucratic monster called welfare. To me, the men in Washington created it for a purpose, even if it is a political purpose: it was made to address certain problems. Nobody could imagine all of the negative things that would happen to this system and how people would come to use it in a different way. It has shaken the work ethic and idea of justice for many Americans. The system is very old and it is abused and it breaks down. That is what the refugees have said most clearly to these bureaucrats; that the system is broken."

In terms of numbers admitted, the United States has been the most generous nation participating in the resettlement of Southeast Asian refugees. Assuming annual admission rates continue and at the same level, this figure will exceed 1 million by the end of 1990; in comparison, France would have accepted only 150,000 refugees. This generous U.S. refugee admission policy can be seen as part of the American tradition of welcoming the homeless and oppressed. It reinforces visibly, sometimes dramatically, the ideals that are seen as important pillars of American values. The United States wants to be seen as a sanctuary for the persecuted. Yet at the same time refugees continue to mention throughout the interviews war guilt and its implications. "You really did not want us, you were forced to take us," said one interviewee.

From a policy perspective, then, it is this generosity toward admission of refugees as demonstrated in the Southeast Asian program that will continue to be closely scrutinized by Congress and the American public in the future. Although no legislator will define it, there are limits to American generosity, obviously relating to issues such as the availability of resources and the numbers of people admitted. There is general agreement that there must be restrictions and limits, but determining them seems to get more complicated each year.

What we know for certain is that continued global political and economic strife can only create new refugee groups seeking some kind of safety in this country. And the thought of a potential mass refugee migration to American shores, as in the 1980 Cuban exodus, remains staggering. Clearly, refugee admission policy is rooted in a tradition of both hospitality and hostility. America can slam the immigration door on any group it chooses not to designate as refugees. This door that can open can also slam shut, with tragic consequences—as we have seen during World War I and World War II, and even today in the case of refugees from Haiti and El Salvador.

United States refugee policy most certainly will remain an emotionally charged subject. There will be no easy answers to the questions of who gets asylum and refugee status and who does not, especially with regard to admission ceilings. The painful truth is that there will always be some political element of bias and favoritism in the admission process, simply because there will always be refugees who are seen as politically more deserving or in need.

The argument over economic versus political refugee will find no easy solution; so, too, the question regarding those who flee from a Communist dictatorship versus those who flee from a right-wing dictatorship. Again, the truth is that a bias-free admission policy remains, like many of the United Nations treaties, an aspiration to live up to, to try to attain; certain refugee groups will probably always be of greater interest and concern to the United States than others. Such refugee policy issues continue to be critically important to the people whose voices are heard in this book.

The reaction of Americans to the Southeast Asian refugees has, for the most part, been positive. But this acceptance varies according to the degree of contact with refugees and immigrants, familiarity with their history, and the willingness of people to accept cultural diversity in their community.

American refugee policy helped save many thousands of lives; there is something very reassuring about that for all of us. Understanding exactly who these people are, and how they are going to fit into this society, is the next difficult step that is being addressed in communities throughout the country.

The refugees talked about racism. Americans display a growing envy—even anger—about Asians, especially in light of the economic boom of the Japanese world market, its products and banking skills. For many Americans, their own lack of experience with Asian peoples perpetrates myths and stereotypes: Asians are seen collectively as hard-working, motivated, and family-oriented. But most of the refugees who were interviewed saw Americans as lacking curiosity and, frequently, discipline. Several interviewees raised the issue of the traumatic impact of the war on this country and how that affected their own relations with Americans. "They [Americans] never asked me about the Vietnam War or about my previous life, about the fall of Saigon or any questions about how I knew so much English and American slang. They were not curious. You know I worked with many Americans in my country. I guess they want to forget," said Le Van Ton.

These interviews have underlined the notion that the issue of the war does not go away. Refugees who were interviewed continue to point out that there appears to be an unwillingness or inability on the part of the greater American public to see these newcomers as products of the war. "People try very hard to make the issues separate. They are not. You always have the military question, the defeat and loyalty. Well, there is a tie, a very big tie, but Americans want to hide it, to make it easier for themselves, that means not even talking about it. Which goes to my theory that Americans have still not come to terms with the war," said Pauline Van Tho.

Americans have learned a great deal from these refugees about who and where we are today in the world. One of the more telling conversations about American attitudes toward the refugees took place in Seadrift, Texas, with a fourth-generation Texan who labeled the work style of the competing Vietnamese shrimp fishermen as "un-American." When pressed to explain, he said that no American works sixteen hours a day today, that such work behavior was "un-American." Well, perhaps we have gotten complacent and a bit lazy compared to our forefathers; and we need to be reminded about the vitality and strength that exists in these newcomers who want a better life and are willing to work hard, as our forefathers did, only under different and in some ways perhaps even tougher circumstances.

Afterword

Le Xuan Khoa

V*oices from Southeast Asia* is a comprehensive view of what it is like to be a refugee from Cambodia, Laos, or Vietnam who has settled in the United States. Articulating the impressions shared by the refugees themselves—over a ten-year period—the stories they tell in this book express bitter feelings about American "abandonment," the tragic circumstances of exodus, various phases of adjustment and integration, and prospects for the future.

Perhaps most compelling, however, is the clear sense of cultural difference that comes through in these accounts, which left me with a sudden, penetrating recognition. I vividly recall, for example, that one day in 1980—when I was associate director of a mental-health program in Philadelphia and was sometimes called on for help by the police, hospitals, or individual doctors, so that they could deal appropriately with Cambodians, Laotians, and Vietnamese—an elderly Hmong woman was asked to remove her clothing just before her examination by a physician. She refused and burst into tears, deeply shaken by the request. (She remained fully clothed during the medical examination.) What brought this to mind while reading *Voices from Southeast Asia* were the many accounts of fear or bewilderment upon encountering different cultural values or customs. Saelee Sio Lai, for instance, remembers that on her first day of school in the United States, "the teacher looked me in the eyes—the eyes! I was frightened. . . . No one had ever done that to me, except my parents, before I was going to be punished. . . . You only look at people when you are angry, when they do something wrong."

Whereas the so-called "Vietnam Generation" of America remembers the haunting phantom of that war, the refugees describe a very different sense of loss. Heng Mui, when applying for an American passport, was asked to put down her nationality. "I wrote 'South Vietnam.' When she [the INS official] saw the application, she took a pencil and put two lines through the word 'Vietnam' and wrote 'Stateless.' Those two pencil lines scratched through my heart."

Another refugee, former Colonel Mong Pang, who works as a janitor at a church, recalls: "I fought very hard for my country, and now all of that is gone and it will not come back. It is very sad, very sad. . . . When I first started this work, the tears went into the toilet, I was so sad. . . . What do they do with a soldier who has no country?"

Dr. G. Chan talks about his struggle to practice medicine in the United States. "It is as if the U.S. officials opened the gates in this country and let you into the courtyard. But nobody will now open the front door." Like the colonel and the doctor, I too left my profession [professor of philosophy] behind. Before escaping from Vietnam in 1975, I remember talking with my wife and kids about our future in America—that they should not be shocked or ashamed if I had to do menial work. As it turned out, my first job was in a 7–Eleven store. After that I changed to a social worker, community specialist, and finally to refugee advocate. And based on my personal adjustments to each of these, I was able to provide job counseling to many former high-ranking officials from Indochina, including some friends of mine.

All of these refugees—new threads of gold and orange—are weaving their way into the multicolored American tapestry. But first, as Samphy Iep says, refugees must come to terms with their loss: "We all have a part of us that is torn away, something special, precious, that is gone. To be stateless and away from your people, your language and culture, that is a very difficult thing. We do not raise these issues among ourselves. We want to come to peace with this." And, with stoicism as a perennial philosophy of life, these refugees from Indochina have overcome their difficulties to become an emerging minority that can no longer be ignored.

What they bring to American life is profound—and profoundly different from what they encounter here. Monk Dong Ta explains the vast differences in attitude and values: "For us, harmony is everything, life and death . . . a sort of accommodation to whatever the problems might be. It's looking for the path that is least stressful, least confrontational. It might be what you call a shortcut around a law or regulation, but it is really a different way of looking at things, doing things."

Another basic shared value of these Southeast Asian groups is their concern primarily with promoting and protecting one's immediate family unit and then, maybe, the local community. Do Van Chi explains: "First I am concerned with my family—what you call extended family, which includes uncles and cousins—and then I might be concerned about neighbors. Usually not. This is the way it is. We protect our family first—all the rest is of a second concern."

The importance of work is stressed in Southeast Asian cultures, often more tied to one's self-worth than in American society. As Monk Phen Anonthasy observes, "When a person does not work, he gets depressed. It is like the air he breathes is being taken away."

Education, too, is greatly valued by Indochinese. In traditional Vietnamese society, scholars rank first in the social class system. Intellectuals are always honored and respected. At the University of Saigon, I had students who undertook a double major, completing two degrees at the same time. Besides the pride and honor involved, they were practicing a Confucian saying that "One can find happiness and joy through studying all the time." In fact, here in the U.S., I know of one Vietnamese student who completed seven degrees at M.I.T., one of which was a Ph.D.

The high value of education is stressed early in our lives. Children are constantly reminded about the importance of being educated and acquiring a good social standing, thereby honoring the whole family. Tutoring his children is a father's personal responsibility, and an elder brother or sister must set a good example for his or her siblings. As Ho Xuan Tam recounts, "There was always pressure to study. I can remember my father helping me with my studies when I was first in this country; he had difficulty with the language, but somehow he always understood my assignments. It was always a big ritual after dinner to study with him. . . . He was very, very proud when my older sister got a scholarship to study pre-med last year at Stanford. It was as if he got the scholarship. So this is pretty much what I'm going to do—go to Stanford."

The refugees have learned during their struggle to build a new life in America, and they have gained a deep appreciation of the generosity, hospitality, and volunteerism of the American people. But refugees don't always understand Americans. The concept of community spirit, for example, is strange. Monsignor Dominic Luong explains how the idea of giving to others appears to the Vietnamese community: "This idea of charity beyond the community is a foreign concept. It just doesn't happen unless the community is urged, usually forced, to do it. But it does happen. You just need to ask for it in the right way. . . . The idea of giving to strangers will work, but it is on a case-by-case basis. The generosity is there, you just have to ask for it in the right way." And in my own experience at IRAC [Indochina Resource Action Center], I found that we could raise money within the refugee community very quickly—over $100,000—for our first asylum conference in 1988. People were so motivated and we were so confident of their support that we went right ahead in organizing that conference, even before the money was there.

In their encounters with new values, refugees are gaining a better understanding of a truly democratic system in which nobody—not even the President—has the right to act above the law. They are learning an unfamiliar respect for differences of opinion, how to "agree to disagree."

Also in the course of the adjustment process, we are now beginning to see the development of solidarity, mutual assistance, and support among the exiles from the three countries of Indochina, which traditionally have been hostile to each other. Former refugees from Cambodia, Laos, and Vietnam are now united in their concern for friends and relatives and compatriots overseas. Mary Trang's fears—"What I am afraid of is that the United States will close its doors to my people"—are echoed by many others. And, as actress Kieu Chinh explains: "To be a refugee here means that you always think about those who remain. It enters every aspect of your life, whether you are aware of it or not. . . . You can't enjoy your home too much, thinking about those friends and family in concentration camps. It haunts you."

The emerging generation, especially, represents the enormous potential, in human and financial resources, necessary for the reconstruction and peaceful coexistence of Vietnam, Cambodia, and Laos. As a member of the Indochinese-American community, I think that the 1990s pose great challenges for us: peace in Cambodia, normalization of relations between the United States and Vietnam, and consolidating and empowering the community—economically and politically. The necessity for significant and constructive change is fueled by new realities that are quickly evolving in the world landscape. We stand, perhaps, at one of those historical watershed periods, in which the flow of events is rapidly accelerating. We are confronted with the heavy responsibility of making urgent but wise choices, whose consequences may be far-reaching. The challenge to the affected countries of Southeast Asia, to the international community at large, and to the overseas Indochinese community in particular is whether we can realize the tremendous opportunity at hand, for us to work together to achieve truly durable solutions which will firmly establish and protect the rights of refugees—and which, by doing so, will serve the broader interests of building peace, democracy, and prosperity in a long-troubled part of the world.

Photo: Horst Faas, AP/Wide World Photos

APPENDIX A

A History of Vietnam, Cambodia, and Laos

Vietnam

The Socialist Republic of Vietnam runs for about 1,000 miles along the eastern coast of mainland Southeast Asia. Its principal geographic features are the Mekong River in the south, the Red River in the north, the northern mountains along the border with China and the central highlands. Vietnam has an area of 127,259 square miles and a population of approximately 62 million people. There are about sixty different ethnic groups in Vietnam, the largest being the lowland Vietnamese who constitute about 80 percent of the population, and live primarily in the deltas of the Mekong and Red rivers, where rice farming has been the main economic activity for centuries.

◁FACING PAGE
Some of the few who survived a battle between Viet Cong and South Vietnamese forces huddle near the jungle town of Dong Xoai. After government rangers recaptured the town, bodies of approximately 150 civilians and 300 Vietnamese government troops were found.

Vietnam achieved independence in A.D. 939 after almost a thousand years of Chinese dominance. The new country then entered a 900-year period of expansion termed the "March to the South." In the early sixteenth century a period of political instability ensued which continued into the period of Western colonization. The first Western contact with Vietnam was in 1535 when Portuguese ships arrived to set up trading posts to gain access to the increasingly important markets of Southeast Asia. The Dutch, English, and French followed, attempting in vain to establish a Vietnamese trading center. In 1858 the French forcibly achieved their goal by seizing the central Vietnamese port of Danang. In 1867 they established "Cochin China," bringing the southern part of modern-day Vietnam under their direct jurisdiction, and by 1883 they were in charge of all of Vietnam, establishing an "Indochinese Union" which consisted of Tonkin (northern Vietnam), Annam (central Vietnam), Cochin China, and the kingdoms of Laos and Cambodia.

French colonization had two goals in Indochina: to civilize the Vietnamese in the ways of the West, and to increase French political and economic status around the world. Initially, they permitted Western-trained Vietnamese to administer the day-to-day affairs of the country. As time passed, however, the French became increasingly involved in the local administration of their colony and moved from a policy of "association" to one of "collaboration."[1]

French colonialism had both a positive and negative impact on the region. The infrastructure was greatly improved, the amount of rural areas under cultivation was increased, and the import of capital and subsequent government policies led to the success of light industries in the cities. The French did not encourage an indigenous commercial and manufacturing sector, however, thinking that it might provide too much competition with their own ambitions. In general, living standards gradually rose for the Vietnamese until the worldwide depression of the 1930s. Since Vietnam was now connected to the world economy, particularly through the export of rice and rubber, the depression had more effect than would otherwise have been the case. The deteriorating economic conditions led to peasant discontent and the growth of nationalist movements.

The Indochinese Communist Party (ICP) was formed in 1930 by Ho Chi Minh. He was the son of a government official in central Vietnam and was educated at the French-administered National Academy in the ancient Vietnamese city of Hue. He later traveled to Europe and in 1920 joined the French Communist party. After training in Moscow, he returned to Vietnam to form the ICP. The most important event in Asia during this period was the militaristic expansion of Japan. In 1941, the Japanese entered Vietnam, using the Vichy French as front men for their plans for a "Greater East Asia Co-prosperity Sphere." Under Japanese rule, the ICP had an opportunity to formulate the lessons they had learned from the Communists in China. The revolutionary strategy of the newly created Vietminh was to work in rural base areas, securing them with support from the peasants, then seizing the cities from the countryside.

In March of 1945, the Japanese granted independence to the Vietnamese and Emperor Bao Dai was placed back on the throne. Following the defeat of Japan, Ho Chi Minh wrote to President Truman, asking him to support his country's independence from France. His letters went unanswered, however, as Truman did not want to alienate the French or allow a Communist government to take power in Southeast Asia.

By August of 1945, within two weeks of V-J Day, most of the villages and cities in northern and central Vietnam were controlled by the Vietminh. On September 2, the formation of the Democratic Republic of Vietnam (DRV) was announced in the northern city of Hanoi. "Initiative and surprise" were credited by its leadership for the sweeping victories. In the south, French residents, Vietnamese nationalists, and the British military continued to hold power and were responsible for diluting the effect of the Communists in that area.

The French wanted to regain influence over their former colony after the war and went about creating a new administration in the south. An accommodation between north and south was attempted, and in 1946 the French and the Vietminh signed an agreement whereby the French recognized the DRV as a "free state." In return, the Vietminh agreed to accept a continuing French presence and agreed to join a "French Union." The victory of the conservatives in France, however, made the acceptance of an accommodation less likely, and by the end of 1946 talks gave way to fighting.

In 1949, the Chinese Communist Party (CCP) came to power. The CCP encouraged the Vietminh and provided them with military assistance. In the spring of 1950, the United States also became involved, announcing a military assistance program for Indochina with the purpose of containing Communist activity in the region. The aid program was formalized in December by the Mutual Defense Assistance Agreement with France and the French Associated States of Indochina. By the fall of 1950, the Vietminh won an important victory over the French by forcing them out of Chinese border areas, allowing a more steady flow of arms across the border. In 1951 the Vietminh officially adopted the Chinese "New Democratic Model" consisting of a two-stage process: a bourgeois democratic revolution in which major industries would be nationalized while smaller capitalists would be allowed to operate, and a proletarian socialist revolution.

In 1954 French forces were defeated at the battle of Dienbienphu. This battle was critical in causing the French to reexamine their chances for a military victory and set the stage for the upcoming talks in Geneva. The French, Emperor Bao Dai, the Vietminh, the People's Republic of China, the Soviet Union, and the United States were represented at the talks. China and the Soviet Union wished to avoid another engagement with the West so soon after the Korean War, and pressured the Vietminh to accept a political compromise. It was agreed that Vietnam would be divided along the 17th parallel into a French and a Vietminh zone of influence—an official recognition of a North and a South Vietnam. The agreement also called for nationwide democratic elections in July 1956, and allowed for a period of three hundred days when Vietnamese citizens would be allowed to pass freely from one zone to the other. A large refugee migration did take place with one million northerners moving to the south.

In November 1954, the French announced that they would withdraw completely from Vietnam, ending their control of the South Vietnamese economy, withdrawing their troops, and transferring responsibility for training the Vietnamese Army to the United States. Ngo Dinh Diem was appointed prime minister of the Government of Vietnam (GRV) at the urging of the United States. Diem had been a government minister in the pre–World War II Bao Dai government and, like Ho Chi Minh, came from the Vietnamese elite. His major base of support was from his fellow two million Catholics in the south, and he consolidated his power rapidly through the use of local organizations.

Part of the American plan in Vietnam was to encourage land reform. It was felt that an adequate land reform program would take the steam out of the Communist insurgency. Advisers were sent to South Vietnam in 1955, but due to lack of planning and the lack of desire from the South Vietnamese to implement the program, this showed few positive results. In the summer of 1955, Diem, with backing from President Eisenhower, announced that there would be no elections held with the DRV. The rejection of elections led Hanoi to increase its efforts to "liberate" South Vietnam and in 1959 the DRV Central Committee called for a more active approach. The North Vietnamese felt that, with the lack of domestic support for Diem, the time had come to take the offensive, and a program of protests and selective assassinations began.

In late 1960, the National Front for the Liberation of South Vietnam was created by the Communists as an anti-Diem front consisting of many Communist and non-Communist groups in the South. Diem's reaction was to clamp down on all groups, thus isolating himself from moderate groups in South Vietnam and from the goals of U.S. policy. In November 1963, he was assassinated by a United States–backed military coup, and a Military Revolutionary Council under General Duong Van Minh was created to run the country.

In 1964 the United States became more deeply involved when an intelligence-gathering patrol in the Gulf of Tonkin was attacked by North Vietnamese PT-boats. President Johnson asked for a congressional resolution to expand the war and on August 7, 1964, the Tonkin Gulf Resolution was overwhelmingly passed. By March, the United States was conducting a major bombing campaign in North Vietnam and had landed two battalions of marines at Danang. In May, U.S. troops in South Vietnam began their "search and destroy" missions against the southern Communist Viet Cong, and by the summer were using B-52 bombers in a campaign of industrial-target bombings in North Vietnam.

By the beginning of 1965, most of the rural areas in the south were held by the Communists. Although the political situation in South Vietnam was improving under the leadership of Nguyen Van Thieu and successful land-reform measures were underway, neither the South Vietnam rural "pacification" program nor the bombing of the north seemed to be leading to victory. In January 1968, during a New Year's truce, the North Vietnamese and the Viet Cong launched the Tet Offensive. The military gain for the Communists was negligible but the psychological impact on U.S. policy-makers was considerable; negotiations now became an increasingly important factor in United States policy.

The American public grew frustrated and doubted the validity and purpose of the war. Antiwar protests, public draft card burnings and massive public marches on the capital forced President Johnson not to seek reelection in 1968. The war had turned a tide.

In 1969, the new administration under President Nixon began to pursue a policy of "Vietnamization." The goal was to build up South Vietnamese troops while allowing the United States to withdraw gradually but steadily from an increasingly unpopular and apparently unwinnable war. At the same time, the secret bombing of neighboring Cambodia was instituted to disrupt Communist supply lines into Vietnam.

Opposition to American involvement in this war, which had existed since the beginning of the involvement, began to escalate. In November of 1969, it was reported that four hundred and fifty unarmed South Vietnamese civilians had been massacred in the town of My Lai, and in May of 1970, four Kent State University students protesting the war were killed by National Guardsmen. Antiwar movements continued to grow. In June of 1971, the Pentagon Papers were published, detailing the history of the U.S. involvement. The increasingly visible opposition added fuel to the desire of the Nixon administration to put a quick end to the war.

The next two years saw an on-again, off-again peace process, with the United States using the discontinuance of bombing campaigns as added incentive for the leaders in Hanoi. Finally, in January 1973, an "Agreement on Ending the War and Restoring Peace in Vietnam" was signed in Paris by the United States, North Vietnam, South Vietnam, and representatives of the Viet Cong. The agreement called for the release of American prisoners of war, U.S. withdrawal from Vietnam, a cease-fire, the end of military activities in Cambodia and Laos, and the formation of a National Council of Reconciliation and Concord whose purpose was to supervise the cease-fire and to arrange elections for South Vietnam. The Communists continued to press south, however, and after a series of victories beginning in January, entered Saigon in late April 1975. A Provisional Revolutionary Government of South Vietnam was created, leading to the formation on July 2, 1976, of the Socialist Republic of Vietnam.

The victory had been easier than expected and the Communists had to move quickly to consolidate their achievements. Security was their first concern and a Military Management Committee was created under the leadership of General Tran Van Tra, former leader of the revolutionary forces in the south. Indoctrination was a primary concern, achieved through reeducation and work camps to which several hundred thousand people were sent.

After security, the economy remained the major concern. In the cities, all GVN property, banks, foreign enterprises, and other "comprador bourgeoisie" holdings were promptly confiscated. In the country, because half of the population of the south had moved to the cities during the war, the success of the new agricultural programs was dependent on the return of the peasants to the countryside. New Economic Zones (NEZs) were created, based on models which had been used in the north. Some Vietnamese joined the NEZs voluntarily, but many were forced back to the country. This demographic shift never lived up to its expectations due to bad management of the NEZs and the continuing high-level political disagreements on the pace of change in the south.

In 1976, the Second Five-Year Plan was announced, the first Five-Year Plan since 1961 and the first economic plan for the whole of Vietnam. Its major goals were the development of heavy industry, promotion of agriculture, and promotion of the socialist transformation in the south. It was hoped that the Western nations as well as the People's Republic of China and the U.S.S.R. would contribute to this effort, and projections were made accordingly. There was reason to assume at this time that the Western countries would in fact contribute. Even the United States was considering an aid program following the dropping of war reparation demands by Vietnam. In March of 1978, however, there was a sweeping nationalization of business and industry in the south leading to the emigration of several hundreds of thousands of refugees, including a large number of well-trained ethnic Chinese.

The plight of the "boat people" and Hanoi's drift into the Soviet sphere of influence contributed to the deterioration of Vietnamese-Chinese relations. In March of 1978, Hanoi joined the economic group COMECON and in June the first Soviet ships docked at the former U.S. naval base of Cam Ranh Bay. By July, the Chinese cut all economic aid to Hanoi, and in November, a Treaty of Friendship and Cooperation was signed between Vietnam and the U.S.S.R. containing a military-assistance clause which Beijing felt was meant to refer specifically to them. In February and March of 1979, the China-Vietnam rift peaked as China launched an attack to "teach a lesson" to Vietnam for the invasion of Kampuchea.

In the fall of 1978, the Kampuchea National United Front for National Salvation (KNUFNS) was created under the leadership of an ex–Pol Pot supporter and leader in the eastern provinces, Heng Samrin. In December of 1978, the Vietnamese and the KNUFNS invaded Cambodia. Within three weeks, the Vietnamese had taken the Cambodian capital of Phnom Penh, establishing the People's Republic of Kampuchea shortly thereafter.

Although the West did not support the infamous Pol Pot regime, it could not afford to overlook the overthrow of a sovereign government. The Cambodian invasion, the refugee problem, the importance of establishing relations with China, and the close ties between Moscow and Hanoi ensured that there would be no economic help from the West and that Vietnam would have to rely almost exclusively on the Soviet Union.

From 1975 to 1986, Ho Chi Minh's successors attempted to improve the economy while keeping faith with the goals of socialism. A mixture of capitalist and socialist-oriented laws and strategies emerged. At the March 1982 Vietnamese Communist Party Congress, leaders admitted that they had been "too ambitious" in their five-year plans and endorsed market-oriented "liberal" reforms. At the same time, the inefficient NEZs continued to operate, with 1.5 million Vietnamese living and working in them. In 1983, taxes were raised to cut down on the spread of private industry, but the private market was still active, much of it moving into the underground economy. In 1984, it was reported that the private sector was still dominant in the food, fish, and forestry industries.

Le Duan, Ho Chi Minh's successor as head of the Vietnamese Communist party, died in mid-1986 and in December a major leadership shakeup and a "renovation campaign" began. Ho's lieutenants Truong Chinh, Pham Van Dong, and Le Duc Tho were encouraged to step down, and Nguyen Van Linh, an economist credited with encouraging decentralization in the south, was made party chief. In addition to the three top party leaders, the shakeup included three other Politburo members and nine new members in the day-to-day policymaking Secretariat. In the Central Committee, fifty-four members left while eighty-one new members joined. Of the twenty-two ministries in Vietnam, seventeen have had new leaders since mid-1986.[2]

Linh permitted economic liberalization and some degree of political tolerance. In February 1987, the Central Committee announced several measures meant to steer the country away from the socialist transformation and toward the development of the economy. These changes included tax breaks, bank loans, the allowing of businesses to set their own prices, and the borrowing of foreign currency to import raw materials. In April, higher cash incentives and bonuses for workers were announced as was the end of discrimination against private enterprises, excessive central planning, and the laws governing moonlighting for governmental employees. The south has been allowed to develop its own economic policies separate

of peasants marched on Phnom Penh to protest French taxes. These protests had little effect on French control. Taxes went increasingly into the pockets of French officials, and public order, education, and medical services were neglected in lieu of the gain of personal wealth. Even French successes, such as a vastly improved infrastructure (9,000 kilometers of roads and 500 kilometers of railroad line were built between 1900 and 1930), were more beneficial to French and Chinese merchants than to the local population.

Following the worldwide depression of the 1930s, the economy began to improve and more Cambodians ascended to government positions. The level of education increased, helping the French by maintaining the growing bureaucracy, but also creating a new class of Khmer intellectuals. Cambodia's first high school, the Collège Sisowath, the Institut Bouddhique, and the newspaper Nagara Vatta were the most important intellectual achievements heralding the "awakening" of the Cambodians.[6] World War II had a great impact on events in Indochina in general, and in Cambodia in particular. The Vichy French government welcomed the Japanese and ruled with Japanese "guidance" for the next four years.

The death of King Monivong (ruled 1927–1941), who had been ruling with French support for the previous fourteen years, left two factions fighting for the monarchy. The Vichy government supported the great-grandson of King Norodom, Norodom Sihanouk, who subsequently became king. Sihanouk had not been trained for his new position, and was dependent on French advisers to help him run the country. In March of 1945, the Japanese removed the French from their posts. They encouraged Sihanouk to sever his ties with the French and declare an independent government. The new government was named after the Cambodian pronunciation of the French word, Cambodge–Kampuchea.

Under this "independence," Japanese forces remained in Cambodia but permitted the Cambodians to regain some important symbols such as the Buddhist calendar and Khmer names for government ministries. They also allowed intellectuals to organize, form anticolonial groups, and hold rallies. The end of World War II brought the defeat of the Japanese and the return of the French. The intellectual awakening precluded a return to business as usual, though, and France would never again have the degree of control it enjoyed before the war.

In 1946, the Cambodians were allowed to form their first political parties. The Democrats won handily in the September Consultative Assembly election, winning fifty of the sixty-seven seats. They considered this victory to be a mandate for change and attempted to draw power from the monarchy and to the assembly.

The French presided over these events, but slowly came to realize the costs of retaining their colonial possessions. The success of revolutionary groups in Vietnam and escalating Cold War tensions prompted the French to look to the United States for help. In order to convince the United States that they were fighting for democracy, not merely protecting colonial territories, the French began to give more control to the Cambodians.

With this loosening of control came the rise of several political groups. Former leaders of the Issarak movement created the Unified Issarak Front, supported by the Indochina Communist party (ICP), which was founded in 1930 by the Vietnamese revolutionary Ho Chi Minh. In 1951, the Front became the Khmer People's Revolutionary party (KPRP). The party grew rapidly and by 1952 had two thousand members.[7]

Due to the emergence of these new forces, the government in Phnom Penh controlled only one-third of the country. Sihanouk saw his power waning and in June took steps to halt his decline. He declared himself prime minister, appointed his own cabinet, and dissolved the assembly. He also put pressure on the French in a worldwide publicity tour, claiming that he was the only alternative to a Communist takeover and that the French must allow more direct rule. As a result of these moves, the French granted him authority over foreign and legal affairs and over the armed forces. The KPRP and democratic forces lost popular and foreign support, and temporarily retreated from the political scene. In 1954, King Sihanouk became Prince Sihanouk, abdicating to his father in order to become more politically active from a less exalted position.

Following the Geneva Conference of 1954 and the international recognition of Sihanouk's leadership, KPRP cadres went into self-imposed exile in Hanoi. Because of the retreat of the old leaders, new leaders with few prior contacts with the KPRP or the Vietnamese were able to move into leadership positions. These were former members of the Khmer Students' Association (KSA), exposed to Communism and nationalism while on scholarships to France.

These former students and other factions of the KPRP met in Phnom Penh in September of 1960. This meeting changed the future direction of the KPRP as the students, under the leadership of Ieng Sary and Saloth Sar (alias Pol Pot) gained the upper hand, advocating an immediate armed struggle to overthrow the government of Cambodia. Sihanouk called the new group the Red Khmers, or Khmer Rouge.

Throughout the 1960s, the Khmer Rouge was constantly harassed by Sihanouk's forces and largely disappeared from public view, some at the hands of the government and some by choice to keep a lower profile. Further preventing the ascension of the Communists was Sihanouk's "Buddhist socialism" program which nationalized foreign trade and banking and quieted much of the criticism from the political left. Sihanouk's reforms were limited, however, and such peasant concerns as health and agricultural development went largely unnoticed by the government and the elite.

The United States and the Vietnam War

The United States had been providing aid to Sihanouk throughout the 1950s and early 1960s, including 30 percent of the police and military budgets.[8] In 1963, Sihanouk began to reduce U.S. ties, cutting the aid and meeting with leaders from North Vietnam. Alienated from Sihanouk, the military began to make their own political plans. In October 1966, General Lon Nol was elected premier of the National Assembly.

But peasant protests continued, and in 1967, the Cambodian government, wanting to build sugar plantations in the economically deprived province of Battambang, failed to adequately compensate the peasants for the land they took. At the same time, aggressive tax-collection efforts were launched and two collectors were killed by area peasants. Rebellions broke out overnight throughout the province. Lon Nol and Sihanouk were able to quell the unrest after declaring a state of emergency, but only after 10,000 people were killed.[9]

These uprisings and the repression that followed had the effect of making the peasants increasingly susceptible to Communist propaganda, convincing many that armed struggle was indeed the only hope for change. Sihanouk continued to believe that he could walk an increasingly difficult tightrope between Cambodian liberals and conservatives, and between North Vietnam and the United States. He felt that talks with the North Vietnamese were the best way to control the increasing rate at which they were violating Cambodian borders in an attempt to set up supply lines and depots.

The educated elite, Lon Nol, and the generals disagreed. On March 17, 1970, Lon Nol led a coup, ousting Sihanouk from power. There is evidence both for and against the direct role of the United States in the coup, but what is certain is that the United States moved quickly to support the new government once it had been installed.[10] Khmer paramilitary units, under the supervision of the United States Special Forces, were sent immediately to Phnom Penh. U.S. president Nixon saw the new anti–North Vietnam government as an opportunity to further the "Nixon Doctrine" and quickly set about arming them in a fight against Communist forces in North Vietnam. It was his intention to "do everything possible to help Lon Nol."[11] In April, the U.S. Army began to attack Communist forces in Cambodia. The attacks lasted only two months and had limited success. The supply and command centers that the United States had hoped to destroy simply moved farther into the interior.

Although U.S. ground forces left Cambodia in June of 1970, U.S. efforts in general were increased as the Lon Nol government became totally dependent on American supplies. In 1973, President Nixon pledged "all-out support" for the Khmer Republic and dramatically increased the bombing campaign which had been underway since 1969. From 1969 to 1973, the United States dropped three times the quantity of explosives on Cambodia as were dropped on Japan throughout the whole of World War II. Of the 540,000 tons of explosives dropped between 1969 and 1973, 250,000 tons were dropped in 1973 alone.[12] The results of the bombing were an increase in the acceptance of KPRP propaganda against the "imperialists" and the devastation of much of the Cambodian countryside. By the end of the war in 1975, there were 450,000 casualties and hundreds of people dying from starvation every day.[13]

The North Vietnamese entered Cambodia in full force shortly after Lon Nol's coup, taking ten major cities in the first ten days of battle. The government's response was to create the "Lon Nol Line" dividing Cambodia in half in an attempt to protect the western half not yet taken by the Vietnamese. After several battles in the early 1970s, the North Vietnamese army solidified its positions in eastern Cambodia and was able to turn its attention more fully toward South Vietnam. Fighting in Cambodia was taken on increasingly by the People's National Liberation Armed Forces of Kampuchea (PFLANK). PFLANK suffered tremendous setbacks in the summer of 1973 as a result of U.S. bombing, but when American domestic political pressures forced the end of the Vietnam War, they gained strength, until in January of 1975 they launched the "Mekong

River Offensive." The offensive lasted until April 17 when Communist forces moved in to take the Cambodian capital of Phnom Penh.

Democratic Kampuchea

The first major action of the Khmer Rouge was to empty Phnom Penh and other Cambodian towns. In their attempts to totally change society and restore the agricultural base, they conducted this exodus in brutal fashion. Often the old and sick and those who could not continue were simply left to die on the roadside. Estimates of those killed during the four years of Khmer Rouge rule range from one to three million people. The Khmer Rouge also acted quickly against former Khmer Republic officials and soldiers, and others who would not conform to the new order or who were seen as part of the old. They concentrated on destroying the old values of king, colonialism, capitalism, and religion, and building the new socialism from "year zero."

The country was divided into seven administrative zones and although conditions varied from zone to zone, life was difficult for all. The state maintained complete and direct control: "Economic activity was entirely managed by the state apparatus. There were no markets, no currency, no independent exchange; in most places no private garden production or independent food gathering, and by 1977 there was a policy, even more strictly enforced, of communal cooking and eating. Movement outside the basic unit, village or co-operative was forbidden without written authorization, which was rarely granted."[14]

Education and medical facilities were almost nonexistent, since most of the teachers and doctors had already been eliminated or had fled the country as part of a larger refugee emigration.[15] Agricultural productivity actually increased in some areas, but it was so badly managed that it did nothing to improve the quality of life for the Khmer people. Throughout this period there was a great deal of infighting between the various factions in Democratic Kampuchea (DK). In 1978, Ieng Sary, now deputy prime minister for foreign affairs, announced that members of the old-guard Communist groups were involved in a coup with support from the Vietnamese. Sary and Prime Minister Pol Pot moved quickly to consolidate their power. Between 1976 and 1978, at least ten leaders of the KPRP were executed.[16] The last group to resist the Pol Pot/Ieng Sary consolidation was in the east, led by Heng Samrin and Hun Sen. When Pol Pot's forces entered this zone, they escaped to Vietnam and began to seek the help of the Vietnamese in the overthrow of the Pol Pot regime.

Fighting had been going on between the DK and the Vietnamese since the KPRP came to power in 1975. Border disputes spread rapidly and, combined with Vietnamese reaction to the radical policies of Pol Pot, led to all-out confrontation in December 1978. In less than a month, the Vietnamese and their Khmer allies were in control of Phnom Penh.

People's Republic of Kampuchea

The goal of the People's Republic of Kampuchea (PRK) has been to return Cambodian life to normal, to undo the damages of DK rule. The government of President Heng Samrin and Prime Minister Hun Sen has relied heavily on foreign aid from Vietnam and the Soviet Union to accomplish this, but the economy remains in shambles. Although conditions have improved since the Pol Pot years, Cambodia remains one of the world's poorest countries with a per capita gross domestic product of $80 and an infant mortality rate of 216 deaths per thousand, the second worst in the world.[17] One major reason for the inability of the government to deal with these issues is the drain on the economy created by civil war.

The Coalition Government of Kampuchea

The Khmer Rouge were routed by the Vietnamese in 1978, but moved into base camps along the Thai-Cambodian border and soon began to rebuild their forces. Fearing the increasing strength of Vietnam, the Thais and the Chinese assisted the Khmer Rouge with a program of nonmilitary and military aid. In July 1982, two other opposition forces, the Sihanoukist National Army (ANS), led by Prince Sihanouk, and the Khmer People's National Liberation Armed Forces (KPNLAF), led by former prime minister Son Sann, joined forces with the Khmer Rouge to form the Coalition Government of Democratic Kampuchea (CGDK) in a consolidated attempt to overthrow the present regime. This new group gained international credibility, retaining recognition and receiving aid from the United Nations as the legitimate government of Cambodia, and aid from the Association of Southeast Asian Nations (ASEAN) and the United States.

In 1990, support from the international community for the CGDK continues. Fighting between the CGDK and PRK forces, common in the dry seasons from 1979 to 1985, has slowed considerably, and more effort has been put into diplomatic positioning with the withdrawal by 1989 of the 140,000 Vietnamese troops still in Cambodia.

Despite attempts at reconciliation, two main obstacles remain. The first involves the future role of the Khmer Rouge, whose international credibility is weakening. Increased fighting between the Khmer Rouge and its coalition partners, and moves to create a Khmer Rouge–controlled area within western Cambodia through the repatriation of refugees, are contributing to the resurrection of outlaw status for the Khmer Rouge. When the United Nations passed its annual resolution condemning Vietnam and declaring its support for the CGDK on November 3, 1988, it added a stipulation that Cambodia must not return to "the universally condemned policies and practices of a recent past"—an indirect but clear reference to the Khmer Rouge.[18] On November 8, Hun Sen, Sihanouk, and Son Sann met in Paris to establish a new "working commission"; the Khmer Rouge was pledged to triple its current aid to the Sihanouk and Son Sann forces in 1989, further distancing the Khmer Rouge from its coalition partners.[19] The Khmer Rouge retains a powerful guerrilla army of 30,000 to 40,000 troops, however, and any lasting settlement, most experts agree, must include them.

The second problem concerns the timing involved in creating a new government. Hun Sen and the Vietnamese insist that they must retain power during an election involving the various parties. The CGDK maintains that such an election would be fraudulent and that the PRK must relinquish power to an international group in preparation for the elections. These are tremendous obstacles to peace and prosperity for Cambodia, but in contrast to the last twenty years, there is at least now some hope. Caught in the middle of international struggles and consequences, the Khmer people have been at the mercy of external events and severe nationalist reaction for over one hundred years. French colonialism, the Vietnam War, the Pol Pot years, and the invasion by Vietnam have exhausted a once-proud country. Ironically, it is now international pressure in which the best hope lies. Vietnam, China, the United States, the Soviet Union, and the ASEAN countries, including Thailand, all see a stable Southeast Asia as being in their national interest and all have a stake in the creation of a peaceful and prosperous Cambodia.

Laos

Laos is a mountainous, land-locked country whose only natural line of communication and transportation is the Mekong River, which runs along the western edge of Laos and forms the border with Thailand. But even the river, due to unnavigable stretches, has historically divided the country into three distinct areas: Luang Prabang in the north, Vientiane-Savannakhet in the center, and Champassak in the south. Rarely, and only under strong central leadership, such as the fourteenth-to-seventeenth-century Kingdom of a Million Elephants (Lan Xang), has any sort of unity been achieved. The Lan Xang period is regarded as the height of early Laotian civilization, and could have provided a foundation for its national development except for the reemergence of internal divisions, encouraged by outside interference and the cultural, political, and social shocks of Western colonialism.

According to Theravada Buddhism, the Lao form of Buddhism established in the seventh century, the right to rule was based not on the divine right of a particular lineage, but instead on the concept of karma. Any ruler having reached the appropriate stage could claim leadership. There were no centralized bureaucracy or feudal relationships and therefore no nationwide institutions. Also retarding the growth of nationalism in Laos was the lack of a firm agricultural base, provided in Thailand and Vietnam by extensive rice plains.

Because of its internal divisions and lack of natural resources, Laos has always been prone to outside interference and has traditionally been dominated by its powerful neighbors. Before Western colonization, this outside pressure came alternately from Thailand, Burma, Vietnam, or China. Each of these outside powers supported a particular regional leader, thus preventing the development of a united Lao state.

Colonialism

Limitations on Lao growth were always perpetuated by the Western powers. The French invaded present-day Vietnam in 1859 and established a Cambodian Protectorate in 1863. Northern Laos, with the exception of its traditional religious and administrative center of Luang Prabang, was controlled by Vietnam at the time and thus became part of the French Empire. Southern and central Laos were controlled by Thailand, but when the Thais attacked northern Laos in 1883, the French retaliated and established a protectorate over those territories as well. In 1887, after being rescued by the French from Chinese invaders, King Oun-Kham asked for French protection and thus Luang Prabang also became part of the French Empire.

The French saw in Laos not the opportunity to build a modern state, but instead a satellite to the empire they were building in Vietnam. Most of the members of the civil service in nineteenth-century Laos were Vietnamese brought into the area by the French. The French forced upon the Laotians a Western-style parliamentary government which had no foundations in Laotian administrative history. As a result, "the forms of Western parliamentary democracy were adopted without its content."[20] The country was controlled by a powerful bureaucratic elite. Traditional borders and historical divisions were ignored and the southern city of Vientiane was selected as the national capital in 1900.

The rate of development in Laos was a disappointment to the French. They set out to build a modern infrastructure in the hope of providing a market for Vietnamese goods. High taxes were partially responsible for the lack of Lao cooperation as was the lack of knowledge by the French of traditional Laotian social and political structures. Most Laotians simply acquiesced in French rule without being enthusiastic contributors.

Perhaps the greatest influence the French had on modern-day Laos was accidental. In World War II the Japanese, anxious to obtain natural resources and to expand their sphere of influence, fought several battles in Indochina. A truce was reached early in 1941 after which the Vichy French, fearing the spread of influence from Thailand, encouraged the Laotians to band together. The National Renovation Movement was created and interest in traditional Lao culture was rekindled. These efforts by the French to create Laotian pride were more successful than intended and led to a new feeling that independence from all foreign powers could be achieved.[21]

The French were not prepared to give in to this nationalism, however, and with the defeat of the Japanese they moved quickly to reestablish their dominance. The Lao Issara government, created by Prince Phetsarath in October 1945, was overthrown by French troops, and in May 1946, Laos became an associated state within the French Union. In 1947, Laos was recognized as a constitutional monarchy, and the French recognized the king of Luang Prabang as the legitimate ruler. Gradually, however, the Laotians gained more control. In 1949, the Franco-Lao General Convention was signed, giving the Laotians de jure, if not de facto, independence, and in October 1953, the Franco-Lao Treaty was signed, giving all power of government to the Laotians.

The Pathet Lao

In 1935, the new Indochinese Communist Party led by Vietnamese Ho Chi Minh had only two Laotian members.[22] It was not until after World War II when the Laotians began to see themselves as one nation that any national movements at all began to take hold.

When the Lao Issara government was overthrown by the French, its leaders escaped to Thailand to plan the future of their movement. By 1949, its leadership had split over the issues of cooperation with the new government and the level of ties with the Vietnamese. The majority chose to join the new government in Vientiane, but Prince Souphanouvong, a member of the royal family long involved with the Vietnamese, went to Viet Minh headquarters and founded the Lao Resistance Front. Souphanouvong became prime minister of his newly declared government, naming Kaysone Phomvihane as his minister of defense. The name they gave to the new government was the Resistance Government of the Land of the Lao, or Pathet Lao.

In 1953, the Viet Minh and the Pathet Lao fought the French in northern Laos and almost captured Luang Prabang. As a result of the attack, the Pathet Lao now controlled large parts of northern Laos, and when the French were defeated by the Viet Minh at Dienbienphu, the Pathet Lao became an increasingly important political entity. The 1954 Geneva Agreements on Indochina led to a readjustment of political forces in Laos. The Vietnamese demanded equal representation for the Pathet Lao and the coalition Royal Laotian Government (RLG). Although this point was not conceded by the Western powers, the RLG pledged to "reintegrate the Pathet Lao into the political life of the community."[23]

In 1955, Souphanouvong created the Lao People's Party (LPP) and began the slow and methodical process of consolidating and expanding his power in Laos. In 1956, his half-brother Souvanna Phouma became prime minister and declared his intention to bring the Pathet Lao—under their newly formed political party, the Lao Patriotic Front (LPF)—into a broad-based coalition government. He was successful, and in November 1957 Souphanouvong was invited to join the new government, assuming the post of minister of planning, reconstruction, and urbanization.

The first Lao coalition government had widespread domestic and international backing, but the United States, in the height of the Cold War and with an increasing interest in Southeast Asia, feared the inclusion of Communists. Aid was withheld and antigovernment right-wing groups were formed with American support. The Souvanna government fell in the summer of 1958 and an anti-Communist government took its place. Fighting started again between RLG forces and the Pathet Lao and the coalition broke apart.

American military aid increased as a result of this fighting, and special forces were sent to further American interests. A staged election was held in 1960 with the help of the CIA and its agents in the Ministry of Defense. The United States–backed government did not have a substantial base of support, however, and in August 1960 a coup was staged by a captain in the Royal Lao Army. He declared a neutralist government and asked Souvanna to head the country once again.[24] The CIA reacted by providing large amounts of military aid, and in December 1960, right-wing forces attacked Vientiane. The Souvanna government fled north and two governments now existed simultaneously.

In 1962, President Kennedy, realizing the lack of support for the Vientiane government, withdrew military support. He reasoned that a neutralist coalition government was the best way to calm events in Laos and to deny Vietnamese access to the strategic Ho Chi Minh trail. With U.S. support withdrawn, neutralist forces again gained the upper hand. The second coalition government was formed in June of 1962.

Outside events once again conspired against the Laotians, however, and in less than a year the coalition had deteriorated. Assassinations were common and fighting between the Pathet Lao and the neutralists erupted once again. By this time, the United States was inexorably involved in the war in Vietnam and efforts to revive the coalition were doomed. The Pathet Lao stepped up their activities and their cooperation with the Viet Minh, and in April 1964 the United States began what was to be an extensive bombing of Communist forces in Laos. Between 1965 and 1973, two million tons of bombs—i.e., much more tonnage than was dropped on Japan during World War II—were dropped on a country with an area of 91,000 square miles; 750,000 people, 25 percent of the population, were directly affected and forced to flee their homes.[25]

The bombing, and the increased U.S. presence over the next few years. led to a strong increase in Pathet Lao support and organization, both at government and grass-roots levels. Political and logistical support from the Vietnamese continued, giving them expanded use of the Ho Chi Minh Trail. One month after the 1973 Paris agreement on Vietnam, and the exit of American forces from Indochina, the Laotians also negotiated an agreement, the Agreement on the Restoration of Peace and Reconciliation in Laos. It became obvious to the RLG government that without U.S. support their already slight hopes of total victory were not going to be realized. Thus, the third coalition came into being, and again, Souvanna and Souphanouvong were its leaders.

After the United States pulled out of Vietnam, military successes followed quickly for the Viet Minh. Saigon and Phnom Penh were taken by Communist forces in April 1975, lending encouragement to the Pathet Lao and adding support to their cause. Roads were seized, protests were held, many RLG officials resigned, and revolutionary committees and people's courts were formed. In May 1975, protest meetings were held in Vientiane and Luang Prabang. In June, the United States Agency for International Development (USAID) offices were seized and the United States suspended all relations with Laos. In August, Pathet Lao forces took over the Vientiane local administration, and held a ceremony for the "Vietnamese specialists" who had contributed so much to their cause.[26]

The government and the economy became increasingly paralyzed. In November, Souvanna and Souphanouvong convinced King Savang Vatthana to step down, and the Lao People's Democratic Republic (LPDR) was created. When it became clear in 1975 that the Pathet Lao was going to take control of Laos, many Laotians fled, crossing the Mekong River into Thailand. The first to leave were those who had fought against the Pathet Lao in the Vietnam War. This included Vietnamese who had settled in Laos before 1954 and had cooperated with the French, and the Hmong people from northeastern Laos who had cooperated with the Americans. The Hmong had been recruited by the CIA to fight their "secret war" in Laos—at one time 30,000 Hmong were under U.S. command.[27] The next group to leave were the civil servants, technicians, and educated among the Lao population. Many others left simply because they were in the path of the vast exodus of people.[28]

In the period from May 1975 to June 1985, 310,000 Laotians crossed the border into Thailand. The extent of the emigration has ebbed and flowed with events inside and outside the country. Large increases occurred in the harsh years of 1975–1978, then leveled off as conditions improved.

In 1984 the figures increased again, due mostly to the "pull factor" of family-member emigration. Recently, the exodus has slowed again as the Thai government has made it more difficult for refugees to enter their country. The exodus has reduced the population of Laos by 10 percent, which is a serious situation because many of those who left were the most highly trained people in the country.

The exodus was due in part to the harsh policies of the new LPDR government. Borrowing on the Vietnamese model, and not taking local conditions into account, the Laotian People's Revolutionary Party (LPRP) moved too quickly in its quest to control all facets of Laotian life.[29] Many trained people were sent to reeducation camps and although no organized resistance was formed, the Communists lost all hope of gaining the active support of the people which they so badly needed.

The Lao People's Democratic Republic

The main focus of the LPRP since coming to power, however, has not been on politics and ideology, but on economic growth. When the LPRP was created on December 2, 1975, it saw as its goal the creation of a modern socialist state. That this achievement would prove difficult was obvious not only because of the structural difficulties in reorganizing the government bureaucracies but also because Laos had never really been a modern state of any kind. The leaders formed a structure modeled on the Soviet and Vietnamese system, with former secretary of state Kaysone Phomvihane as secretary general and Souphanouvong as president. The country that the LPRP took over was in dire economic straits. The United States had built a large, superficial economy around Vientiane, and when aid to Laos was cut off in 1975 this economy went bankrupt. These conditions, combined with the close of the Thai-Laotian border in November 1975, amounted to what was a virtual boycott of Laos. The government reacted by penalizing Lao businessmen, on whom they blamed the crisis, and by mass nationalization. The economic problems came to a head in 1976 when, combined with a severe drought, the economy came to a virtual standstill. At this point, LPRP officials reversed their previous policy, asked the International Monetary Fund (IMF) for aid, and began to look for other solutions to their problems.[30]

Today Laos is involved in developing its New Economic Management System. Basically, this is the same idea now being tried by the Communist world in general, mixing capitalism and socialism to try to stimulate the economy. This has come about partly as a result of domestic conditions and pressure from international lending organizations, and partly from coaxing by the Vietnamese. This new effort has had only limited success, however, and charges of corruption and inefficiency are common.

Laos is still heavily dependent on foreign aid. Improvement is made more difficult by the entrenched bureaucracy. Like similar situations in China, the Soviet Union, and Vietnam, it has proven very difficult to bypass those whose livelihoods are based on the continuation of a system based on "a government of men not laws."[31] Efforts continue, however, to correct these problems. The Fourth Lao People's Revolutionary Congress was held in November 1986. New members of the Politburo, the Secretariat, and the Central Committee were chosen and the second five-year plan was announced. Prime Minister Phomvihane attacked the inefficiency, charging party officials with being "narrow-minded and selfish" and citing "subjectivism, haste . . . and a desire to wipe out the non-socialist part of the economy overnight" as the main problems facing the country.[32] At the June 1987 Central Committee Plenum, the Council of Ministers announced that prices would no longer be set by the government but by supply-and-demand. The effect this will have on the growth of the economy remains to be seen, but international loan agencies are sure to look favorably on these changes.

Ties with Vietnam remain the most important factor in Laotian government policies. The "special relationship" continues to determine not only Laotian policies but its daily activities as well. Economic, social, technical, and commercial agreements are common and with the exception of the foreign affairs departments, all government departments have Vietnamese advisers.[33]

In the past decade, Vietnam has provided technical and monetary assistance for 544 infrastructure projects throughout the country. The Vietnamese Central Office for Laotian Affairs maintains considerable power within Laos under such agreements as the 1977 Treaty of Friendship and Cooperation and, more recently, the 1986 Technical and Scientific Cooperation Agreement. Laotian foreign policy is shaped by its eastern neighbor, and ties with the West are complicated by its support for Hanoi's Cambodian policy. Occasional border incidents with Thailand also limit Laotian opportunities, particularly in the area of trade.

Laos is still subject to its larger, more powerful neighbors. Vietnam and Thailand have reassumed the roles they once played, as the United

States and France have been forced to bow to nationalist movements. Conditions are still harsh for the Laotian people: GNP per capita is only $184, life expectancy is forty-six years, foreign debt amounts to $400 million, and communication and transportation networks have not substantially improved in the last forty years.

The key to the future success of the LPDR lies in its relationship with its neighbors, particularly Vietnam. If the Vietnamese are able to reach an accommodation in Cambodia and are allowed to become part of the international community, then Laos will follow, enabling it to get the aid it so badly needs. If the Vietnamese continue to isolate themselves, then Laos will remain isolated as well, and will continue to have to wait for the time when it can truly call itself a modern nation.

NOTES

[1]Duiker, *Vietnam: Nation in Revolution*, p. 30.

[2]*Asia Yearbook*, 1988, p. 121.

[3]Ibid., p. 122.

[4]*Asian Survey*, January 1989, p. 131.

[5]Chandler, *History of Cambodia*, p. 143.

[6]Ibid., p. 164.

[7]Ibid., p. 185.

[8]Etcheson, *Rise and Fall of Democratic Kampuchea*, p. 63.

[9]Ibid., p. 71.

[10]For more information on the role of the United States in the Lon Nol coup see Shawcross, *Sideshow*, chap. 8, and Etcheson, *Rise and Fall*, chap. 6.

[11]Etcheson, *Rise and Fall*, p. 89.

[12]Ibid., p. 101.

[13]Lawyers' Committee for Human Rights, p. 2.

[14]Vickery, *Kampuchea*, p. 31.

[15]For more information on Cambodian refugees see Shawcross, *Quality of Mercy*, chaps. 3 and 4.

[16]Vickery, *Kampuchea*, p. 31.

[17]Chanda, "Economic Change in Laos, 1975–1980," *Asian Survey*, January 1988, pp. 108–9.

[18]*New York Times*, "U.N. Adopts Anti-Khmer Rouge Policy," November 4, 1988.

[19]*New York Times*, "Sihanouk Hints at U.S. Military Aid," October 14, 1988.

[20]Stuart-Fox, *Laos*, p. 31.

[21]Brown, *Apprentice Revolutionaries*, pp. 31, 32.
[22]Brown, "Communist Seizure," p. 129.
[23]Stuart-Fox, *Laos*, p. 33.
[24]Ibid., pp. 33, 34.
[25]Ibid., p. 36.
[26]Brown, "Communist Seizure," p. 41.
[27]*National Geographic*, May 1988, p. 44.
[28]Brown, "Communist Seizure," p. 179.
[29]Ibid.
[30]Chanda, Economic Change," p. 36.
[31]*Asian Survey*, January 1988, p. 221.
[32]*Asia Yearbook 1988*, pp. 69, 70.
[33]Ibid., p. 70.

REFERENCES

Asian Survey, January editions, 1981–1989.

Asia Yearbook, 1988. "Laos." Far Eastern Economic Review, 1988.

Banks, Arthur, S., ed. *Political Handbook of the World*. Binghamton, N.Y.: CSA Publications, 1988.

Becker, Elizabeth. *When the War Was Over*. New York: Simon & Schuster, 1986.

Bowman, John S., ed. *The Vietnam War: An Almanac*. World Almanac Publications, 1985.

Brown, MacAlister. *Apprentice Revolutionaries: The Communist Movement in Laos, 1930–1985*. Stanford, Calif.: Hoover Institute Press, 1987.

———. "The Communist Seizure of Power in Laos." In *Contemporary Laos*, Martin Stuart-Fox, ed. New York: St. Martin's Press, 1982.

Chanda, Nayan. *Brother Enemy: The War After the War*. New York: Harcourt, Brace, Jovanovich, 1986.

Chandler, David P. *A History of Cambodia*. Boulder, Colo.: Westview Press, 1983.

Norindr, Chou. "Political Institutions of the Lao People's Democratic Republic." In *Contemporary Laos*, Martin Stuart-Fox, ed. New York: St. Martin's Press, 1982.

Colbert, Evelyn. "U.S. Policy Toward Vietnam Since the Fall of Saigon." In Joseph Zasloff, ed., *Postwar Indochina: Old Enemies and New Allies*. Center for the Study of Foreign Affairs, 1988.

Duiker, William J. *Vietnam: Nation in Revolution*. Boulder, Colo.: Westview Press, 1983.

————. "Vietnam Since the Fall of Saigon." In *Papers in International Studies: Southeast Asia Series*. Stanford University Press, 1980.

Etcheson, Craig. *The Rise and Fall of Democratic Kampuchea*. Boulder, Colo.: Westview Press, 1984.

Freeman, James A. *Hearts of Sorrow: Vietnamese-American Lives*. Stanford, Calif.: Stanford University Press, 1989.

Haines, David W., ed. *Refugees in the United States: A Reference Handbook*. Westport, Conn.: Greenwood Press, 1985.

Johnson, Stephen T. "Vietnam's Politics and Economy in Mid-1987." In Joseph Zasloff, ed., *Postwar Indochina: Old Enemies and New Allies*. Center for the Study of Foreign Affairs, 1988.

Joiner, Charles A. "Laos in 1986." In *Asian Survey* XXVII:1 (January 1987).

————. "Laos in 1987." In *Asian Survey* XXVIII:1 (January 1988).

Kiernan, Ben. *How Pol Pot Came to Power*. London: Verson, 1985.

————, and Chanthou Boua. *Peasants and Politics in Kampuchea 1942–1981*. New York: M.E. Sharpe, 1982.

Lawyers' Committee for Human Rights. *Kampuchea: After the Worst*. New York and London: 1985.

Mason, Linda, and Roger Brown. *Rice, Rivalry and Politics: Managing Cambodian Relief*. Notre Dame, Ind.: University of Notre Dame Press, 1983.

Morris, Richard B., ed. *The Encyclopedia of American History*. New York: Harper & Row, 1976.

Santoli, Al. *To Bear Any Burden*. New York: E.P. Dutton, 1985.

Shawcross, William. *The Quality of Mercy*. New York: Simon & Schuster, 1984.

————. *Sideshow: Kissinger, Nixon and the Destruction of Cambodia*. London: Andre Deutsch, 1979.

Sihanouk, Prince Norodom. *War and Hope: The Case for Cambodia*. London: Sidgwick & Jackson, 1980.

Stuart-Fox, Martin. *Laos*. Boulder, Colo.: Lynne Rienner, 1986.

Van-es-Beeck, Bernard J. "Refugees from Laos, 1975–1979." In Martin Stuart-Fox, ed., *Contemporary Laos*. New York: St. Martin's Press, 1982.

Vickery, Michael. *Cambodia 1975–1982*. Boston: South End Press, 1984.

————. *Kampuchea: Politics, Economics and Society*. London: Frances Pinter, 1986.

APPENDIX B

Table 1

Summary of U.S. Refugee Admissions, 1975–1990,
Indochinese and Total

Fiscal Year	Southeast Asia	All Countries Total
1975	135,000	146,158
1976	15,000	27,206
1977	7,000	19,946
1978	20,574	36,507
1979	76,521	111,363
1980	163,799	207,116
1981	131,139	159,252
1982	73,522	97,355
1983	39,408	61,681
1984	51,960	71,113
1985	49,970	68,045
1986	45,454	62,440
1987	40,105	64,821
1988	35,347	76,086
1989	55,680	105,688
1990	51,500	111,000
Total	991,979	1,425,777

Source: U.S. Department of State, Bureau of Refugee Programs, as of August 6, 1990, Summary Sheet.

234

Table 2

Indochinese Refugees: Departures to U.S. and Third Countries
(Excluding Orderly Departure Program)
Cumulative since April 1975

	Total
Australia	123,433
Belgium	4,517
Canada	127,998
Denmark	4,128
France	165,579
FRG	24,104
Italy	3,102
Japan	3,263
Netherlands	6,631
New Zealand	8,911
Norway	6,208
Sweden	3,737
Switzerland	9,714
United Kingdom	18,260
Other*	290,265
Total Third-Country	799,850
Total U.S.	857,494
Grand Total	1,657,344

Source: U.S. Department of State, Bureau of Refugee Programs, p. 10 Summary Sheet, as of December 31, 1989.

*Almost all are Vietnamese resettled in the People's Republic of China.

Table 3
Indochinese Refugee Population, 1990

State	Number	State	Number
California	365,100	Rhode Island	7,600
Texas	69,500	North Carolina	7,600
Washington	43,600	Tennessee	6,500
Minnesota	33,900	Indiana	4,400
New York	33,300	Alabama	3,400
Pennsylvania	29,700	Arkansas	3,300
Illinois	29,600	Kentucky	3,200
Massachusetts	28,900	Nebraska	2,700
Virginia	23,400	Nevada	2,500
Oregon	20,700	South Carolina	2,500
Florida	15,900	New Mexico	2,300
Wisconsin	15,500	Mississippi	1,900
Louisiana	15,400	Idaho	1,900
Ohio	12,700	District of Columbia	1,800
Colorado	12,600	Maine	1,800
Michigan	12,600	South Dakota	1,100
Georgia	12,200	Montana	1,000
Kansas	10,900	New Hampshire	1,000
Maryland	10,900	North Dakota	1,000
Iowa	10,200	Vermont	700
Utah	9,500	West Virginia	400
Oklahoma	9,400	Delaware	300
Missouri	8,500	Guam	300
New Jersey	8,500	Wyoming	200
Connecticut	8,300	Alaska	100
Hawaii	8,000	Other Territories	*
Arizona	7,700	Total	925,400

Source: Office of Refugee Resettlement, U.S. Department of Health and Human Services, January 31, 1990.

*At the close of fiscal year 1989, 20 states were estimated to have populations of Southeast Asian refugees of at least 10,000 persons.

APPENDIX C

Additional Readings

Brown, Frederick Z. *Second Chance: The United States and Indochina in the 1990s*. Colchester, Vt.: Council on Foreign Relations. 1989.

Broyles, William, Jr. *Brothers in Arms: A Journey from War to Peace*. New York: Knopf. 1986.

Bui Diem. *In the Jaws of History*. New York: Houghton Mifflin Company. 1987.

Chanoff, David and Doan Van Toai. *Portrait of the Enemy*. New York: Random House. 1986.

Cohen, Barbara. *The Vietnam Guidebook*. New York: Harper & Row. 1990.

Doan Van Toai and David Chanoff. *The Vietnamese Gulag*. New York: Simon & Schuster. 1986.

Dommen, Arthur J. *Conflict in Laos: The Politics of Neutralization*. New York: Praeger Publications. 1971.

———. *Laos: Keystone of Indochina*. Boulder, Colo.: Westview Profiles. 1985.

Farmbry, Kyle, ed. *The String Bracelet: Reflections of and by the Young People of Southeast Asia.* Washington, D.C.: Intercultural Productions. 1989.

Haing Ngor with Roger Warner. *A Cambodian Odyssey.* New York: Macmillan. 1987.

Hayslip, Le Ly. *When Heaven and Earth Changed Places.* New York: Doubleday. 1989.

Indochina Chronology (published quarterly). Berkeley, Calif.: Indochina Studies Program, Institute of East Asian Studies, University of California at Berkeley.

Komer, Robert W. *Bureaucracy at War: U.S. Performance in the Vietnamese Conflict.* Boulder, Colo.: Westview Special Studies. 1985.

Lawyers Committee for Human Rights. *Inhumane Deterrence.* New York. 1989.

———. *Refuge Denied.* New York: 1989.

Ng Shui Meng. *An Analysis of the Situation of Children and Women in Laos.* New York: UNICEF/Vientiane. 1987.

Nguyen Tien Hung and Jerrold L. Schecter. *The Palace File.* New York: Harper & Row. 1986.

Palmer, Laura. *Shrapnel in the Heart: Letters and Remembrances from the Vietnam Veterans Memorial.* New York: Random House. 1987.

Pike, Douglas. *PAVN: People's Army of Vietnam.* Novato, Calif.: Presidio Press. 1986.

———. *Vietnam and the Soviet Union: Anatomy of an Alliance.* Boulder, Colo.: Westview Press. 1987.

Reynell, Josephine. *Political Pawns: Refugees on Thai-Kampuchean Border.* Oxford: Refugee Studies Programme, University of Oxford. 1989.

Santoli, Al. *New Americans: An Oral History.* New York: Viking Press. 1988.

Shaplen, Robert. *Bitter Victory.* New York: Harper & Row. 1986.

Someth May, ed., with an introduction by James Fenton. *Cambodian Witness: The Autobiography of Someth May.* New York: Random House. 1986.

Szymusiak, Molyda. *The Stones Cry Out: A Cambodian Childhood, 1975–1980.* New York: Hill & Wang. 1986.

Truong Nhu Tang with Doan Van Toai and David Chanoff. *A Viet-Cong Memoir: An Inside Account of the Vietnam War and Its Aftermath.* New York: Vintage Books. 1986.

Vietnam: A Country Study (Area Handbook Series). Department of the Army. 1989.

1977   United States admits 7,000 Southeast Asian refugees.

1978   United States admits 20,397 Southeast Asian refugees.
              Vietnam invades Cambodia, forcing thousands to flee into
              Thailand. Persecution of Chinese-Vietnamese in Vietnam
              creates a mass exodus.

1979

JANUARY 7   Vietnamese capture Phnom Penh; Heng Samrin becomes
              new leader. Over 100,000 Cambodians crowd Thai border
              in search of safety.

JAN.–JUNE   Each month 5,000 Lao refugees flood into Thailand; num-
              bers decrease to 2,000 per month by end of summer.

JUNE 8–12   Thailand forces 44,000 Cambodians back into Cambodia,
              resulting in extensive loss of lives.
              United Nations holds major Conference on Indochinese
              Refugees.

OCTOBER 10   60,000 Cambodians flee en masse to Thailand.

OCTOBER 20   Thai government moves 30,000 Cambodians deeper into
              interior to protect them from border conditions.

DECEMBER   U.S. government estimates that more than 350,000 Cam-
              bodians died of starvation in 1979.
              Khao I Dang refugee camp in eastern Thailand has popula-
              tion of more than 160,000 Cambodians.
              A total of 76,521 Southeast Asian refugees are admitted to
              the United States.

1980

JANUARY 4   Increased Thai-Cambodian border war continues to pro-
              duce refugees.

JANUARY 15   Thai government stops registering new arrivals into Khao I
              Dang, hoping to deter refugee flow.

JUNE 17   United Nations begins voluntary repatriation program for
              Cambodians with very little success.

JUNE 23	Vietnamese army begins major attack against Cambodian border camps, driving 75,000 Cambodians into Thailand.
JULY	President Jimmy Carter signs into law the Refugee Act of 1980.
	Flow of boat people from Vietnam now reaches 70,000 per month.
DECEMBER	163,799 Southeast Asian refugees are admitted to the United States.

1981

MAY	United Nations resumes massive food distribution program to Cambodians on Thai border.
JUNE	Authorized to establish annual ceilings by the Refugee Act of 1980, United States sets Southeast Asian refugee ceiling at 165,000, but actually admits 131,139.

1982

MAY	United Nations creates Border Relief Operation to coordinate all services to Cambodians on border.
DECEMBER	73,522 Southeast Asian refugees are admitted to the United States.

1983

OCTOBER	Vietnamese army increases offensives against Cambodian resistance forces along Thai border, drawing thousands of civilians into the fighting.
DECEMBER	United States admits 39,408 Southeast Asian refugees.

1984

MAY	Temporary camps for 230,000 Cambodian and Laotian refugees living between Cambodia and Thailand are established by United Nations.

DECEMBER   51,960 Southeast Asian refugees are admitted to the United States; 10,000 numbers are made available for persons under Orderly Departure Program from Vietnam.

1985

JANUARY   United States announces formation of a high-level indepen-dent panel to review Indochinese refugee situation. Policy changes are to be recommended for future admissions.

DECEMBER   United States admits 49,970 Southeast Asian refugees.

1986

JANUARY   Vietnam suspends Orderly Departure Program interviewing and blames backlog of 60,000 applicants on United States and other Western countries.

MAY   U.S. Panel of Indochinese Refugees recommends continua-tion of program but a shift toward regular immigration channels for Southeast Asians seeking admission solely for family reunification. Panel recommends that all Cambo-dian cases in Khao I Dang denied U.S. resettlement by the INS be reviewed and the camp be kept open indefinitely. By the end of May, 154,000 refugees remain in camps in Southeast Asia and 250,000 Cambodians and land Viet-namese remain along the Thai-Cambodian border.

DECEMBER   45,454 Southwest Asian refugees are admitted to the United States.

1987

JANUARY   U.S. government makes request to Vietnamese government to restart Orderly Departure Program.

AUGUST   Vietnamese permit interviewing to begin again for program.

SEPTEMBER   Thai government reiterates plan to close Khao I Dang; serious security problems occur on borders.
Orderly Departure Program processing resumes after 18-month hiatus.

OCTOBER   Hatfield-Atkins bill passes.

DECEMBER   United States admits 40,105 Southeast Asian refugees.

1988

MAY   Asylum crisis widens for all refugees in Southeast Asia with continued reports of shootings of refugees, threatened camp closings, and pirates.

JUNE   Hong Kong begins screening all Vietnamese refugees. First-asylum nations meet and call for "immediate action" on behalf of all resettlement countries.

AUGUST   153,000 refugees are in camps; more than half have been there over three years.

DECEMBER   United States admits 35,347 Southeast Asian refugees.

1989

JANUARY   Renewed artillery action takes place on Thai-Cambodian border causing 20,000 to be quickly moved to "repatriation villages" inside Cambodia.
United States shifts 6,500 refugee numbers from Southeast Asian ceiling to Soviet Union.

MARCH   Six-member Association of Southeast Asian Nations announces that, as of March 14, Vietnamese asylum-seekers arriving in Southeast Asian countries will no longer be automatically eligible for resettlement to a third country.

JUNE   Second International Conference on Indochinese Refugees called by the U.N. Secretary General. Britain issues formal demand for forcible repatriation of Vietnamese asylum-seekers from Hong Kong to begin in October.

AUGUST   Paris Conference on Cambodia.

SEPTEMBER U.N. Conference on Withdrawal from Cambodia.

DECEMBER United Kingdom forcibly repatriates 51 asylum-seekers back to Vietnam amid international protest.

48,000 Southeast Asian refugees are admitted to the United States.

John Tenhula

A former program officer for the National Council of Churches and legal officer for the office of United Nations High Commissioner for Refugees, a holder of Ph.D. and J.D. degrees, John Tenhula is adjunct professor at Columbia University.

Liv Ullmann

The internationally renowned actress has been devoted to alleviating the plight of refugees and other deprived groups around the world for the past ten years. She has visited thirty countries to interview victims and investigate conditions first-hand, and as vice-president of the International Rescue Committee, the largest U.S. relief group for refugees, in 1989 she helped found the Women's Commission of Refugee Women and Children under the IRC's auspices. A frequent participant in Congressional hearings, Ms. Ullmann recently testified before the U.S. Senate about human rights violations she had found during her 1990 visit to detention camps in Hong Kong.

Le Xuan Khoa

Formerly Deputy Minister of Culture and Education of the government of the Republic of Vietnam, Le Xuan Khoa completed his post-graduate studies at the Sorbonne and was a philosophy professor at the University of Saigon before coming to the U.S. in 1975 as a refugee. A distinguished author and a tireless advocate of refugee affairs, Professor Khoa is currently president of the Indochina Resource Action Center (IRAC), a national organization based in Washington, D.C. Dr. Khoa was selected by the Board of the Asian and Pacific American Civil Rights Alliance (APACRA) as the recipient of the 1988 Civil Rights Award.